OUTDOOR DOMESTICITY

RICARDO DEVESA

---

*On the Relationships
between Trees, Architecture
and Inhabitants*

To my father, a builder of houses; and my mother,
a grower of trees.

View of the pergola with the
pre-existing trees at La Casa,
Frigiliana, by Bernard Rudofsky

Index

Foreword

María Teresa Muñoz

The pure artifact, which every work of modern architecture aspired to become, stands in opposition by its very essence to the natural realm, to what is not man-made. That is how the philosopher Theodor W. Adorno opens his reflections on natural beauty in modernity, compiled in his *Aesthetic Theory*, published posthumously in 1970. A meditation on natural beauty is fundamental to any aesthetic theory, Adorno points out, but great art and its interpretation shut the door anything that was once attributed to nature; they put aside any thought of what happens beyond their aesthetic immanence. And yet, those two poles, the natural and the fabricated, invoke one another: nature refers us to a mediated and objectified world, whereas the work of art calls up nature as it represents immediacy. In another passage from the same work, Adorno refers to the feeling of bad conscience that surfaces in the modern sensibility when faced with contemplating an old wall, a country house or, ultimately, a landscape. But nature appears as all-powerful only when there is no room for natural beauty, like in agricultural professions where nature is seen as an object of action. In those cases, Adorno concludes, natural beauty has no place.

One of the chinks exploited by the backlash against modernity beginning in the mid-20th century was precisely the recognition of the active role that nature could play in architectural works. Nature contributes to the built object the definition of a precise place, as well as the passage of time. Aldo van Eyck referred to this as the substitution of a generic space and time with a specific, concrete place and moment. That being said, reflections on nature had emerged in America long before the advent of modern architecture in Europe, with the figure of Frank Lloyd Wright and his connection to 19th-century American intellectuals. Nature, for Wright, was above architecture, which must submit to it – if not by emulating its forms, then by building them from the inside out, like in any organic process. Henry David Thoreau, in his 1854 work *Walden*, even questioned the need for a house, since man is capable of living in nature by taking advantage of the elements that are present in the landscape.

Ricardo Devesa's book is presented as the individual study of five houses spanning a chronological range of almost a century, all built in Europe except one, which was built in America but by a European architect. The book's aim is to contrast a singular element, the tree, isolated from the landscape, with an architecture that is also singular, the detached house. Houses and trees, or trees and houses, contrast precisely because they are presupposed to be different, because of their diversity. The tree, the natural element, is identified with what exists before and will exist after the architecture, the construction of the house; it is an indisputable pre-existing element that conditions the design decisions, beyond the formal determinations of the designer. In addition, the tree provides a temporal dimension that is unlimited and cyclical, contrasting with the limited timespan of the architecture. In the houses studied by Ricardo Devesa, architecture appears in contrast to trees as an object that, once built, is devoid of evolution or movement; it even aims, in keeping with the goal of all modern architecture, to eschew the possibility of decay, aging or destruction.

Devesa writes of a necessary coexistence between tree and house, a coexistence based on the individuality of both elements. The focus, moreover, is never a generic tree or group of trees, but rather a cypress tree, a carob tree, an olive tree or a jacaranda. The more difficult and expensive the tree is to maintain during the process of building the house, the more it is appreciated for its special value or the difficulty involved in preserving it. Both Le Corbusier and Marcel Breuer emphasized the views of trees, including partial views, from the windows of their houses, treating the trees as aesthetic objects, whereas Bernard Rudofsky made holes in the walls for the branches of the trees to pass through, creating the equivalent of a frame for a painting. The irregular geometries of the trunks or branches act as a counterpoint to the simplicity and volumetric regularity of the house's forms, which adapt to, but also make use of, the trees to construct special enclosures, sometimes outdoors.

Thornstein Veblen, in his work *The Theory of the Leisure Class* from 1899, refers to the fact that the aesthetic condition of an object is mediated by its rarity and the difficulty of obtaining or maintaining it. Everyday objects, but also flowers and trees or shrubs, are appreciated all the more when they are rare, or when they offer a special beauty to a place and, consequently, a certain distinction to the people who possess them. In the cases examined in this book, we might also say that the natural elements lend a certain rarity and aesthetic value to the architecture with which they coexist, either because of their consideration as aesthetic objects, as in the case of Le Corbusier or Breuer, or as indicators of an intended ruralism or vernacular quality superimposed onto the artificiality of modern architecture, as in the case of Rudofsky, the Smithsons or Navarro Baldeweg. In the first group, the role of trees is restricted to mere visual enjoyment, and they are identified with architectural elements like pillars; the second group takes into account the trees' more utilitarian role as climatic conditioners, providing shade and protection.

The architecture's delegation of a distinctive character onto the natural elements that accompany it is far removed from the theses of modernity, which claimed a universality and formal neutrality that stood in opposition to the search for any particular character. That was, however, the aim of English and American landscape designers and architects of the 19th century, who pursued a perfect coexistence between house and landscape, especially the contiguous landscape, and they placed a value on artificial, man-made landscapes over and above pristine nature. In the examples presented by Ricardo Devesa, the rational enjoyment of the forms of modern architecture gives way to a more sensitive attitude towards the indeliberateness of forms and the passage of time inherent in natural elements. The presence and even prominence of the trees in these houses invites a more relaxed and contemplative attitude in their inhabitants, beyond the mere utilitarianism of their spaces and forms.

The almost monographic treatment of each example, without interferences between them, presuming that the conclusions will provide a certain degree of generality, warrants some consideration. In the first place, the selected works were all designed by architects who offered their own reflections on the subject of trees or vegetation, whether pre-existing or planted subsequently. In that sense, the study of each of the houses is mediated by the explicit objectives of their designers. Second, Ricardo Devesa focuses above all on the process, the design and construction of the architecture, whatever its duration, in which trees condition the development of the built forms, sidestepping the role that the trees may play in the eventual transformations of the house or its aging. The tree, here, is a static element, although its organic condition is sometimes evident in the seasonal changes it undergoes throughout the year.

Without observing a chronological order, La Casa in Frigiliana by Bernard Rudofsky, from the early 1970s, kicks off the book, an example of "architecture without architects", followed by two emblematic examples of modern architecture: Marcel Breuer's Caesar Cottage from the early 1950s and Le Corbusier's Villa La Roche from the 1920s. A purist villa by Le Corbusier, in which the architect defends paying special attention to trees, follows the study of a Breuer house that represents a certain formal weakening of modern architecture, making room for new elements like patios or porches. The only example by a Spanish architect, Villa Pepa, built by Juan Navarro Baldeweg in Alicante in the 1990s, introduces a personal discourse by this architect/artist, which draws on the activation of sensory stimuli that natural elements can also awaken in the inhabitant or the observer of the architecture. And finally, the Hexenhaus, built in Germany by the British architects Alison and Peter Smithson, features the longest construction period of all the cases, from 1986 and 2001, and the incorporation of many of the surrounding trees as well as architectural elements like pavilions, bridges or exterior stairways.

A more exhaustive discourse on houses and trees would have required a broader catalogue of cases and would also have obliged establishing relationships between the different examples and perhaps even the formulation of a taxonomy. That was Ricardo Devesa's aim in the second part of his doctoral dissertation, which is not included this book. By offering the reader only the five examples, without a chronological or geographical order, and each one discussed in depth, Devesa delegates to the reader the possibility of discovering possible commonalities between them or, on the contrary, maintaining them as separate universes, each with its own specific conclusions. There is a concerted effort in the book to balance the five discourses while, at the same time, avoiding forcing an eventual confluence between them. Ricardo Devesa adds the idea of outdoor domesticity to the title, which implies giving trees a role beyond their simple dialectical presence as a natural element. Trees construct an exterior for each of the dwellings, a context that conditions the critical reading of these works of modern architecture, now activated by the presence of nature. In all of them, including Le Corbusier's villa, we find instances of breaking up the box, the compactness of the built volumes, which are forced to disperse to accommodate the natural elements. The interconnection between volume and space, which was one of the objectives of many of the artistic avant-gardes of the 20th century, gives rise here to a new concept of habitation that is less universal, but more free. These unique homes built by European architects throughout the 20th century certainly resonate with some examples of American organic architecture, in which the coexistence of architecture and nature occurs seemingly without friction. But if we look at them carefully, we discover how much the formal self-absorption of modern architecture has conditioned them, each in a different way, into an uneasy dialectic with the natural realm. The trees that can be seen through windows, that cross through a hole in a wall, that climb the walls of a patio or drop leaves onto a glass roof, in all cases they undergo a kind of metamorphosis, a process of estrangement, that is necessary to coexist with an architecture that can never fully merge with them.

Introduction
Ricardo Devesa

Relationships of Contiguity between Houses and Trees

There have been relationships of contiguity between houses and trees since ancient times; originally because trees were a source of food and energy; then formal and spatial relationships emerged, as well as meanings and mythologies. These connections eventually became explicit in architectural design, largely since the advent of modernity. This was perhaps because the house was one of the central architectural programs during that period in history; or it could have been due to a growing sensitivity regarding aspects of the environment and the landscape in relation to a project's surroundings. In any case, trees have been deliberately incorporated into modern houses since the moment they were granted status as a prominent part of spatial and environmental design.

The designs in this book all incorporated pre-existing trees into the houses from the moment the architect visited the site or learned of their existence. Thus, in many cases, this decision is present in the earliest preliminary sketches: the trees are shown in the topographic surveys of the site, situated precisely in the terrain with indications of their formal properties - diameter of the crown, height and relative position of the trunk - as well as their botanical characteristics and the specific climatic and even perceptual benefits that are offered by each species.

The attention to and emphasis on the existing trees on the site appear in the design briefs, where the architects discuss their adequation and inclusion in the houses. There are a wealth of reflections on trees' contributions to domestic life. In that sense, our starting point is the clearly established attention to trees and their active integration into houses as integral elements of domestic

02

03

Previous page:
01 Farnsworth House,
Mies van der Rohe, 1951

02 Snellman House,
Gunnar Asplund, 1917

03 Eames House,
Charles and Ray Eames,
1948

04

04 Kaufmann House,
Frank Lloyd Wright, 1937

architecture, an interest that has been shared by a large number of contemporary architects.

Each period in the history of architecture has had its own particular analogies between architecture and trees. The architects of each period have forged different formal and symbolic links between natural and architectural elements. Vitruvius situated the origins of architecture in the chance event of a fire caused by tree branches rubbing together. In the late 19th century, with the rise of new relationships between architecture and nature, various new articulations and reconsiderations emerged regarding vegetation and the built environment.

In early modernity, there was a rash of designs which, unprecedentedly, connected houses and trees. Some paradigmatic 20th-century houses are exemplary in terms of their defining relationships with trees. Examples include the Snellman house (Djursholm, Stockholm, Sweden, 1917) by Gunnar Asplund; the Villa Mairea (Noormarkku, Finland, 1937) by Alvar Aalto; the Kaufmann House (Bear Run, Pennsylvania, USA, 1937) by Frank Lloyd Wright; and the Farnsworth House (Plano, Chicago, USA, 1945), by Mies Van Der Rohe.[1] In other cases, a group of trees was the determining factor in the design, such as the row of pre-existing eucalyptus trees at Charles and Ray Eames's house in California (Pacific Palisades, USA, 1948).

As we have said, this interest in annexing the trees already on the site is often reflected in the earliest sketches or in the site plans, which detail their positions and characteristics. Drawings that are well known for this characteristic include those by Josep Antoni Coderch for the Ugalde house (Caldes d'Estrac, Spain, 1951); those by Le Corbusier and Pierre Jeanneret for the Villa La Roche (Paris, France, 1923), which will be analyzed in depth in the corresponding chapter; and those for the extension of the Huarte house (Formentor, Mallorca, Spain, 1968) by Francisco Javier Sáenz de Oíza.

Occasionally, the trees on the site are harnessed for the construction of the house, as was the case, for example, in the Elza

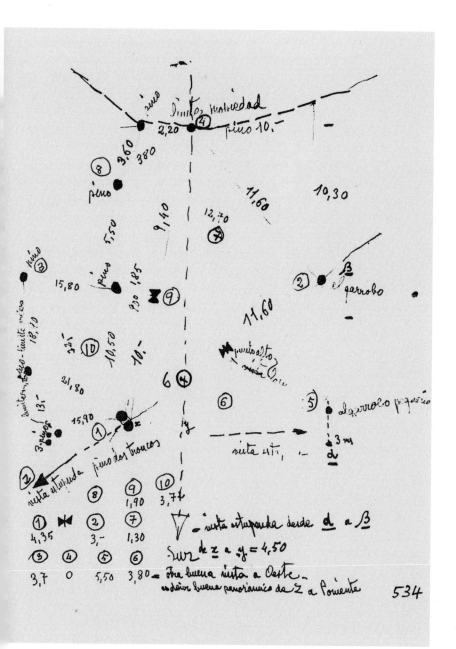

05 Notes on the site for the Ugalde House, José Antonio Coderch, 1951

Berquo house by Vilanova Artigas (São Paulo, Brazil, 1967), where
the architect used the tree trunks as pillars for the courtyard, or
in John Lautner's Pearlman Mountain Cabin (Idyllwild, California,
1957). In contrast, other architects have suggested phenomenological rather than compositional relationships with trees. Alison and
Peter Smithson were pioneers in this regard, as we will see later.

The very concept of the house is transformed following the
connections with the trees that arise. The connections between
the two become an opportunity to forge a dialogic relationship
between apparent opposites: artificial versus natural; interior
versus exterior; what is pre-existing on the site versus what is
created by the architecture as an inhabited place; even permanence versus transitoriness. Rethinking houses based on trees is,
thus, the aim of this research - specifically, looking at the effects
of incorporating trees on the idea of place, on time in architecture
and, finally, on extending the domestic sphere into the outdoors.

How Do Houses Change as They Incorporate Trees?

We define a house as a building that encloses habitable interior
spaces that can accomodate a private domestic program. However, houses combined with trees cannot be limited solely to isolated indoor spaces. Their province is expanded to incorporate
the adjacent outdoor space. In that sense, the outside cannot be
detached from the experience of habitation. The house concept
is expanded when connections are forged with the elements that
characterize the site - in this case, trees. By this, we do not mean
that architects should place as much attention on landscaping as
on the interior spaces of a house. The ties you can forge between
houses and trees extend beyond the design of a garden. The correspondences between the two are deeper and more complex
on a formal, spatial, symbolic and perceptual level, as we will see
in the case studies later. Ultimately, the network of connections,

06 Elza Berquo House, Vilanova Artigas, 1967

correspondences and coexistences between houses and trees expands the notion of domesticity.

The qualities of the trees enrich the experience of the domestic space. A tree grows, sprouts, spreads and stands tall, climbs and blooms. Additionally, a tree can be pruned or shaped, it can fall or whither, or be cut down and die. Similarly, it can produce new shoots, or another can be planted in its place, it can sprout and grow again. Trees, as living entities, record the passage of time. Standing next to a house, a tree offers a record of life implacably running its course. In this book, we will reexamine the temporal values of permanence that are wielded in architecture. We will see how the inevitable contingency of all earthly existence can be incorporated into design.

Trees can endow architecture with all their intrinsic natural properties: their adaptation to the change of the seasons, to climatic conditions and atmospheric agents. If architects forge relationships between trees and their designs, they will be able to incorporate attributes beyond the stable, immutable and enduring qualities that are characteristic of architecture. As a result, the presence of trees in houses will reveal the ephemeral nature of all human constructive action on earth.

There is, however, a tendency to continue looking at trees as natural elements after they have been incorporated into an architectural design or a garden. This is a mistake: from the moment a tree is associated with a man-made space, it becomes another artificial element in the design and, therefore, a cultural element. Cultivated. One more construction material - incidentally, the most ecological and sustainable one there is.

Trees, here, are considered a raw material and a valuable component of the construction because of everything they add to the house - in other words, due to the spatial, temporal, phenomenological, topological, programmatic and symbolic conditions they contribute to the design process.

Defining a tree by its morphology and formal structure makes it of interest to architects. Reduced to its spatial features, a tree has two clear elements: the trunk and the crown, structured in branches, leaves, flowers and/or fruit. As a formal structure, upright and lush, a tree can be incorporated into the architectural design process like similar formal architectural elements, such as supports, beams and ceilings, offering a range of different spatial qualities.

Finally, and no less importantly – although it does not fall within the purview of this research – each tree species is associated with a certain symbolism. Trees are connected with cultural readings and mythological narratives, with artistic interpretations and popular, religious or pagan rites. Ultimately, houses and trees, together, reveal how we inhabit a particular landscape.

Trees in the Mythological and Technical Origins of Architecture

Tree, like fire, are present in many of the explanations about the mythological origins of architecture.[2] Architectural designers, thinkers and theorists, without a doubt, have been drawn to the intrinsic spatiality of trees. We see this, for example, with Marcus Vitruvius Pollio (1st century BC) or the abbot Marc-Antoine Laugier (1713-1769) in a more naturalistic and symbolic vein. However, trees have also served as the foundation for explaining the origins of architecture in other more explicitly technical approaches, such as those offered by Eugène Viollet-le-Duc (1814-1879) and Gottfried Semper (1803-1879).

The primitive hut, made from tree trunks and branches, entered the architectural debate in the second half of the 18th century. A critical revisiting of the principles of architecture led to the adoption of the primitive hut as an imitative archetype. One of the most representative examples of this model is, without a doubt, the famous cabin that Laugier cites in his text *An Essay on Architecture*.[3] In its many illustrations, the hut is represented as being built entirely from trees.

The reference to trees is also present in an essential element of classical architecture: the column. The analogy between the column and the tree trunk, cited time and again by treatise writers, explains, for example, the decrease in thickness at the top of the shaft of a column. This similarity becomes literal in the column shaped like a tree trunk used by Bramante in the loggia of the Basilica of San Ambrosio in Milan, a gesture that seems to suggest its arboreal origin. We might also read a literal allusion to trees in an element used profusely during the Baroque, the Solomonic column, evocative of the Temple of Jerusalem. In any case, the trunk of the tree has been a source of inspiration for support elements in architecture on many occasions.

Trees are also represented in many designs by French Enlightenment architects. For example, in his Cenotaph for Newton, Boullée placed a crown of trees on the terraces around the base of his great dome. Ledoux's city of Chaux is also outlined in trees. Even in some of the architectural fantasies and delusions represented by Jean-Jacques Lequeu (1757-1826), the tree appears as an architectural inspiration and as a spatial structure capable of giving rise to a habitable place.

The arboreal origin of the structures of Gothic cathedrals were also formulated in this same naturalistic vein. The grove was a model for medieval temples, where the columns and the ribbing of the vaults evoked the interlacing trunks and branches of the forest. Their bright and colorful stained glass windows resemble the leaves and flowers of trees as light filters through. The tree as a spatial form, and its visual and perceptual effects, are architecture's original, natural and primitive points of reference.

Gottfried Semper, in his text *The Four Elements of Architecture*,[4] completely broke with the tradition started by Vitruvius and picked up from the 15th century by a series of writers who resorted to mythical narratives or stories to explain the origins of architecture. Semper, in contrast, based his perspective on anthropological research and an observation of the evolution of construction techniques. His proposal, also backed up by the

07 The Vitruvian primitive hut from *Essai sur l'architecture* by Marc-Antoine Laugier, engraving by Charles Eisen

analysis of numerous primitive constructions, explained the evolution of architecture through materials, construction techniques
and the characteristics of the societies in which they developed.

Semper's identification of the basic elements of architecture
made it possible to break with the aesthetic norms of classicism.[5]
This helps us understand the profound differences between the
traditional definition of architecture, as a representational art –
similar to painting and sculpture – and the definition offered by
Semper or Viollet-le-Duc, which situates it as a purely formal and
spatial art.

Based on the work of these 19th-century theorists, the concept of imitation in architecture was dismantled and the naturalistic attitude that upheld an opposition between nature and
the work of man faded away. This shift in attitude led to new
models in the relationship between architecture and its natural
surroundings. In that vein, this research studies the formal and
spatial, phenomenological and temporal connections between
houses and trees.

Purpose

The purpose of this text is to revisit and update the hypotheses of
20th-century domestic design based on a targeted analysis of the
incorporation of trees into the design of houses. The investigation
sparks a series of questions: for example, what notions or ideas
of place are architects proposing when they decide to integrate
an existing tree into the design for a house? How can time be
incorporated into architecture based on trees? What spatial con-
sequences are derived from establishing formal correspondences
between houses and trees? And how can we extend the house
into exterior spaces in order to generate outdoor domesticity?

The goal was not to develop a manual for domestic architecture, not to mention gardening or landscaping. The instrumentalization of the case studies focuses on formulating a series of
architectural principles and relational logics linking houses and
trees, resulting in three contributions to architectural design the-

ory. It is empirical theory, formulated, therefore, based on the relationships described, examined and experienced in the five case studies under analysis. The overall contribution lies in expanding and revisiting the concepts of place, time and domesticity.

The Five Case Studies

This research originally began with 10 case studies. They were united by the aspect that one or more pre-existing trees had an impact on the ultimate form of the house. They included Mies van der Rohe's Farnsworth House, where the diameter of the pre-existing tree canopies defined the boundaries of the project, and Charles and Ray Eames's house, which was built in relation to the existing eucalyptus trees on the site. After this first selection, a long search began for other projects in which trees were a focus of attention in the design of a modern house; it uncovered more than 100 relevant cases.

What at first might have seemed a rather peculiar, even exotic, attitude on the part of a handful of modern architects, little by little ended up revealing that many of the best designers of the 20th century had incorporated pre-existing trees into their houses as essential elements in their definition and occupation. Following this extensive compilation of houses with trees, there was a clear need to narrow down the list of examples to be analyzed.

The first reduction was based on how they could be grouped, since the possible taxonomies could be as varied as the number of researchers who might set out to classify and analyze the same examples. The second reduction came in the decision to work on just a few qualitative examples, precisely to engage in an in-depth analysis as opposed to simply compiling a catalog of cases.

The criteria for selecting a limited number of cases focused on obtaining a collection of examples that was sufficiently representative, both in terms of the different connections between houses and trees, and in relation to the chronological span of the 20th century. Moreover, the selected projects were also important with regard to the unique vision that the architect's complete work could contribute to the incorporation of trees into architectural design. The third condition was a consequence of the previous point: that is, architects who had published their thoughts and ideas regarding this question were favored. Therefore, all the selected architects had to have formulated theories to support their understanding of architectural design. Furthermore, they needed to have written about their interpretations of the role of trees either in their own projects or as part of their vision of architecture as a whole.

Finally, upon moving forward with the analysis of some of the examples, it was clear that there were almost always a series of recurring themes. These served as the foundatin for the conceptual hypotheses according to which all the case studies were approached. They dealt with formal relationships and the expansion of the domestic realm beyond interior spaces, the ties with the idea of place, and the treatment of time in architecture.

The five final case studies subject to analysis were: Villa La Roche (Le Corbusier and Pierre Jeanneret, Paris, France, 1923), Caesar Cottage (Marcel Breuer, Lakeville, CT, USA, 1952), La Casa (Bernard Rudofsky, Frigiliana-Málaga, Spain, 1969-72), Hexenhaus (Alison and Peter Smithson, Bad Karlshafen, Germany, 1984-2001) and Villa Pepa (Juan Navarro Baldeweg, Xaló-Alacant, Spain, 1992).

Although the entire span of the 20th century is covered by the five cases, the order of their presentation is not chronological but synchronous. This results in jumps in time from more current cases to older ones and vice versa, resulting in conceptual deductions that remain individualized yet connected to one another and complementary.

Thus, the sequence of the examples ranges from an attitude where the order of the architecture prevails over the trees to a design approach in which the inhabitants' experiences and the changes shown by the trees over time take predominance. Beginning with Rudofsky's La Casa and ending with Alison and Peter

Peter Smithson's Hexenhaus follows a specific logic. For Rudofsky, La Casa was designed toward the end of his life. In that sense, it was a testing ground for the reflections that resulted from his travels and later exhibitions and books. The design in relation to the trees also shaped his ideas about outdoor rooms conditioned for habitation. Likewise, we can observe how he employed and invoked architectural archetypes as the basis for its composition.

In Breuer's Caesar Cottage, which emerged during a period of re-evaluating the principles of the International Style, there was a desire to capture a more subtle connection with trees, since the architectural order remains unaltered by their natural order. The house intercepts the tree, and the tree crosses through the house, but each element maintains its idiosyncrasy.

In the Villa La Roche and the Villa Le Lac, we see how Le Corbusier and Pierre Jeanneret align the spaces – and their openings – with three existing trees. In this case, the architectural order is adapted to the geometric order of the trees; as a result, the trees also become an integral part of the composition of the house.

Villa Pepa, by Juan Navarro Baldeweg, sits halfway between the three houses that precede it and the Hexenhaus that follows. Navarro articulated the house around the existing trees, plus another three trees that he planted himself, generating a wealth of formal symmetries and fluctuations between them. However, because the architect is also an artist and he depicted the house in some of his paintings, his art provides complementary readings of the project: the tree functions as a perceptual element and, above all, as a record of time.

Finally, in Alison and Peter Smithson's Hexenhaus, the reference to trees comes from phenomenological and figurative approaches. However, it is an excellent example of how architecture can be connected to the ancient forest around it. In that sense, the connections between the Hexenhaus and the trees are more perceptual than merely compositional and formal. They are more atmospheric and temporary.

The five case studies, presented in this order, make up the first, analytical section of this text, from which a series of theoretical contributions are then derived with a bearing on modern domestic architectural design.

Endnotes

1 See the work by Luis Martínez Santa-María, which deals mainly with the relationship between modern houses and trees in *El árbol, el camino, el estanque, ante la casa*. Barcelona: Fundación Caja de arquitectos, 2004. Arquithesis no. 15. See also the study on Mies and his relationship with trees by Cristina Gastón. *Mies: el proyecto como revelación del lugar*. Barcelona: Fundación Caja de arquitectos, 2005. Arquithesis no. 19. For the relationship with trees in Le Corbusier's work, seeJosep Quetglas. "Point de vue dans l'axe de l'arbre", in *Massilia 2004 bis. Le Corbusier y el paisaje*. Barcelona: Associació d'idees, 2004.

2 This section draws on the ideas outlined in the article by Gerardo Arancón and Miguel Ángel García-Pola entitled "El árbol y la arquitectura", published in the newspaper *La Nueva España, Diario Independiente de Asturias*, on Wednesday, January 11, 2006.

3 Marc-Antoine Laugier, *An Essay on Architecture*. Los Angeles: Hennessey & Ingalls, Inc., 2009. See, especially, Fabio Restrepo's doctoral dissertation on the illustration of Laugier's myth of the hut in *Ceci est mon testament: Marc-Antoine Laugier* under the direction of Dr. Juan José Lahuerta Alsina and Dr. Helio Piñón Pallares, defended on June 12, 2011 at the Universitat Politècnica de Catalunya. This Enlightenment naturalism offers images in which the tree itself, without any architectural additions or manipulation, appears as *L'abri du pauvre* [The poor man's shelter], an engraving Ledoux included in the first volume of his *L'Architecture*.

4 Gottfried Semper, *Die Vier Elemente der Baukunst*, Braunschweig, 1851; English translation: *The Four Elements of Architecture*, by Bernard Maybeck, 1890, and by Harry Francis Mallgrave and Wolfgang Hermann, eds. Cambridge-New York: Cambridge University Press, 1989. Semper used the word *Baukunst* – the art of building – as opposed to *Architektur*, which also exists in German. See Hano Walter Kruft, *A History of Architectural Theory*. New York: Princeton Architectural Press, 1994: "For Semper the roots of art and architecture were always to be traced to the applied arts." See Antonio Armesto (ed.), *Escritos fundamentales de Gottfried Semper: El fuego y su protección*. Barcelona: Fundación Arquia, 2014.

5 Semper captured this in his book, *Style in the Technical and Tectonic Arts or Practical Aesthetics* (1860-1863), where he aimed to construct a new theory of architecture based on finding its constitutive laws, as though it were a natural science: he was looking for the primeval formal structures. See *Style in the Technical and Tectonic Arts, or, Practical Aesthetics*. Los Angeles: Getty Research Institute, 2004. The influence of Semper's theory was very significant in Germany, Austria and North America, beginning in the second half of the 19th century, and it is clear in the work of several major 20th-century architects including Gaudí, Kahn, Le Corbusier, Loos, Mies van der Rohe, Scarpa, Utzon and Wright.

Bernard Rudofsky

LA CASA

The habitable garden, the inhabited patio, or the atrium occupied by plants and trees form for Rudofsky a true open-air room. He used them continuously in his designs for houses to achieve an outdoor domesticity.

Compendium of an Architectural Vision

"La Casa" is the name Bernard Rudofsky (Moravia, 1905; United States, 1988) gave to the house he designed for himself and his wife Berta in the village of Frigiliana (Málaga) between 1969 and 1972. The couple spent their summers there until Bernard's death. In 2006, Berta sold it to its current owner, who, upon beginning renovations, prompted the Andalusian government to protect the property and its surroundings. But, why are the surroundings of La Casa so important, to the point that both the house and its environment need to be protected?

Rudofsky designed the house respecting the existing trees, the orography of the site, as well as the terraced slopes and the rock formations that project from the ground that is leveled off by dry stone walls. In fact, the blueprints show the diameter and position of each tree, and the locations of all the rocks and terraces. Moreover, the design brief, published in the 1977 issue of *Arquitectura*, asserted that the house "emerged from the circumstances" of the terrain.[1]

But Rudofsky did not just maintain the trees; he also established relationships between the trees and certain areas of the house employing an immense spatial, symbolic and sculptural richness. He considered how the spaces of La Casa could respond to the harsh summer climate – the time of year when the couple would be living there. This is evident in a letter he sent to Isamu Noguchi in which he writes: "Our house is built in keeping with Yoshida Kenko's recommendations, with summer in mind. In winter, you can live anywhere, but a poor house is unbearable in summer."[2] Adapting the house to the seaside summer in Málaga, using the native trees and a series of open architectural elements – pergolas, porches, courtyards, pools, Rudofsky was able to protect the house from the wind and the direct sunlight. Without planning a garden as such, he managed to create shaded areas with natural humidity among the pre-existing pines, carob trees and olive trees, defining habitable outdoor spaces for the summer months.

Previous page:
01 *Triclinium* on the kitchen terrace, La Casa

02 La Casa, view of the west façade

03 La Casa, view of the east façade

04 Aerial photograph of the site

Building La Casa gave Rudofsky a great opportunity to put into practice all the reflections and theories on domestic life he defended so assiduously in lectures, books and exhibitions. In fact, as a result of his frequent travels around the world,[3] - especially in the Mediterranean but also in Japan and India - he accumulated a huge quantity of photographs, which he himself had taken, of examples of vernacular architecture from different cultures and countries. This constant learning process, fed by traveling and living in multiple places, led him to write an enormous number of articles, which he eventually compiled into books such as *Behind the Picture Window* (1955), *The Kimono Mind* (1965), *Streets for People* (1968), *The Unfashionable Human Body* (1971) and *The Prodigious Builders* (1977).

Equally important were the exhibitions he curated for the MoMA, including: *Are Clothes Modern?* (1944), *Textiles* (1956), or the well-known *Architecture without Architects* (1960-65). With the latter, Rudofsky began a real international revitalization of vernacular architecture, contrasting with the radical - and widespread at the time - International Style. In that vein, Rudofsky centered his activity as an architect on discussing the meaning of progress and on updating vernacular architecture as "a point of departure for the exploration of our architectural prejudices".[4]

In the 1980s, he organized two other exhibitions: *Now I Lay Me Down to Eat* (1980, Cooper-Hewitt Museum) and its German version *Sparta/Sybaris* (1987, MAK in Vienna). In them, he reflected on different aspects of dwelling, including ways of sitting and the spaces dedicated to hygiene, as well as bedrooms and even the appropriate shoes and clothing for wearing at home.

These exhibitions, along with the books and catalogues he published, and the nearly 20 house designs he completed, either by himself or with associates, helped him establish a veritable theoretical corpus on the house and habitation. The analysis of La Casa in Frigiliana will determine the meaning of the relationships between domestic architecture and trees, not only present in the architects' designs but also in his thought and theoretical formulations, based on a critical revision of archetypes and thousand-year-old traditions of dwelling.

La Casa Adapted to the Trees and the Surroundings

Located on a cliffside typical of the coastline, La Casa sits on a small hill with views over the Mediterranean. There were a series of stone walls on the plot, running north-south, forming a terraced descent toward the east with areas for farming. Olive trees were originally planted on those terraces, but after the farming activities ended, the species characteristic of the Mediterranean woods recolonized the landscape.

The built section of the dwelling sits lengthwise along the north-south axis at the highest point of the plot. It is a single story, although it is made up of a series of stepped-back volumes "determined by ten old olive trees that could be preserved by inserting the house in between them", according to the design brief.[5] In addition to this construction, Rudofsky incorporated a series of five three-dimensional structures, like staggered pergolas, following the descending terraces leading toward the sea. As he describes it, "the half-dozen different levels weren't chosen at random; they are simply fitted onto the terrain, which is fundamentally rocky".[6] In that sense, the architect "not only rejected the old custom of cutting down trees and leveling the ground, he made a concerted effort to preserve the rural character of the landscape".[7]

The construction consists of two main volumes connected by a central porch – which, in turn, extends toward the east in tiered three-dimensional structures. The volume to the north is occupied by the more public areas: entryway, guest bath, living room, dining room, kitchen and storage. The rooms to the south, on the other hand, house the private areas: bedrooms, bathrooms and solarium. Finally, this volume is joined to the studio, the storage area and, adjoining the patio, the garage.

The different built volumes adapt to the terrain as it slopes down southward: the highest level corresponds to the living room

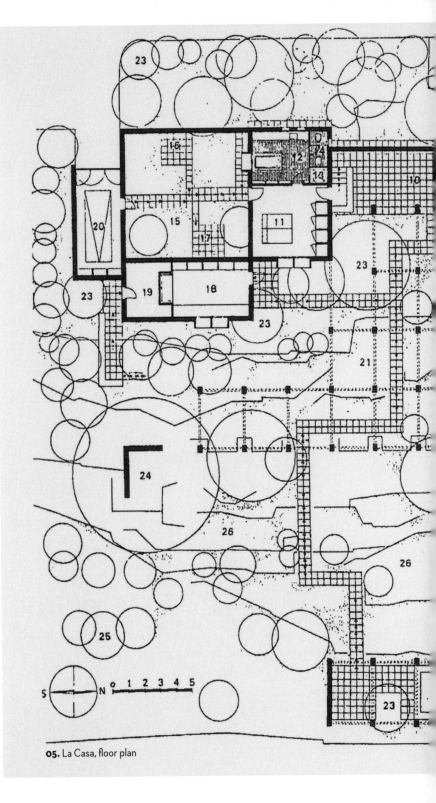

05. La Casa, floor plan

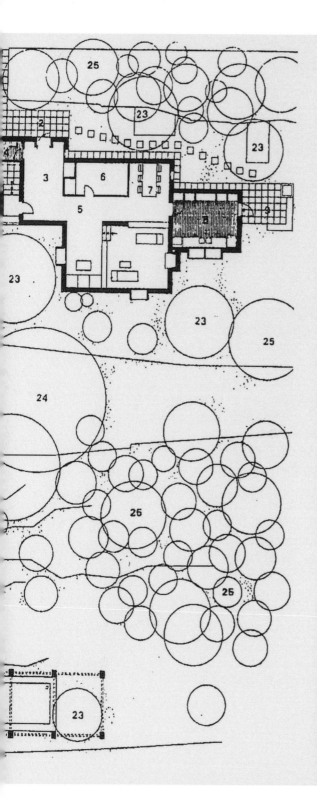

1. Front path
2. Entrance
3. Vestibule
4. Washroom
5. Living room
6. Storage
7. Dining room
8. Kitchen
9. Terrace
10. Porch or covered walkway
11. Bedroom
12. Bathroom
13. Shower
14. Toilet
15. Patio
16. Morning terrace
17. Afternoon terraces
18. Studio
19. Storage
20. Garage
21. Pergola
22. Pool
23. Olive trees
24. Carob trees
25. Pine trees
26. Rocks

and dining room, the second connects the entryway, the porch and the bedroom with the bathroom. The lowest level is the studio and the patio. Finally, the garage is located at the southern extreme. However, the ground level of each of the rooms is different. In fact, there are three steps between the entryway – which is on the same level as the dining room and the kitchen – and the porch level. The same thing happens between the porch and the bedroom. There is another considerable difference in level when you cross from the patio towards the garage.

The construction creates a broad spatial diversity in alternating the ceiling heights of each room, along with the ground levels of the different volumes. Despite this variety, both in plan and in section – intended to create a picturesque and vernacular quality – there is a continuous axis of circulation lengthwise that connects all the rooms together. Thus, the doors to the different spaces are all lined up in a sequence, stringing together the rooms and spaces with their different heights along a single linear path. Plus, this organization in a sequence moves from interior to exterior spaces without the need for hallways, crossing from one threshold to the next without interruption.

This lengthwise axis for circulation through the built volume meets up with another perpendicular axis. It runs beneath the five framed structures, made of thick prefabricated columns and beams. The preexisting trees and terraces outline the path's location and length. Whereas the lengthwise axis is straight, there is a zig-zagging movement followed by the paved path, with its stairs and landings. The central porch area is at the top. On a level that sits 18 meters below the porch, Rudofsky added a pool, or *alberca*,[8] under one of the five framed structures. The relationship between the central porch and the pool is defined by the stepped path and the five structures, following this crosswise axis.

The two perpendicular axes correspond to two different types of habitation: one, the longitudinal axis, creates interior rooms; the other, the transversal axis, lays out "exterior rooms" in relation to the existing trees. To condition these outdoor rooms, Rudofsky

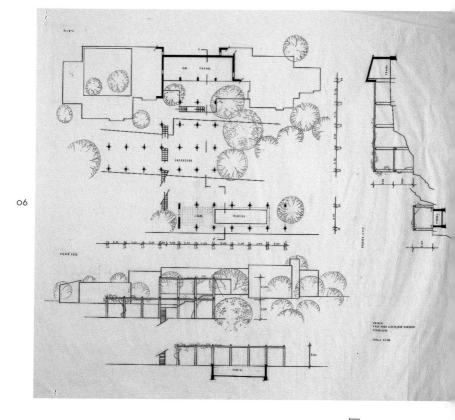

06

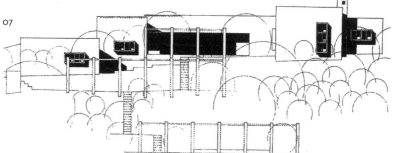

07

06 La Casa, layout of the five three-dimensional structures

07 La Casa, east elevation

built the five pergolas and a series of walls – parapets or wind-breakers – and he paved part of the ground to create paths and terraces.

Skeletal Architecture

The five, tiered three-dimensional structures are arranged according to a grid measuring 2.75 meters wide by 3.5 meters deep, and their height varies depending on the ground level. In other words, the five frames maintain the same distance between columns and the same bay width. The porch located in the middle of the built volume of the house provides the modular pattern for these grid structures, made up of four modules, although in that case it has a roof. Thus, the five open-framed modules coincide with the house's central porch. The final pergola, although detached, is consistent with the basic grid and the overall composition of the house as a whole. These structures generate a three-dimensional framework for the surroundings,[9] conferring a human scale to the site.

The two structures closest to the house contain two modules. The next one has four, and the last one six. The four frames are aligned along their north side, skirting around an olive tree and a carob tree to the right, both of which are drawn and numbered on the site plan. To the south, the four structures stretch out across the terrain according to the number of modules in each, letting some of the olive branches reach across the three-dimensional frame. The paved path between the four pergolas runs in a zig-zag pattern from one module to the next. The paving material, which is that same as what was used for the interior of La Casa, highlights the lack of a differentiation between interior and exterior uses.

The fifth and final structure sits at the lowest level of the plot and is six modules long. Of the six, the two southernmost modules include a paved terrace, leaving a tree pit for the existing olive tree. The pool occupies three more modules in length and the entire width of the structure. The final module frames

08

09

08, 09 La Casa, pool

another olive tree, planted in unpaved ground. To the extreme south, Rudofsky replaced the two columns with a whitewashed wall, which acts as a windbreaker and offers sun protection.

These five structural porticoes arranged across the natural landscape with its stepped terraces are adjusted to avoid cutting down any of the trees on the site, and they adapt to the existing changes in level in the same way as the covered pavilions do in the built volumes of La Casa. These structures recall the green-houses used for centuries by lemon farmers in Gargnano, Italy, known as *limonaie*. Rudofsky photographed them often on his many travels through Italy.

Rudofsky included a few photographs of the *limonaie* near Lake Garda in his MoMA exhibition *Architecture without Archi-tects* (1964). One of them was even printed on the cover of the exhibition catalogue. Later he added two more photographs of the greenhouses to the publication that expanded on the theo-retical written content developed for the exhibition, titled *The Prodigious Builders* (1977). It shows how he was impressed by them, to the extent that he built similar frame structures for La Casa, and also used them earlier in several garden projects he

10 The *limonaie* in the Gargnano Valley (Verona, Italy). Photograph by Bernard Rudofsky for *Architecture Without Architects*

10

designed: one for the painter Nivola (1950) and another for the Carmel family (1962-64). In both cases, he included a porticoed structure which took over the garden, organizing it and allowing for human occupation of the site.

In the short text that accompanied the photographs of the *limonaie* in the MoMA catalogue, Rudofsky added the following D.H. Lawrence quote, taken from his text *The Lemon Gardens*:

> All summer long, upon the mountain slopes steep by the lake, stand the rows of naked pillars rising out of the green foliage like ruins of temples: white, square pillars of masonry, standing forlorn in their colonnades and squares [...] as if they remained from some great race that had once worshipped here.[10]

The structures at La Casa let the trees reach through the three-dimensional frames they define, like what happens in ruins. Plus, Rudofsky made it so those areas could be inhabited like real rooms. In fact, he covered them in summer with semi-transparent fabric - or the canvas used for harvesting olives - to provide shade. With this simple system, he adapted the exterior spaces in accordance with what he saw and photographed on his travels to different countries, for example the covered streets of Japan, Arab bazaars, or the canopies in certain streets of Seville.[11]

Indeed, Rudofsky used the different forms and types of green roofs - grape vines, awnings, thatch, trellises - as archetypes. These natural roofs were supported by lightweight architectural structures, with the potential to regulate temperature, light and humidity, in addition to providing - through the plants and trees surrounding them - a multitude of scents, colors and even sounds. He summed it up quite eloquently as follows:

> What toldos are to the Spaniard, the *pergola* is to the Italian. The corresponding English terms - arbor, bower, covered way - are helpful but neither exhaust its meaning nor give an adequate idea of the pergola's many applications. Unlike an awning, a pergola is a three-dimensional affair, if ever so incorporeal - a pavilion without walls and

ceiling. It stands at the threshold of architecture as Nature's lobby, or, to turn the simile around, as the farthest penetration of architecture into the realm of Nature.[12]

Rudofsky was interested in the spatial component offered by the pergola. In fact, he thought of such structures like open-air pavilions – like real domestic rooms, despite their lack of walls or roofs. For him, greenery was inseparable from architecture, and thus natural from artificial:

> Raising a pergola is a joint undertaking of man and nature; it is planted rather than planned, with roots for foundations. The vines and calabashes, wisterias and ramblers are as much constituent parts of the structure as pillars and poles. Birds and butterflies supply the ever so volatile ornaments. No marble halls bear comparison to a fully orchestrated pergola with its vegetal arabesques, its sounds and scents.[13]

Walls Breached by Trees

Rudofsky managed to save 10 olive trees, two carob trees and several pine trees that were growing on the site. Of the two carob trees, Rudofsky treated the one located further south in a unique way, enclosing it between two walls forming a right angle in the southwest corner. His intention, among other things, was to protect it from the wind and prevent it from possibly toppling, since it sat near a drop off in the terrain.

Of course, the two walls enclosing the carob tree are not arranged at random; they are laid out to coincide with the two perpendicular axes which make up the orthogonal organization of La Casa as a whole. In this way, he incorporated the carob tree within the architectural order of the design. The walls have another characteristic feature: because the walls were built in such close proximity to the tree trunk, they make way for the branches to pass through via small holes. The holes look like windows, giving the walls a domestic air – like another room, although occupied by the carob tree.

11 Illustration of a pond with a pergola from *Hypnerotomachia Poliphili* (1499), reproduced by Rudofsky in his article "The Conditioned Outdoor Room"

12 15th-century illustration of a walled garden, reproduced by Bernard Rudofsky in his article "The Conditioned Outdoor Room"

In fact, this solution implemented for the carob tree was not an isolated instance in Rudofsky's work. He incorporated existing trees into the domestic realm in nearly all his designs for houses and gardens, developing an expanded idea of what could be considered as belonging to the domestic sphere. One good example is the garden he built for the painter Nivola, located in an old vegetable garden. The architect described it in the following terms:

> Here is an unconventional garden without gardening. The meager vegetation was left untouched. A few walls, posts, screens and pavements were carefully placed to set off the individuality, the "calligraphic subtleties of some old apple trees, pines and bushes of beach plum.[14]

Rudofsky also approached this intervention in relation to the existing trees as a jumping off point for the design. To that end, he arranged a series of basic architectural elements which interacted with the apple trees, pine trees and plum trees. He built a solarium, a barbecue, two benches, two three-dimensional frame structures, a fountain, paved terraces and three free-standing walls to act as screens.

All the architectural elements are once again governed by a grid, where the existing trees, which were unregulated prior to the design, become subject to the composition formed by the elements occupying the garden. We might say that the architecture incorporates and arranges the trees through its regularization, thus highlighting their individuality, while articulating them within the overall composition.

Nivola painted a series of colored murals on the walls of the solarium, as well as on two of the free-standing walls. However, the wall that was built against an old existing apple tree was left unpainted according to Rudofsky's specific instructions. The architect writes about this desire to set it apart, preventing the painter from turning it into a mural:

13, 14 La Casa, carob tree protected by the corner walls

A free-standing wall, plain and simple, with no special task assigned, today is unheard of. In a garden, such a wall assumes the
character of a sculpture. Moreover, if it is of utmost precision and of
a brilliant whiteness, it clashes - as it should - with the natural forms
of the vegetation and engenders a gratuitous and continuously changing spectacle of shadows and reflections. And aside from serving as
the projection screen for the surrounding plants, the wall creates a
sense of order.[15]

As a result, a random apple tree is individualized, and the new
combination of wall and tree takes on a sculptural character. At
the same time, the wall built facing the tree incorporates the tree
into its geometric order - an order that governs the entire exterior
space and, thus, all the preexisting trees. Rudofsky used the same
approach in those relationships with the apple tree as he did with
the two walls that surrounded the carob tree at La Casa.

Rudofsky was also enchanted by the effects of reflected light
and the projected shadows of branches and leaves on the surface
of the wall. Despite being recognizable for their natural outlines,
as the forms were framed against the flat stretch of the wall they
appeared as abstract figures, decontextualized from the tree.
They even seemed like ornamentation, as Rudofsky commented:
arabesques that changed over the course of the day and the year.
In short, "an ever-changing spectacle".

The architect reflected his interest in the shadows projected
around La Casa through his photographs of the shadows cast
by the olive trees on one side of a pillar. He also took pictures of
the exterior faces of the walls that flank the carob tree. Similar
images were also taken in prior projects such as the Frontini and
Arnstein Houses, which Rudofsky built in Brazil in the years before designing Nivola's garden.

Rudofsky asserted that "a wall has, apart from its utilitarian
and aesthetic virtues, a unique quality which radiates comfort far
beyond and above bodily comfort". On the one hand, we might
say that it is the comfort of being rooted in a place. In his designs,

15

16

17

15 Floor plan of Nivola's garden, Amagansett, New York, 1949

16 Nivola's garden, free-standing wall with a hole for the trunk of the apple tree

17 Photographs by Bernard Rudofsky of different types of tree branches from the Frontini and Arstein Houses, São Paulo

Following page:

18 Nivola's garden, free-standing wall with a hole for the trunk of the apple tree

18

this feeling of being rooted, grounded in a place, occurs because the walls are associated with the existing trees. That association, therefore, lets us generate a meaningful place. On the other hand, because the walls and trees are part of a new shared order, the inhabitant has a sense of orientation within the new place. The grounding and orientation given by the walls, organized according to a geometric composition, and their relationship with the trees, lets us feel the emanation of the comfort Rudofsky talks about.

The idea of having the tree branches pass through the walls probably comes from his collaboration and contact with Gio Ponti in Milan, where he was director of the magazine *Domus* from 1937 to 1938. While he was living there, Rudofsky designed two hotels with Ponti: one in Dalmatia (Croatia) and the other, the Hotel San Michele, in Anacapri (Naples). Neither was built due to the breakout of the Second World War, which forced Rudofsky to emigrate to South America. The solution employed for the rooms in the Hotel San Michele was an update of previous designs for seaside houses done with Ponti.

In the rooms of the hotel they designed together, there was always a outdoor space, like a patio, in order to "take advantage of the sun and the stars as if one were in another room, this one without a ceiling," according to Ponti. And he continued, "All of them have a patio with protecting walls creating a small enclosure taking in a few pine trees and olive trees."[16] In fact, one can see, literally, how in the drawings of the plans, sections and perspectives, holes were left in the walls to let certain branches pass through the walls into a different space, inverting the relationship between inside and outside, from one side of the wall to the other.

As a result, the ensemble takes on "a peculiar monumental quality",[17] as Rudofsky wrote about the old apple tree in Nivola's garden. It is a monumentality that he also found fascinating in old, or even collapsed, houses which have been overtaken by vegetation, as he captured in some of his photographs - for example, the ones of Morocco published in several of his books. In fact, he was always fascinated by ruins, "not by the ivy-covered, romantic sort, but by the intimate, classical kind, the roofless houses of antiquity".[18] In other words, by what they revealed about domestic life and the inhabitants' intimate realities.

The solarium he built for Nivola's garden is actually a roofless room – a pool, although without water. Privacy is guaranteed in its interior, expressly for anyone who might want to sunbathe. The solarium can only be accessed via a ladder leaned up against the outside wall. Inside, in contrast, Rudofsky added a built-in staircase against the wall, which provides a path down to the ground inside. The result: four low walls which monumentalize the act of sunbathing.

Again, we can see the genealogy of this solarium through Rudofsky's photographs, based on a vernacular construction from the island of Pantelleria called the *giardino*. Plus, he wrote a series of notes in his book *The Prodigious Builders* (1977), in which he described "a kind of miniature fortress, scattered about the vineyards." They represent "a single-tree orchard, whose sole purpose is to protect a lone lemon tree [...] from the furious winds". Such structure do not only exist in Pantelleria, Rudofsky continues; there are also similar constructions around certain fig trees, for example, on the island of Hierro in the Canarian archipelago. For the architect, the *giardino* "achieves the simplicity of a heraldic device" which "embodies the archetype of the paradise (a Persian word meaning circular enclosure)".[19]

Thus, for some cultures, the tree is considered heritage to be preserved and protected, either through an enclosure or a simple wall attached to it. When a tree is encircled or a simple wall is built near it, the tree is given a symbolic, sacred, monumental and even foundational value for the new place.

The Patio: A Room without a Ceiling
Rudofsky felt a deep enthusiasm for patios as inhabitable spaces. In a number of articles, he reflected on the merits of patios as full-fledged domestic spaces, even drawing up blueprints and developing theoretical proposals on the subject. Likewise, they were

19

19 Perspective for a house by the sea, designed by Gio Ponti

20 Perspective for a room at the San Michele Hotel, designed by Bernard Rudofsky and Gio Ponti, Anacapri, 1937

21 Floor plan for a house by the sea, designed by Gio Ponti

NELL'ALBERGO DI SAN MICHELE
ALL'ISOLA DI CAPRI

20

FACCIATA SUL MARE

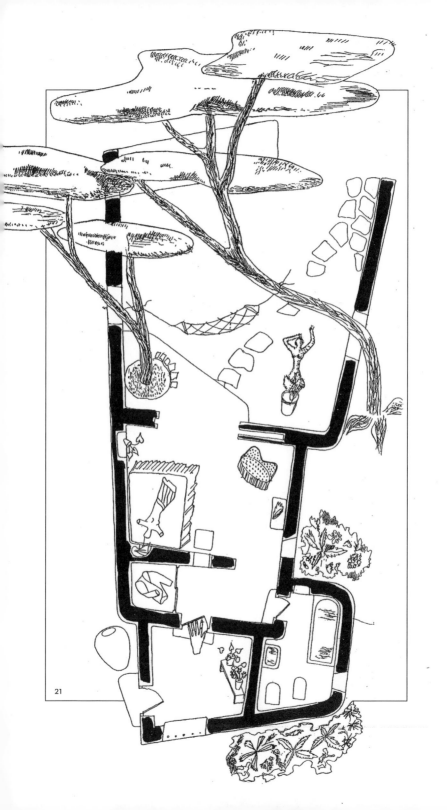

23

22 La Casa, shadows of branches cast across one of the pillars of the pergolas

23 Photograph of a *giardino* on Pantelleria island, by Bernard Rudofsky

central, essential rooms in the houses he designed. As he wrote, "The patio is one of the oldest architectural contrivances. It can be found in every great civilization."[20] He considered the patio an indisputable architectural archetype. He did not look at it as a simple garden of trees, dirt or a lawn, but rather as an enclosure used by many "primitive" cultures as a dwelling and living space.

A drawing he published in *Domus* in 1938 – which was also used in 1946 as a cover for the magazine *Interiors* – shows a square patio, in which the usual furniture from a domestic interior is arranged on the grass. The natural elements of tree and grass confirm that it is an exterior space, that it is outdoors. However, they are also responsible for making the patio inhabitable by providing shade, humidity, a microclimate; they climatize it.

This drawing establishes a clear parallel with the terrace of the Beistegui apartment (Paris, 1931) by Le Corbusier, which, although it is covered in grass, cannot be described as a simple roof garden. The presence of a fireplace reveals it is as another room in the apartment; although it doesn't have a roof, it is associated with an inhabitable space. In 1938, Rudofsky also added a fireplace to the patio in one of his designs, a house for his wife Berta in Procida. It was not until 1941, however, that he brought the idea to life in the Frontini House.

The drawing is a demonstration of what dwelling meant for Rudofsky in terms of outdoor rooms. In another article for *Domus*, Rudofsky drew a two-story patio occupied by two large trees. Part of the space is covered by a temporary awning. What is really surprising, however, is that he added a painting hanging on one of the patio walls, as though it were, again, another room in the house, with the same status as any other interior.

He compiled these reflections in a single chapter titled "The Conditioned Outdoor Room",[21] published in his book *Behind the Picture Window*. Here, Rudofsky offers a defense of exterior spaces surrounded by walls as spaces suitable for living in, which can be conditioned for daily use. For him, just as the interior spaces of a house need to be conditioned (historically with fire-

24 Solarium in the garden of Nivola House, by Bernard Rudofsky

25 Photograph of the wall of a house in Morocco, by Bernard Rudofsky

26 Photograph of a courtyard in Thera, Santorini, Greece, by Bernard Rudofsky

Interiors

27 Cover of the magazine *Interiors*, illustration by Bernard Rudofsky, 1946

28 Patio of the Frontini house, by Bernard Rudofsky, São Paulo, 1941

29 Terrace of the Beistegui apartment by Le Corbusier, Paris, 1931

30 Sofa-pergola, illustration included in the article by Bernard Rudofsky "The Conditioned Outdoor Rooms"

31 Sketch by Bernard Rudofsky illustrating his vision of the patio as an outdoor room, published in *Domus*

30

31

places, cross-ventilation, etc. and currently with air-conditioners, humidifiers, radiators, etc.), exterior spaces can also be conditioned using vegetation and the trees we find in gardens, which serve as a buffer against changes in climate conditions. Moreover, he suggests that exterior spaces can also be conditioned through the use of certain architectural elements, such as free-standing walls – acting as screens, pergolas, awnings, benches and trellises.

Climate control is Rudofsky's first consideration when conditioning exterior spaces. Climate, however, implies something more than mere temperature control. It also impacts diet, temperament, and even sexual appetite. In that sense, he wonders about the relationship between climate and the experience of dwelling.

> Does climate control really end at the doorstep? Emphatically no! It is but a question of making oneself at home out of doors. In a superbly layed-out house-garden, one ought to be able to work and sleep, cook and eat, play and loaf. No doubt, this sounds specious to the confirmed indoor dweller and needs elaboration.[22]

Rudofsky wondered about the uses of domestic gardens at the time (recall that the book was published in 1955, in the post-war era, in the United States, where the American dream consisted of a house with a yard in the suburbs). In response, he compared the gardens in front of houses to a formal parlor, used only occasionally: "Evidently, the current variety of gardens is not intended as more than an ornament. Like the parlor of our grandmothers, the garden is an object of excessive care. Like the parlor, it is not meant to be lived in."[23]

Rudofsky also criticizes the fact that the two spaces have no relationship between them, despite the possibility of huge windows ("the great advance of modern architecture"), since the glass acts as a separation rather than a way of joining them together.

> Paradoxical though it may sound, the use of glass walls in recent years alienated the garden. Even the 'picture window' as the domes-

32 Courtyard of the
Arnstein house, by Bernard
Rudofsky, São Paulo, 1939-41

33 Japanese House, photograph by Bernard Rudofsky,
used as an illustration for

Chapter 9, "The Importance
of Trivia," in his book *The
Prodigious Builders*

tic version of the show-window is called, has contributed to the estrangement between indoors and outdoors; the garden has become a spectator garden.[24]

The paradigmatic example of this impossible relationship between interior and exterior is the Farnsworth House by Mies van der Rohe. Rudofsky might have had it in mind, since the large glass panes frame the adjacent landscape, cutting it off, and, in turn, turning it into a "spectator garden" – or, as Peter Eisenman described it, a denaturalized representation of the landscape, a sign representing nature.[25] In contrast, when Rudofsky uses panes of glass, he treats them as screens, or sliding planes, providing a direct connection to the garden, the patio, or the natural ground.

Rudofsky discovered how these relationships and uses of gardens and patios existed in traditional Japanese houses. He also cites the courtyards in Roman villas and, especially, those in Pompeian houses. In the latter case, he was truly surprised by the vegetation that had taken over and the effects it created on the surface of the walls. From there, he built up his theory about patios as outdoor rooms:

> These ancient fragments are the nearest thing to a type of outdoor rooms which, I believe, will be or ought to be, a permanent fixture of domestic architecture. [...] Most of what comprises Pompeii today is a labyrinthine configuration of space; indoors that reverted to outdoors, gardens of a poetic sort, opening and closing on ever new vistas. Traces of painting and reliefs on the walls underscore the intimate, room-like atmosphere. A most engaging element is the libertine vegetation.[26]

In addition to the picturesque image of a patio occupied by plant life, he also praised the climatic advantages of the presence of green, which can be achieved in a space that is open to the elements. He expressed it as follows:

> Small walled outdoor spaces will maintain temperatures better than unenclosed spaces, which are buffeted by the wind. Plus, in

full sunlight, the walls act like radiators [...] By means of light-, temperature-, and humidity-controlling elements, perfectly conditioned settings are achieved for the different hours of the day and the transitions of the seasons.[27]

By conditioning outdoor spaces through the use of a combination of vegetation and architecture, domestic gardens become livable, private rooms:

> Domestic gardens as we have known them through the centuries were valued mostly for their habitableness and privacy, two qualities that are conspicuously absent in contemporary gardens. [...] These gardens were an essential part of the house; they were, mind you, contained *within* the house. One can best describe them as rooms without ceilings. They were true outdoor livingrooms, and invariably regarded as such by their inhabitants.[28]

At the same time, Rudofsky refused to place all the importance on vegetation in the garden:

> Vegetation alone, it seems, cannot supply the commodiousness which makes a garden livable. It depends upon the presence of some inanimate elements: a gate, a bench, a few posts, which constitute, so to say, centers of gravity in an agitated sphere of forms and colors, sounds and smells. [...] One sometimes gets as much pleasure from a naked pergola as from the stoutest tree.[29]

For Rudofsky, architecture was essential in making a garden habitable. The "inanimate elements" help condition the outdoor spaces for living, in correlation with the vegetation, and give them an order that contrasts with the chaos of nature. "The habitable garden could thus become additional living space and, in a sense, a nobler version of the house."[30]

The habitable garden, the inhabited patio, or the atrium occupied by plants and trees form true outdoors room in Rudofsky's eyes. He used them continuously in his designs for houses, from the house in Procida – one of his first projects – to his late sketches for an ideal house, in which each room is connected to a landscaped patio.

The house in Procida, widely published in *Domus* as the prototype for a country house for a single woman (it was actually a house for Berta, who would become his wife), defended the use of a central atrium:

> The courtyard is the real living room. The ground is grass with a few marguerites and veronica: in spring there will be violets and orchids. The sky, with its endless changes, serves as a ceiling. Protection from the summer sun can be found under a stretch of canvas. A fireplace allows for enjoying the long afternoons in spring and even autumn. Dogs, cats, and doves find a refuge here.[31]

The central courtyard was meant to be the heart of the house. A real outdoor living room. In contrast, what should have been the main interior living room was designated as a music room, and he proposed only using it as a proper living room in case of inclement weather. Likewise, Rudofsky installed two adjacent fireplaces, one in the patio and another in the music room, which shared a chimney. However, the two spaces are not directly related either through a door or a window. They are linked only through the access porch, between the patio and the outdoor garden. In that sense, he imagined the patio floor covered in grass, to create a continuity with the natural ground of the exterior garden: "The garden should come inside, not stop at the door."[32]

For Rudofsky "the floor is the noblest part of the house". In various articles, he praised the mosaics from Roman houses, or the tatamis from Japanese houses. That is why he represented the textures of the pavements in detail in his plans. His attention to the finishes of the pavements was not limited to sensations. He was also impressed by the richness of the floorings in the houses of those ancient cultures, precisely because they demonstrated that "it is possible to eliminate nearly all the furnishings in a home to reveal its floor".[33]

The same text included a sketch of a patio entirely filled with wild trees, above a grass-covered ground. In the middle of that wild patio, he drew a pair of chairs and a small table, as though it were a tearoom. It is a domestic scene. The jungle-like presence of the trees is contained by the order of the patio walls. The "outdoor room" is the house's real living room, despite that ambiguity in the drawing regarding whether or not there is a roof.

Rudofsky also added a patio to La Casa, with a square floor plan, connected directly to the bedroom and the garage through two separate doors. Both are aligned along the north-south longitudinal axis, which crosses through the whole house. Thus, this outdoor room is connected with the axis of the composition of the house's built volume. The floor of the patio adapts to the natural level of the terrain, descending toward the garage. Only two crossed paths are paved, coinciding with the north-south and east-west orientations. There are two terraces opposite one another on the east-west axis, arranged in a swastika shape. Two existing olive trees were preserved on the east side of the patio. In that sense, this outdoor area is no different from the sketches presented earlier, which served as the foundation for his theoretical conception of these "rooms without ceilings": the presence of trees, a natural ground combined with paved areas, and a direct connection with interior spaces.

On the other hand, the legend that accompanies the plan lays out two uses for the patio: the eastern half for use as an afternoon terrace – given its ideal orientation to receive sun from the west – and the western half as a morning terrace – receiving morning sunlight from the east. In other words, it can be used throughout the day, and is thus considered the true living room of La Casa. Moreover, the space is also the largest room (7.8 meters on each side), larger even than the living-dining room inside.

Rudofsky and his wife used the patio as another room in the house, beyond its use a private and protected place where they could sunbathe. In fact, on the patio, he and Berta were entirely protected from both the wind and the neighbors' sightlines, guar-

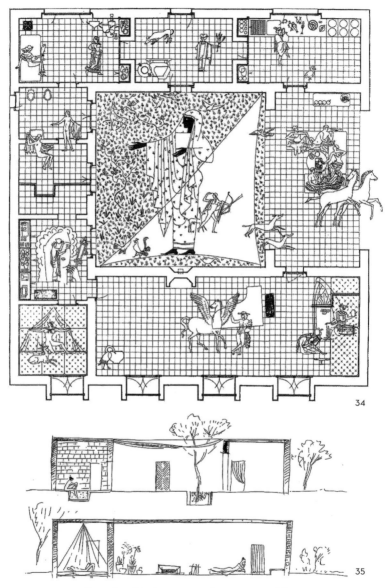

34 Floor plan of the house in Procida, Naples, designed by Bernard Rudofsky, 1938 **35** Cross sections of the house in Procida

anteeing them total privacy. It is no coincidence that the space is associated with the private uses in the house: the bedroom and the bathroom.

Ultimately, as he did in the design for the house in Procida and the houses in São Paulo, as well as the example in Frigiliana, Rudofsky always proposed a domestic use for the patios, pleasantly occupied by trees, plants, fireplaces, terraces and even furniture more characteristic of an interior room. In this way, the architect conditions the exterior spaces as rooms without ceilings, gardens that are domestic spaces for the daily enjoyment of the inhabitants.

The Porch: Nucleus of the House

The porch is another of the architectural elements highlighted by Rudofsky as a relational space between interior and exterior. The central space in La Casa ties together the rooms in two ways: lengthwise, between the day and night areas in the covered volume; and crosswise, in relation to the exterior space outlined by the three-dimensional portico structure of the garden. This covered space, closed on three of its sides and open to face the garden, forms the intersection of the two main axes of the composition. It forms the central nucleus, both for the covered volumes, and between those volumes and the exterior spaces.

As we saw earlier, Rudofsky built similar porches for his projects in Procida, as well as in the Arnstein House in São Paulo. Likewise, in both cases, he used this architectural archetype as a point of connection between the interior, the patios and the garden. However, one of the first porches he designed was for the Campanella House in Positano (1936) together with the architect Luigi Cosenza. A central open porch on one side helped articulate different areas of the house, while also acting as an architectural frame for contemplating the landscape of the bay. The space was, in consequence, the main room in the house.

Similar to the Villa Oro (also built in collaboration with Luigi Cosenza in Positano, 1937), the Campanella House sat on a cliff

36

37

above the sea. Before building the house, he had to put in a re-taining wall to the west to support the land clearing. The terrace resulting from the clearing is located to the east and is open to the landscape, framing it with a large double-height opening. Rudofsky affirmed that the intent of this central porch was "to blend interior and exterior in a single spatial continuum in direct contact with nature".[34]

In the Campanella House, except for the bedroom, located to the south, all the other functions are situated under the dou-ble-height porch roof, or opening toward it. Thus, the volume in the north houses the kitchen and the fireplace on the ground floor and the living room above; the living-dining room and stairway are under the roof. In the southern block, there is a lookout point/balcony on the ground floor, and a bedroom above. In the middle of the porch, the architects left two existing trees: a magnolia and a fig. As a result, the space again becomes the room that houses the private life of the inhabitants, in relation to the trees on the site, becoming a truly rooted place.

Plus, there is a kidney-shaped hole in the roof of the porch to let the tree branches reach through it (a solution that recalls what Le Corbusier did in the *Esprit Nouveau* pavilion). The hole is like the impluvium in the atrium of a Roman house. Thus, this room in the house can be considered an "outdoor atrium".

The design for the Campanella house, therefore, proposed inhabiting a largely open space, almost always exposed to the elements (except for the bedroom). The project is a manifesto on the part of the architects advocating for a domestic life in continuous contact with the pleasures of sun, breeze, trees, and landscape. It is a vision of the domestic realm that contrasts with what we take for granted: the house as a refuge or a cave, as an interior closed off from any relation or overlap with the exterior.[35]

36 Patio of La Casa, by Bernard Rudofsky, Frigiliana, 1972
37 Porch of La Casa

38

39

40

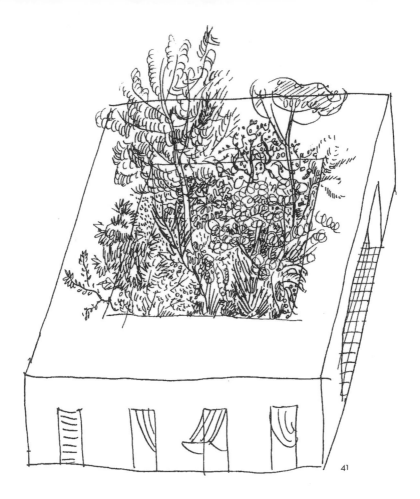

41

38 Sketch for the atrium of a house. Interior perspective, design by Bernard Rudofsky, 1934, published in the article "Variazoni", *Domus* 124, 1938

39 Bamboo pergola in the Arnstein house

40 View of the patio of the Frontini house, from the first-floor terrace

41 Sketch for the atrium of a house

42 Patio of the Arnstein house, by Bernard Rudofsky, São Paulo, 1939-41

42

In Search of a New Way of Living

"What we need is not a new way of building but a new way of living": that was the title of an article Rudofsky wrote for *Domus* no. 123, in March of 1938. The text was illustrated with drawings of the house in Procida. The article becomes, in truth, an early declaration regarding the redefinition of modern domesticity as referring to and rooted in the ancestral customs of habitation.

Rudofsky explains some of the design decisions he took for the house in Procida, such as his recommendations on the use of stairs. According to him, they aren't suited to daily life. He argues that they should only be used in monumental architecture. For that reason, the house in Procida – and nearly all his domestic designs – are limited to a single story.

He also reflects on the use of windows, lamenting "how wretched and profoundly bourgeois they are". In truth, he is referring to the fact that they tend to be at an uncomfortable height for the human body, since they are more determined by how we wish to appear than by the relationship we should have with our habits. "Ancient houses had few if any windows. The only opening deemed appropriate for a room was a door, because it was a passageway."[36] He justifies the fact that all the windows in the Procida design reach down to the ground, providing passage from the rooms to the outdoors. In other words, they allow for a continuous circulation between rooms.

He invoked the same considerations years later for La Casa in Frigiliana when he built windows with bays projecting toward the exterior, with the sole purpose of providing indirect light. Indeed, the exterior projection of the window frame, built using "'tabique' – the clever local technique of suspending bricks in the air", was justified as protection against direct sunlight. In the same vein, he added braided wicker shades on the outside of the windowpanes. Thus, the windows in La Casa did not establish any sort of relationship with the exterior. The doors, in contrast, as

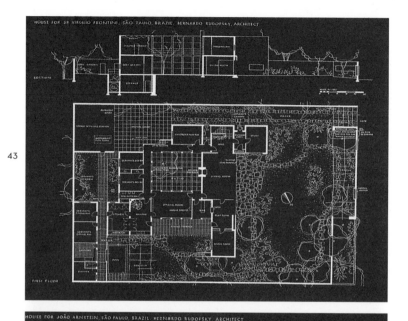

43

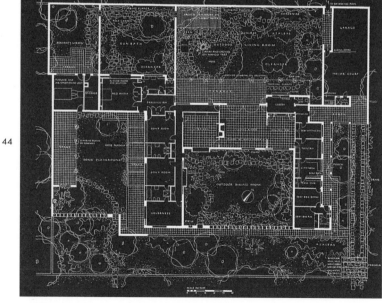

44

43 Floor plan of the Frontini house   **44** Floor plan of the Arnstein house

45

46

45 L'Esprit Nouveau Pavilion, Exhibition of Modern Decorative and Industrial Arts, Paris 1925, designed by Le Corbusier

46 Photomontage of the model of the Campanella house

Rudofsky had learned from ancient houses, are the true openings and connections with the outside.

Further along in the text, he makes a comparison between modern bathrooms and those of ancient Rome, when daily hygiene involved a relaxing bath, usually in a shared setting. In the house in Procida, the bathroom is a large room, with a sunken bathtub at its center. The other bathroom furnishings are located in a different adjacent room. A similar configuration also appears in La Casa in Frigiliana.

Rudofsky then reflects on the modern bed, burdened by headboards and footboards, metal legs or carved wooden columns, which, according to him, interfere with our rest. In its place, he offers a solid stone platform, a *clinium* to recline on. In the same vein, he laments that tables and chairs are designed as independent pieces and are specialized for each particular function. Instead, he proposes built-in alternatives which, along with the solid sleeping platform, create a U-shaped bench similar to the Roman *triclinium*.[37] He observed this type of bench or *podium* – made of stone, plaster or similar materials and usually found adjoining the wall near the front door of country houses or in hallways – in Pompeii. Along with the photographs he took of these built-in furnishings, he made a number of sketches including notes on their correct use, and he did research based on ancient murals and mosaics.[38]

As a result of this research, Rudofsky defends the ancestral form of eating – given that, according to him, eating in a reclined position aids in digestion – like the ancient Greeks and Romans reclined when taking their meals. In fact, going forward, he used the triclinium in several of his house designs. For the house in Procida, he included two of them: one on the open porch, between the patio and the garden, as a dining area; and the other, under an outdoor pavilion in the garden, a small auxiliary porch.

He also built a *triclinium* in La Casa in Frigiliana, just outside the kitchen, as an outdoor dining room for breakfast and lunch. The terrace is defined by a paved floor, which modulates a con-

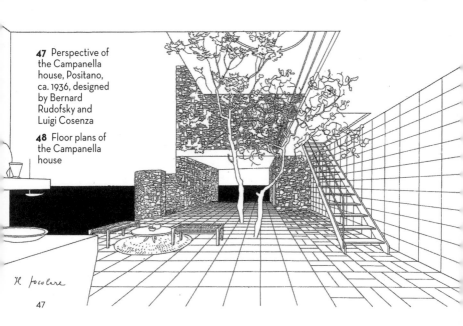

La doccia   *Il solario*   *la passerella*

47 Perspective of the Campanella house, Positano, ca. 1936, designed by Bernard Rudofsky and Luigi Cosenza

48 Floor plans of the Campanella house

Il focolare

47

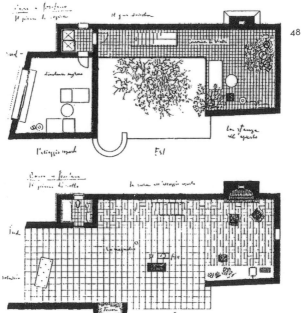

48

49 Perspective of the house in Procida,
1935, designed by Bernard Rudofsky

tinuous U-shaped bench. Rudofsky also added two more built-in benches against the façades: one in front of the door to his studio, in the shade of two olive trees; and the other as an edge for the small walkway that leads out of the back storage area.

As a result, the architect proposes a very limited use of furniture for his house. In fact, much of it was built-in, including the shelves in the main living room, the benches in the kitchen and bathroom, the bookshelves in the study, and even the handrail on the stairs descending from the entryway to the exterior porch, where there is also a built-in table for working or setting down objects.

The text by Rudofsky is a manifesto for a lifestyle based on customs of the past. In it, he proposed occupying the house with the minimum possible furniture, coinciding with some of Adolf Loos's ideas on "The Abolition of Furniture".[39] In that sense, his theory of dwelling was based on Epicurean and pleasure-centered modes of life. But at the same time, he advocated for a more restrained and austere lifestyle. Thus, he aimed to live both spartanly and hedonistically at the same time.

The Meanings of the Tree

Rudofsky put in writing his considerations on the role of trees in architecture in the chapter called "Brute Architecture" in his book *The Prodigious Builders*,[40] in which he defends trees as sacred elements. In his text, he reveals the symbolic status he associates with trees, their mythological connotations present from ancient cultures through to our times. In fact, Rudofsky asserted that life in the trees has always existed, since "trees form a natural roof" for man. He felt it was only natural for humans to feel the desire to hoist themselves up to live among the trees:

> Quite apart from their symbolical connotations, trees are among the most inviting, not to say poetic, of ready-made domiciles. To dwell aloft in an arboreal rigging and gently sway in a breeze, with the sun-

50 Floor plan of a *triclinium*, published by Bernard Rudofsky in his book *Now I Lay Me Down to Eat*. This layout consists of three beds, each for three people, set around a table, leaving the fourth side open for serving

51 Photograph of a *triclinium* in Pompeii, Italy

Following page:
52 *Triclinium* on the kitchen terrace, La Casa

53

54

53 Built-in table and porch railing, La Casa   **54** Built-in benches against the façade of the studio, La Casa

light percolating through a leafy canopy, appeals to an infinite number of creatures, including some of the less inhibited kind of man.[41]

Rudofsky gave the example of houses in the trees, including the people who live in African baobabs. He also included historic illustrations of nest-like houses in China and the elevated houses of the Orinoco River delta in Venezuela. For him, however, trees were not just used historically as houses by different cultures in different countries; rather, they inspired the foundation of all sacred spaces. In that sense, in the aforementioned article, he writes the following:

> The sacred grove was by no means a substitute for a temple. The wood *was the temple*, its trees the columns and the firmament its roof. The word *templum* signifies a section, a district, a visual field on earth or in the sky; by extension, a piece of land dedicated to a godhead, a holy precinct. Most houses of God, whether temples, mosques or churches, betray their vegetable origins. [...] Thus what we call a temple is actually the abstraction of a grove; the thicket of columns recalls the thicket of trees.

Thus, for Rudofsky, the tree as house or as temple amounted to the same thing. The fact that, at the same time, it could be a living space and a sacred enclosure was something he had very much in mind in both the garden and houses he designed and built, where the delights and advantages of the existing trees on the sites were incorporated into the projects. At the same time, the enclosures that formed the patios and three-dimensional structures were conceived as veritable temples of domestic life. It should not surprise us that his final project, called the Ideal House, was a series of rooms associated with tree-filled patios. Ultimately, for him, dwelling was equivalent to living with, near, under or atop a tree.

For the same reason, it does not shock us that Rudofsky developed a tree pavilion for the garden he was commissioned to design for the Carmel family in Michigan (United States, 1962-64).

55

55 Nest-like houses in the Pacific islands, illustration published by Bernard Rudofsky in *The Prodigious Builders*

56 19th-century engraving showing the elevated dwellings of the Orinoco delta, an illustration published in *The Prodigious Builders*

56

In the same garden, he also began by marking the position and exact center of all the existing trees on the site plan and then proposing the construction of three-dimensional porch structures adjoining the existing trees.

For Rudofsky, trees were true human heritage. Through his architectural interventions, he ensured that the trees became an essential part of his houses. Buildings and trees together, linked, intertwined, joined, gave rise to an outdoor space that was conditioned for daily life.

57 House in the trees, 19th-century Chinese illustration, published in *The Prodigious Builders*

Endnotes

1   *Arquitectura* nº 206-207, second quad-rimester of 1977, p. 96.

2   Letter from Bernard Rudofsky to Isamu Noguchi from September 13, 1974 in Andrea Bocco. *Bernard Rudofsky: A Human Designer*. Vienna; New York: Springer, 2003, p. 304. Yoshida Kenk (1283-1350) was a Japanese poet as well as a Buddhist monk. His most well-known work is called *Tsurezure-gusa* (translated into English as *Essays in Idleness*. New York: Columbia University Press, 1998), a collection of 243 short essays, published posthumously. The themes of the essays include the beauty of nature, the transitoriness of life, traditions, friendship and other concepts. It is one of the most broadly studied works of medieval Japanese literature.

3   For the influence of Rudofsky's travels on his ideas and work, see Alessandra Como, "The Voyage and the House: Bernard Rudofsky's Search for Place", in Xing Ruan and Paul Hogben, eds., *Topophilia and Topophobia: Reflections on Twentieth-Century Human Habitat*. London: Routledge, 2007, pp. 150-169.

4   Bernard Rudofsky. *Architecture Without Architects: A Short Introduction to Non-Pedigreed Architecture*. Albuquerque: University of New Mexico Press, 1987, 3.

5   *Arquitectura* no. 206-207, p. 96.

6   Ibid.

7   Ibid.

8   The word *alberca*, usually refers to an artificial tank, with masonry walls, for use in irrigation. However, it also has another meaning in reference to a building, when it is unfinished or has caved in, and it only has walls with no roof. Rudofsky used this archetype to design solariums as well as ponds or pools.

9   *Boletín Oficial de la Junta de Andalucía* no. 159, Seville, 17 August 2009, p. 51. RESOLUTION dated July 27, 2009, issued by the Directorate General for Cultural Heritage, which initiates the process for inclusion of the Rudofsky House, in Frigiliana (Málaga), as a cultural heritage site on the official list of Andalusian Historical Heritage under the typology of Monument.

10 Fragment from the essay by D.H. Lawrence titled "The Lemon Gardens", 1912. In Bernard Rudofsky. *Architecture Without Architects: A Short Introduction to Non-Pedigreed Architecture*. New York: Harcourt Brace Jovanovich, 1977, in Skeletal Architecture, illustrations nº 111 and 112: Exposed pillars of the lemon greenhouses near Lake Garda.

11 For an extended commentary on covered streets, see Bernard Rudofsky, "The Canopied Street" and "The Canopied Street Continued" in *Streets for People: A Primer for Americans*. Garden City, NY: Doubleday, 1966, pp. 69-104 and 201-232.

12 Bernard Rudofsky, "The Importance of Trivia", in *The Prodigious Builders: Notes Toward a Natural History of Architecture with Special Regard to Those Species That Are Traditionally Neglected or Downright Ignored*. New York; London: Harcourt Brace Jovanovich, 1977, p. 296.

13 Ibid, p. 298.

14 Bernard Rudofsky, "The Bread of Architecture", in Andrea Bocco. *Bernard Rudofsky: A Human Designer*. Vienna; New York: Springer, 2003, p. 200.

15 Ibid.

16 Op. Cit, Bocco, p. 273.

17 Op. Cit., Rudofsky, "The Bread of Architecture", p. 200.

18 Ibid.

19 Op. Cit, Rudofsky, "The Vanishing Vernacular" in *Prodigious Builders*, p. 246.

20 Op. Cit., Rudofsky, "Notes on Patios", in Bocco, p. 192.

21 Bernard Rudofsky, "The Conditioned Outdoor Room", in *Behind the Picture Window: An Unconventional Book on the Conventional Modern House and the Inscrutable Ways of Its Inmates*. New York: Oxford University Press, 1955, p. 150-167. The subtitle makes a clear allusion to glass houses with huge picture windows which isolate inhabitants from the exterior, trapping them inside like prisoners.

22 Ibid, p. 157.

23 Ibid, p. 159.

24 Ibid.

25 Peter Eisenman, "miMISes READING", in *Inside, Outside: Selected Writings 1963-1988*. New Haven; London: Yale University Press, 2004, p. 200.

26 Ibid., pp. 162-163.

27 Ibid., pp. 137.

28 Ibid., 159.

29 Ibid., p. 160.

30 Ibid., p. 167.

31 Bernard Rudofsky. "Non ci vuole un nuovo modo di costruire, ci vuole un nuevo modo di vivere. (commento al disegno di una casa all'isola di Procida)". *Domus* no. 123, March 1938, pp. 6-15. Facsimile consulted in Bernard Rudofsky, "What We Need Is Not a New Technology but a New Way of Living. (Comments on the design for a house on the island of Procida)", in Monika Platzer, *Lessons from Bernard Rudofsky: Life as a Voyage*. Basel; Boston; Berlin: Birkhäuser, 2007, pp. 262-270.

32 Bernard Rudofsky. "Variations - On the Floor". Originally published in Italian as "Variazioni", *Domus* no. 124, April 1938, p. 14-15. English translation in Op. Cit, Bocco, p. 183-184.

33 Ibid, p. 184.

34 Original in Gianni Cosenza and Domenico Moccia, eds., *Luigi Cosenza. L'opera completa*. Naples, Electa,

1987, p. 113. English translation in Op. Cit, Bocco, p. 270.

35 For more on the Campanella house as an expression of a lifestyle rooted in pleasure, as opposed to understanding the house as a refuge, see: Alessandra Como, "The Voyage and the House: Bernard Rudofsky's Search for Place", in Op. Cit., Ruan and Hogben, eds., p. 164.

36 Op. Cit., p. 7 in *Domus* no. 123, p. 262 of the work cited.

37 The term *triclinium* was used in ancient Rome to designate the room used for celebrations, where guests were received. However, it was also an outdoor space for eating while reclining.

38 See the article "Table Manners at the Last Supper", in Bernard Rudofsky, *Now I Lay Me Down to Eat: Notes and Footnotes on the Lost Art of Living*. Garden City, NY: Anchor Press; Doubleday, 1980.

39 A suggestion taken from Antonio Armesto on the use of built-in furniture in some of Coderch's designs. See Antonio Armesto, Rafael Diez. *Jose Antonio Coderch*. Barcelona: Santa & Cole, 2009.

40 "Brute Architecture", in Op. Cit, Rudofsky, *The Prodigious Builders*, pp. 49-83.

41 Op. Cit, Rudofsky, *The Prodigious Builders*, p. 54.

Marcel Breuer

CAESAR
Cottage

Breuer spoke out in opposition to the organicist tendencies that looked to natural forms as a source of inspiration for architectural forms. The Caesar Cottage illustrates the contrast of the natural world against the rationality of the built environment, without obstructing a mutually productive coexistence.

A House "Built in USA"

Marcel Breuer (Hungary 1902; United States 1981) designed and
built a small cottage for Harry I. Caesar in Lakeville, Connecticut
between 1951 and 1952.[1] One of the many pre-existing birch trees
on the site was literally intercepted by the house. The edges of
the area of interception were defined by a series of structural
wooden planks. The tree passed through an empty prismatic
space, elevated above the floor level of the cottage. Yet, what
was the architect's real intention in preserving the tree and incorporating it into the enclosure? What ideas about the relationship
between houses and trees were wrapped up in that decision?
Addressing those questions will be the aim of the following analysis, in which it will be relevant to first understand the context of
the period during which this summer house was built.

02

Previous page:
01 Detail of the structure and construction
of the Caesar cottage

02 American cottage published by Peter
Blake in his book *Marcel Breuer: Architect
and Designer,* 1949

The Caesar Cottage was built following the Second World War. By that time, Breuer[2] had built more than 30 single-family homes in different states, at a time that was marked by economic progress in the United States. It was also a moment when new modes of living were emerging, given the need to house 10 million veterans who were returning from the war, mainly in the suburbs of American cities where the domestic program was centered on the nuclear family, a dependence on cars, the mechanization of domestic labor, and the incorporation of a backyard for every house.[3]

Breuer contributed to formulating this modus vivendi when, in 1949, he built the prototype for a single-family home in the sculpture garden of the MoMA in New York.[4] The responses to the decision to incorporate a birch tree into the enclosure of the Caesar Cottage can be found in his domestic designs, in the cultural context of post-war America and in the theoretical contributions compiled in his book-length manifesto Sun & Shadow, published in 1956.[5]

The Caesar Cottage is immersed in the social and cultural context of the 1950s. It was selected for the exhibition Built in USA: Post-War Architecture, held at the MoMA in 1952, along with other notable designs of the moment such as the Farnsworth House by Mies van der Rohe, the Case Study House no. 8 by Charles and Ray Eames, the house Philip Johnson designed for himself, the Tremaine House by Richard Neutra and Frank Lloyd Wright's Friedman House, among others.[6]

The exhibition promoted new built modern architecture in, for and from America. The first call for projects took place in 1944 and the initial idea was to make it a biennial event; in the end, it happened only once more, in 1952, when the Caesar Cottage was included. The exhibition was born as a reaction to the International Exhibition of Modern Architecture of 1932, in which the majority of the designs came from Europe, except for six American architects and seven projects in America.[7] With it, the MoMA aimed "to show the growth of an authentic modern American style, its relationship to the American background and its debt to, as well as its reaction from, the 'International Style'," according to Philip L. Goodwin in the catalog's introduction.[8]

Breuer had two works in the exhibition of 1944, both in collaboration with Walter Gropius: the Chamberlain Cottage and the Ford House. In that exhibition, Frank Lloyd Wright's Kaufmann House became the main point of focus in terms of architecture's relationship with the natural surroundings. In fact, the catalog highlights Wright's new creative activity, put forward as a model, along with "a revaluation of that very dark horse - traditional vernacular building".[9] The chapter titled "A Building and Its Setting", mentions Wright again and the "romantic and emotional" or "organic" relationship he establishes between building and site, with which the new American architecture was associated, contrasted with the "classical and intellectual" approach of Le Corbusier, as a "pure creation of the spirit". The relationship generated by Mies van der Rohe, however, for example in the Barcelona Pavilion, as Elizabeth Mock describes it, "seemed to find the two extremes not wholly incompatible".[10]

Continuing with Elizabeth Mock's text, and moving beyond the different influences, she lays out the following particularity for American architecture:

> The modern American house becomes ever more intimately related to the ground and the surrounding landscape. Living space extends into the garden and walls of glass bring the view into the house. The boundary between inside and outside becomes negligible. Sometimes the garden actually penetrates to the interior, or the house may be set against a rocky hillside. Site irregularities are welcomed.[11]

The relation to the unevenness of the site, its pre-existing characteristics, is valued and upheld as something genuine in the new American architecture, contrasted with the more abstract and rational approach (according to its descriptions) seen with the architecture of the International Style.

Philip C. Johnson

HOUSE FOR PHILIP C. JOHNSON

New Canaan, Connecticut. 1949

The completely open glass and steel house is the major element of an architectural composition which includes outdoor sculpture and a separate blank-walled brick guest house. Spatial divisions in the glass building are achieved by a brick cylinder containing a bathroom, and by low walnut cabinets—one of them containing kitchen equipment. The red brick floor and cylinder are waxed to bring out a cold purple overtone. The steel is painted dark gray; steps and a railing are of white granite.

72

73

Marcel Breuer

HOUSE FOR HARRY A. CAESAR

Lakeville, Connecticut. 1952

A stone pedestal (housing utility and storage rooms) supports a wood box containing living areas, kitchen, and bath. Access to the upper level is by a wood ramp. Cantilevered beams at the narrow ends of the house have diagonal cypress siding bolted to them, thus extending in midair to fences designed to frame the view and insure privacy.

55

03 Pages from the catalog *Built in USA: Post-war Architecture,* featuring the Johnson House, by Philip Johnson, 1949

04 Pages from the catalog *Built in USA,* featuring the Caesar cottage, designed by Marcel Breuer

The substantial difference between the two *Built in USA* exhibitions was the fact that many more single-family homes were presented for the second, largely because of the economic boom after the war. It included younger architects and designs from different states. That being said, and despite the variety of the exhibition, in the catalog Hitchcock defended the surprising "homogeneity of American production. [...] Modern architectural design in America is today more nationally standardized – in a good sense – than is the building industry."[12] In fact, in nearly all the houses there was an open and conscious relationship with nearby natural elements, particularly with a tree or a group of trees, either in the foreground or the background. It is in that sense that the Caesar Cottage is representative of the desired interaction between architecture and the landscape characteristic of a house *Built in USA*.

Sun and Shadow

The revision of the principles of the Modern Movement arose from the appreciation of vernacular architecture and what tradition had to offer *as opposed to* innovation. Marcel Breuer was one of the architects who actively took on this critical role with regard to avant-garde architecture, despite having studied it during his time at the Bauhaus. This attitude was clear during his participation in the symposium organized by the MoMA in February of 1948, intended to respond to the question *What Is Happening to Modern Architecture?*[13]

The debate was sparked by an article published by Lewis Mumford in *The New Yorker*, in which he attacked what Henry-Russel Hitchcock and Philip Johnson had called "modern" and "modern architecture" in their book *The International Style Since 1932*, based on *The International Exhibition of Modern Architecture* organized by the MoMA that same year. Mumford asserted in his article that the curators identified modern architecture with "Cubism in painting and with a general glorification of the mechanical and the impersonal and aesthetically puritanic".[14] Further on he assured that even Sigfried Giedion, one of the leaders of the strictest mechanicists, declared that there was a new position advocating for monumentality, symbolism, and play with design elements such as color, texture, paint and sculpture.

Mumford's article ultimately defended the beginnings of a new style called *Bay Region Style*. According to him, it was born in California and it was an expression of the surroundings, the climate and a coastal lifestyle:

> The style is actually a product of the meeting of Oriental and Occidental architectural traditions, and it is far more truly a universal style than the so-called international style of the nineteen-thirties, since it permits regional adaptations and modifications. Some of the best examples of this at once native and universal tradition are being built in New England.[15]

It was precisely in New England where Breuer and Gropius built their first houses reinterpreting the balloon frame tradition and using traditional materials like stone and wood. They also observed the broad tradition of the American cottage built by the pioneers from England.[16]

It is symptomatic that Breuer titled his intervention for the symposium "On Human Architecture". In it, he seconded Mumford's criticism, saying: "If International Style is considered identical with mechanical and impersonal rigorism, down with International Style! Anyway, the word is an unhappy one, just as unhappy as 'functionalism'."[17] However, Breuer, in an ironic tone, also rebelled against Mumford's defense of a regionalist architecture, which – just by using wood (in the traditional fashion) – was able to surpass functionalism and contribute a certain dose of humanism:

> I don't feel too much impulse to set 'human' (in the best sense of the word) against 'formal'. If 'human' is considered identical with redwood all over the place, or if it is considered identical with imperfection and imprecision, I am against it; also, if it is considered

identical with camouflaging architecture with planting, with nature, with romantic subsidies.[18]

Breuer took up a position against both tendencies: neither functionalist (with a rationalist bent) nor regionalist (inspired by naturalism). Breuer's position was that of remaining unaffected by fashions or imposed styles. Later on, he showed the same attitude when faced with the notion of choosing between one position or another. He made this explicit in his use of the idea of "sun and shadow" to describe his main approach to making polarized architectural decisions.[19] It became the title for his book-manifesto published in 1955: Marcel Breuer: Sun and Shadow, The Philosophy of an Architect, the catalog for the exhibition of the same name, which became his personal collection of architectural design principles and a formal repertoire.

With "sun and shadow", Breuer was alluding to a position that could bring together the abstract principles of the new architecture, along with its sought-after humanization. Rationality could be combined with the use of traditional materials, performance with well-being, life with art:

> The drive toward experiment is there, together with and in contrast to the warm joy of security at the fireplace. The crystallic quality of an unbroken white, flat slab is there, together with and in contrast to the rough, texture-y quality of natural wood or broken stone. [...] The sensation of man-made space, geometry and architecture is there, together with and in contrast to organic forms of nature and of man.[20]

It was in that discourse where Breuer spoke out in opposition to the organicist tendencies that looked to natural forms as a source of inspiration for architectural forms. Conversely, his approach was to contrast the natural world with the rationality of the built environment, ultimately juxtaposing both orders without obstructing a mutually productive coexistence – as was the case, for example, in the Caesar cottage.

05

06

07

05 Pages from the book *Marcel Breuer: Sun and Shadow*, showing the Chamberlain cottage from 1940

06 Pages from the book *Marcel Breuer: Sun and Shadow*, showing the Hanson House from 1950

07 Cover of the book *Marcel Breuer: Sun and Shadow*

Architecture in the Landscape

A year after the symposium, the model house Marcel Breuer built in the MoMA garden was exhibited. The cover of the museum bulletin from 1949[21] shows a frontal perspective drawing of the south façade, opposite the house's main entrance. In the drawing, the house is decontextualized from the real urban situation in which it was exhibited. The illustration contains two large, leafy trees, standing very near to the house. One of them is in the foreground, next to the outdoor children's play area. The other, smaller tree sits behind the façade, in the access courtyard.

With this house, Marcel Breuer revealed several of the latent concerns in post-war American housing, such as the flexibility in responding to basic functional requirements using a volumetric and constructive framework with the potential for expansion. He also showed economy since the construction was carried out with a relatively low budget. But above all, and implicitly, this was where he developed a way of incorporating natural elements from the site into domestic life.

If we compare the aforementioned perspective drawing with the original photographs of the house built in the museum garden, we find that, indeed, the trees were located in exactly the same position as they appear in the drawing. In fact, the trees already existed in the garden, and Breuer took them into account when he decided on the location for the house, making them part of the domestic project he aimed to develop.

With the construction of this prototype, Breuer was not only proposing a new lifestyle for "a man who works in a large city and commutes to a so-called 'dormitory town' on its outskirts where he lives with his family", as Peter Black defined it in the text from the MoMA bulletin. Nor was it his only intention "to demonstrate how much good living and good design can be purchased for how many dollars".[22] The prototype formulated a domestic program in which the trees distributed in the garden, or found in their natural state in the terrain, became a decisive part of this peri-urban lifestyle.

The next precept, published in the book *Marcel Breuer: Sun and Shadow*,[23] highlighted the importance the architect gave to pre-existing elements on the site in determining the form of the house.

> The formation of the land, the trees, the rocks – all these will influence the shape of the house, all these will suggest something about the design of the building. They are an important starting point for any building. The landscape may traverse the building, or the building may intercept the landscape.[24]

How can trees suggest something about the design of a house? To answer this question, we will analyze the corresponding text in the chapter called "Architecture in the Landscape", the epigraph of the second part of the book, in which Breuer demonstrates and explains his theoretical principles.

Breuer starts by distinguishing the types of houses most suited to the topography and features of the terrain. First, he looks at whether the house is at the top of a hill or in the bottom of a valley. According to the position, and for the sake of lighting, the house will have smaller or larger glass surfaces, since "our nerves can't relax if our eye is not comfortable". Beyond the size of the glazed openings, what determines the basic form of a house in relation to the terrain is its position with respect to the ground. In that sense, there is a difference between whether it sits on the land or on "stilts". In other words, if the house is rooted in the ground or raised above it "like a camera on a tripod".

In the first type of house, the inhabitants can walk directly out into the landscape from any of the rooms. The second type, in contrast, provides "a better view, almost a sensation of floating above the landscape, or of standing on the bridge of a ship. It gives you a feeling of liberation, a certain élan, a certain daring."[25] The Caesar cottage, object of this analysis, belongs in the second category. It is a palafitte. And yet, Breuer concludes that the ideal solution is a house arranged in both ways, maintaining contact with the ground, while also rising above it:

08

09

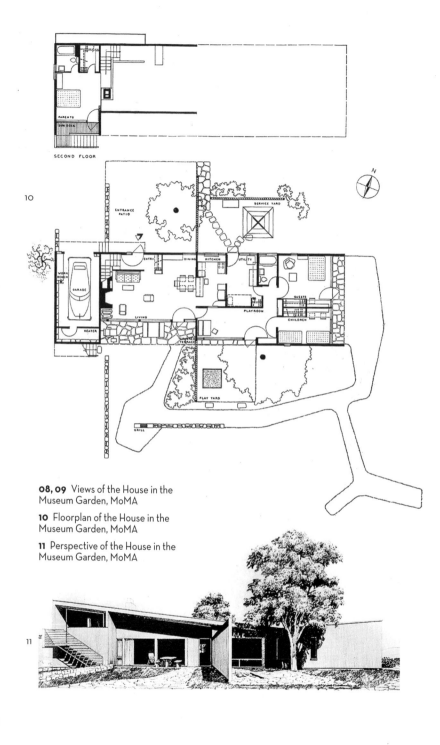

SECOND FLOOR

N

ENTRANCE
PATIO

SERVICE YARD

WORK
BENCH

GARAGE

ENTRY

DINING

KITCHEN

UTILITY

GUESTS

PLAYROOM

CHILDREN

HEATER

LIVING

TERRACE

PLAY YARD

GRILL

08, 09 Views of the House in the
Museum Garden, MoMA

10 Floorplan of the House in the
Museum Garden, MoMA

11 Perspective of the House in the
Museum Garden, MoMA

11

My own favorite solution is one that combines these two opposite sensations: the hillside house. It can be built so that you enter the top floor from the uphill side and the lower floor from the downhill side.[26]

The Caesar cottage also offers the second condition. Plus, if we look at the images Breuer used to illustrate the chapter in question - and most of the images used throughout the book - we find that trees are almost always present. Sometimes, the trees even push their way into the foreground, in front of the house being photographed. Other times they stay in the background, behind the built volume, like a backdrop for the dwelling.

In that sense, the trees appear either as figure or ground for the architecture. They frame it or highlight its relative position, in keeping with a spatial logic: behind/in front; far/near; horizontal/vertical; left/right. The form of the house is revealed, thus, through the dialogue of contrast with the trees. The house intervenes by taking up a specific relative position with respect to the trees. Breuer's architecture defends this relationship between what exists naturally - the trees - and what is manmade:

> A building is a man-made work, a crystallic, constructed thing. It should not imitate nature - it should be in contrast to nature. A building has straight, geometric lines. [...] I can see no reason at all why buildings should imitate natural, organic or grown forms.[27]

In the final phrase, Breuer was possibly alluding to the organic architecture espoused by Frank Lloyd Wright. In any case, he makes it categorically clear that his architecture does not imitate nature; rather it is nature that is organized according to the orderly and geometric laws of architecture, the work of man.

Nonetheless, for Breuer, "Nature and architecture are not enemies - but they are distinctly different." On the contrary, together they can be mutually beneficial, since the presence of a tree can be used in a design to accentuate the geometric order of the architecture; and vice-versa, in the same way, the architecture highlights the biological and organic order of nature. Breuer continues, in the same chapter of his book:

> I feel it is a great mistake either to adapt building forms to organic forms, or to adapt natural forms to the crystallic, geometric forms of architecture, as it was done in the Rococo period.[28]

That is why Breuer does not arrange the trees according to the rational composition displayed by his architecture; he does not include them within the formal laws of the design. Nor does his architecture imitate the forms or figures characteristic of natural elements. Following the previous statement, he asserts, "in the modern garden I would much prefer to see free forms, organic, undisturbed, natural forms – rather than 'charm'."[29]

In fact, at times, the exterior elements in his gardens – like the walls, verandas, balconies and terraces – approach the trees, surround them, mark them off, or even pass through them. In other words, they are arranged more freely, chaotically. However, that does not mean they are independent of the project's geometric logic; only, it is an order that extends over the surroundings, beyond the construction of the house itself. As the architect himself asserts, "whenever that happens, the terrace and the retaining wall is treated as a distinctly man-made thing".

As a result, when Breuer came across trees on the site, he determined to keep them intact, although he also incorporated them into the overall composition of the design. The trees would literally pass through the architecture, like in the Caesar cottage. Although it was the house, which, in keeping with its own laws of composition, was intercepting the pre-existing trees. Both entities, house and tree, thus struck up a relationship, a connection, precisely through the contrast in their orders: natural and artificial. Neither would be altered by the other, although they would both be referenced and reinforced or called into question.

In the Caesar cottage, and in many other houses, we see what Giulio Carlo Argan noticed about the Gropius house, a project executed jointly by Breuer and Gropius in Lincoln, Massachusetts:

The architecture doesn't imitate, nor does it dominate the exterior reality through the authority of its "rational" forms, true and immutable; it penetrates and inserts itself into the landscape in the same way and with the same fluidity as the landscape penetrates and infiltrates its varied perimeter, in its large wide-open terraces and its immense picture windows.[30]

Ultimately, Breuer used this method of arranging the house in relation to trees in nearly all his designs for single-family homes located in natural surroundings, whether amid forests or farmlands. But even when the trees didn't exist on the site beforehand and were planted later on, Breuer followed the same principle founded on setting up a contrast between the two orders: his architecture and nature.

Backdrops and Structural Frameworks

Now, let us look at the morphological relationship between the Caesar cottage and the pre-existing trees. To that end, we'll recreate the route the residents would follow from their arrival by car all the way out to the veranda, looking over the water. The Caesar family, like most middle-class Americans with a house in the suburbs, would arrive by car, coming from the city. They would park near the house, after driving through the existing birch forest. The relationship between cars, houses and sections of undomesticated nature has determined, in large part, modern detached houses.[31]

The vision of the cottage seen from the inside of a car would be similar to that of a drawing Breuer did of a different cottage, in Wellfleet (Massachusetts), in 1948. The house, sitting between the trees, is framed by the headlights, shining on the lake and the nearby hills. Both houses are single-story parallelepipeds, raised off the ground, arranged with their long sides parallel to the shore of the lake. Given the gentle slope of the hill descending toward the east, the point of view is from above the roof of the house, so they appear to be pierced by the tall, thin tree trunks.

The driver would park as close as possible to the house, or even under it, its height allowing, as was the case with Breuer's own house in New Canaan and in many more of his designs. Stepping out of the car, the driver would walk toward the entrance on foot. Along the way, he would be forced to circumvent the trees in order arrive at the ramp that bridges the difference in height between the ground and the raised platform of the house.

The Caesar cottage sits atop six thin pillars made of wood, the same material used for the structure and the building envelope, except for a low volume made of stone, which is used as a storage area for firewood and for a boat for sailing on the lake. The ramp runs perpendicular to the façade, on the side opposite the lake. The entrance sits nearly at the midpoint, as the left side of the ramp coincides with the volume's axis of symmetry.

Reaching the front door of the house requires the inhabitants to look at the façade head on. The perpendicularity of path to access the interior, defined by the ramp and the façade plane, is accentuated by the extended lateral planes and the small, cantilevered overhang of the roof. On the left half of the façade, the inhabitants would see the hills on the opposite shore of the lake out the horizontal window – as well as the dark trunk of an old birch tree passing through the house. On the right half of the façade, in contrast, Breuer placed the entrance (with an opaque door) at the end of the ramp and another horizontal window, half the width of the one on the left, which does not provide views through the house's interior.

Up until the inhabitants reach the bottom of the ramp, they always see the house through the trunks of the existing trees, which they have just walked around. They see the façade as a horizontal plane framed by two sides, the roof and the trees in front of it, as well as the trees behind, glimpsed through the living room window. The distribution of the trees in front of the house's façade monumentalizes the upward sloping path toward the entrance. From this point of view, given its transparency, it seems like the house has no thickness – it is a membrane, a surface floating before us, a backdrop for the trees, which stand in the foreground, facing the inhabitants.

Once they climb the ramp, open the door, and enter the house, the relationship between the planes that define the interior space and the trees they see outside is inverted. The trees appear at the far end of the house, in front of the lake. Now, they serve as a backdrop for the interior space. It is as though the façade we have just crossed has been shifted forward, leaving part of its opacity behind, since this much lighter plane is made of a floor-to-ceiling pane of glass: a huge window that opens onto the lake in front of the multi-purpose space used as a living room and bedroom.

The free-standing concrete chimney sits in front of this window, corresponding with the birch tree that crosses the open volume of the porch outside. The other half of the interior space, which houses the kitchen and a small dining room, opens onto the covered porch, looking out over the lake at a considerable height above the ground level.

The platform which supports this interior space is rectangular, with a proportion of 2 to 1 (two squares measuring 18 feet (5.49 meters) per side, which gives a floor area of 60.2 m2). The platform extends along its entire length toward the lake over a distance equal to half of the base square. The right half (following the direction indicated by the perpendicular axis of circulation in the floor plan) is paved, forming a terrace that is almost entirely covered, except for a skylight located above the kitchen window. The left half, in contrast – in front of the living room chimney – is uncovered and has no floor, although it is clearly outlined by the edges of the wooden planks. This space forms the floating enclosure for the existing birch tree.

Breuer created a third frontal plane, at the end of this path as you exit onto the exterior veranda, also perpendicular to the axis of circulation. In this final section in front of the lake, the surface is outlined only by its edges. The lines of the parallelepiped are formed by the wooden structural beams and supports. These structural elements frame the two exterior spaces that extend

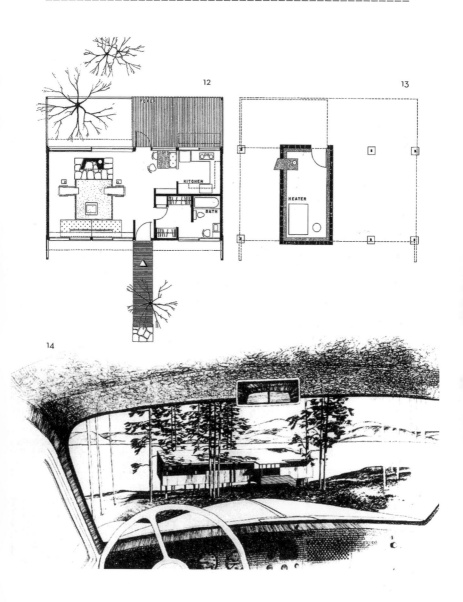

12

13

14

12 Top floor of the Caesar cottage

13 Ground floor of the Caesar cottage

14 Perspective drawing for a cottage
in Wellfleet, Mass., Marcel Breuer, 1948

15 Northeast façade of the Caesar cottage seen from the lake, Lakeville, Conn., 1951-52, Marcel Breuer

16 Front façade of the Caesar cottage

17 Veranda of the Caesar cottage

18 Entrance ramp to the Caesar cottage

19 View of the lake from inside the Caesar cottage

out toward the lake: the terrace and the floorless and roofless enclosure.

In this position, again, we see one of the birch trees in front of the frame and two younger trees behind it, growing right on the edge of the lake. This exterior porch, covered and overhanging, facing toward one or more trees, became a recurring and characteristic element in many of Breuer's houses. An archetypical space that relates directly with the existing trees, just centimeters away: a cantilevered veranda or balcony.[32]

In relation to the birch trees, all the cottage's main façades generate a system of backdrops according to the relative position of the observer. The trees function as figures, and the structural framework of the façades as ground; or vice versa, depending on where you're looking from. Three frontal planes define the sequence as you move through the spaces of the house, aligned tangentially along its axis of symmetry. The lateral planes, in contrast, are made solid, to square off and limit the front and back façades,

Thus, the house is a result of this system of structural frames and backdrops that guide the inhabitants' views in a single direction. The first frame is the most opaque and closed off from the landscape; it shelters and protects the inhabitant. The second is more decisively open to the landscape; it leads our gaze toward the exterior in the direction of the lake. The third is practically dematerialized or reduced to a minimum – the edges – and even disappears in some of the drawings; it stretches out in a cantilever from the built volume, literally floating above the terrain. The openness of the three main façade planes increases progressively as you move toward the landscape of the lake and trees.

Breuer described this formal strategy to regulate the number of openings in his façades in an interview with the magazine *House & Garden* in February 1970: "Usually I have kept the large glass areas to one side of the room, or to one side of the house where there is a view or shelter from weather. Then I made the other walls rather solid." However, when the interviewer asked Breuer to explain further, he replied:

> Mainly, because people need a certain background behind them. Personally, I don't like to sit in a room completely exposed to the landscape. I like to be able to step outside and sit down in the land-scape. But inside the house – probably this is rather an old-fashioned idea – I need some kind of hiding, some kind of protection. Also, I like painting and photos and souvenirs around me, for that you need large wall areas.[33]

Breuer thus made the back and side façades opaque and with narrow windows, adjacent to the roof plane. These façades en-sured privacy in the interior on the east side, where the entrance was located. A house arranged in this way is similar to a chair, which cradles your back, supports your body and sets you up in a position where you are facing single direction.[34]

For the architect, the house is configured as a space that directs the gaze toward selected views of the surroundings. It protects its inhabitants from the elements and from danger, as well as from outside eyes, acting as a sheltering refuge. Plus, the house intercepts the trees, incorporating them into the refer-ential system that intertwines house and inhabitant. By crossing through the trees, the house results from an intersection between the two orders: natural and man-made. Vertical contrasts with horizontal, but neither engages in a figurative emulation of the other. On the contrary, the relationship gives rise to a house that is adapted to a human scale, and a nature that is arranged for human contemplation.

Thus, Breuer defined the domestic space through the relation-ship generated between the façade planes and their degree of openness to the exterior. He used a similar spatial composition in many of his houses, which we can see in his other designs.[35] A formal system based on symmetries and asymmetries, balanced by oppositions between covered/uncovered, opaque/transparent, horizontal/vertical, in front/behind, artificial/natural, corresponding with his abstract principle of sun and shadow.

Paul Klee's Influence on the Caesar Cottage

Although Breuer was educated from a young age according to the functionalist principles of the Modern Movement, in his lecture titled "Where Do We Stand?",[36] given in Zurich in 1934, he outlined parallelisms between vernacular architecture and rationalist maxims. We see the critical view of those principles, albeit timidly, in the construction of the Gane Pavilion for the Royal Agricultural Show in Bristol in 1936. The walls were built in masonry, a pre-modern construction method. From early on, and even in his American period, Breuer incorporated aspects of vernacular architecture combined with the avant-garde.

However, he never fully left behind the fundamental principles of composition he learned during his time at the Bauhaus. Particularly, the abstract methods of composition developed by the artist Paul Klee (1879-1940), who was a professor at the Bauhaus during the 1920s, where he taught Breuer, both in Weimar and Dessau. In some of Breuer's early paintings, we can clearly see Klee's influence. In that sense, what Breuer himself highlighted in his short presentation of Paul Klee's work in the exhibition at the MoMA in New York in 1950, was the following:

> His paintings, free, fluctuating, changing and fantastic, display the strong and constant discipline of the composition: nearly always centric or symmetric. You discovered that the chaos of his studio, filled with many different tools, materials, paints, bottles, easels (he worked on five to eight pictures simultaneously) was in fact in pedantic order – everything in its organized place, neat and clean.[37]

From Klee, Breuer learned the "discipline" of composition: i.e., the rules of a logical construction of form. We find this kind of

20 Divider from the Breuer House II, New Canaan, Conn., 1951, with a reproduction of Paul Klee's *Senecio*

geometric relationships in the exercises proposed by Klee during the years both men coincided at the Bauhaus, as well as in the artist's drawings and paintings and in his writings and publications. Breuer was familiar with that material, and he applied the principles in his architecture and in the furniture and other objects he designed.

If we analyze the floor plan of the house, we find that, as we suggested earlier, its simple composition is based on a square divided into two further squares, organized along a central axis, although without generating perfect axial symmetries.[38] This modulation, derived from the division of the main square into other smaller squares, organizes all the interior partitions, the divisions of the windows and doors, and the dimensions of the interior and exterior spaces. However, the trees are not part of this square-based geometric system. Their location with respect to the house draws on a topological order rather than a geometric one. The

20

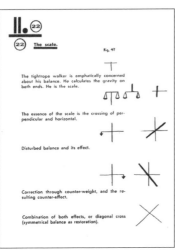

21

22

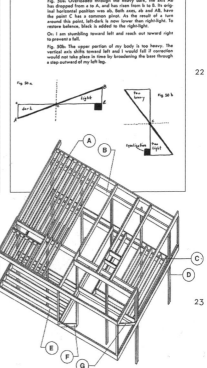

21 Model of the Caesar cottage as seen from the lake

22 Pages from the Paul Klee's *Pedagogical Sketchbook*, 1925

23 Balloon-frame structural diagram of the Caesar cottage

23

24

25

24 View of the Caesar cottage from the lake

25 Sideboard with display cabinet ti 66b, 1926, Marcel Breuer

26 Lattenstuhl slatted chair ti 1a, 1924, Marcel Breuer

26

order of the architecture is independent from the natural order, as we highlighted earlier.

Breuer looked at the relationships of balance that Paul Klee laid out in what became the second Bauhaus book, his *Pedagogical Sketchbook* published in 1925, and applied them to the geometric order.[39] These rules draw on the principle of balance defined by the intersection of a vertical line and a horizontal line, which, when the balance is disrupted, produces an effect of instability in the composition. When this is corrected using counterweights, it achieves a counter-effect that rebalances the whole.

One of Klee's paintings that best demonstrates this asymmetrical balance is *Senecio*, from 1922. Upon careful analysis, we find that, although they are inscribed within a circumference that is subdivided by a regular grid, the forms to left and the right of the central axis are not governed by the principles of symmetry, but by principles of balance and contrast: above/below, close/far, light/dark, square/circle, large/small. Take a look, for example, at the eyes, mouth, neck, eyebrows, the different colored surfaces; it all creates a pendular movement from one side of the painting to the other. A dynamic system, in movement, despite the centricity of the composition.

This same system can also be seen in the composition of the Caesar Cottage. It is evident, for example, in the relationship between the open and closed spaces of the porch. It also appears in the compensation between the living-bedroom and the kitchen-dining-bathrooms. Even in the trees drawn on either side of the central axis: the one that crosses the ramp is on the right, whereas the one that runs through the patio is on the left, balancing the composition, like on a scale, generating relationships in a diagonal that activate all the spaces of the house.

The same thing happens with the vertical planes. Let us look at the façade that faces the lake (in the photograph taken from the water or in the model). In it, we can follow the axes of the composition: the horizontal lines defined by the porch beams; the central vertical axis defined by the post. However, in the apparent symmetrical composition of this elevation, there is a new imbalance, mainly due to the stone volume on the lower level, which is situated to the right of the central axis, leaving the other side, figuratively, in a cantilever. The counterweight, in this case, is achieved through the shifted vertical line of the tree that passes through the roofless part of the porch, from top to bottom, and the chimney and water heater ventilation duct.

We see how Paul Klee's principles of equilibrium and balance were also used by Marcel Breuer, especially in this case. Further proof, perhaps more anecdotic than analytical, is that Breuer had a copy of Paul Klee's *Senecio* hanging on a divider in his third house in New Canaan – a house which was built, incidentally, in the same year as the Caesar cottage.

There is another similarity between Klee's painting and the 17th-century engraving Breuer chose as the initial illustration for his foundational text *Sun and Shadow*. Again, the illustration uses a composition divided along its central axis, which makes the opposites – night and day – enter into contrast, although at the same time they also balance one another out. An abstract principle equivalent to Klee's idea of balance.

Transition from Chaos to Order

Finally, we can address our initial question of the architect's intentions regarding the relationships between people and nature, developed through the design of this house and, by extension, the rest of his work.[40] To answer that question, we'll turn back to the text of *Sun and Shadow*:

> The real impact of any work is the extent to which it unifies contrasting notions – the opposite points of view. I mean unifies and not compromises. This is what the Spaniards express so well with their motto from the bull fights: Sol y sombra. […] And they did not make it sun or shadow. For them, their whole life – its contrasts, its tensions, its excitement, its beauty – all this is contained in the proverb: sol y sombra.[41]

The background of his text is a veiled criticism of the principles of the International Style, as we pointed out earlier. However, Breuer hoped to merge the technological and formal advances of the Modern Movement with basic human needs. Let's look at the example he uses referring to the transparency achieved by the use of large glass surfaces: "Transparency also needs solidity. And not only for aesthetic reasons, but also because total transparency leaves out such considerations as privacy, reflecting surfaces, transition from disorder to order, furnishings, a background for you, for everyday life. Transparency becomes more so next to solidity – and solidity makes it work. Sun and shadow." Indeed, "Neither one-sided over-simplification, nor tuned-down compromise offers a solution. The search for a definite, clear answer that satisfies opposite aims and needs is what takes architecture out of the realm of abstraction and gives it life – and art."[42]

Breuer applied this inherent dualism exemplified by polar opposites in all the elements of his architecture: in "support and weight [...] compression and tension. In the surfaces we use, there is color and texture. There is form and space. There is the building and the landscape."[43] We would add that there are houses and trees. Relationships between opposites that helped Breuer build, for the inhabitants of his houses, a transition from chaos (nature) toward order (architecture); places that are given an orientation by using trees as a system of points of reference. To that end, the house intercepts the trees, and the trees pass through the house.

27

28

27 Engraving used to illustrate the book *Marcel Breuer: Sun and Shadow*

28 *Senecio* by Paul Klee, 1922

Endnotes

1   For more on the cottage typology, see
    Antonio Armesto. "La villa y el cottage
    de Marcel Breuer", in *Ciclo de conferen-
    cias "Profesores. Arquitectos" Escuela de
    Arquitectura de San Sebastián*. Donostia:
    Erein, 2006. Harry I. Caeser was the
    father of Leslie Stillman, wife of Rufus
    Stillman. Rufus was one of Breuer's best
    clients and they became close friends,
    according to Robert F. Gatje in *Marcel
    Breuer: A Memoir*. New York: Monacelli
    Press, 2000, p. 30.

2   Marcel Breuer emigrated to the United
    States in 1937, where he settled in Cam-
    bridge, Massachusetts after accepting
    an invitation from W. Gropius to join
    the faculty at Harvard University. They
    coincided briefly at the Bauhaus, both
    when Breuer was a student (1920-1923)
    and later when he was a master in the
    carpentry workshop (1925-1928).

3   For an interpretation of this model of
    housing and its relationship to post-war
    American culture, see: Beatriz Colomina.
    Domesticity at War. Barcelona: Actar,
    2008. Beatriz Colomina, Annmarie
    Brennan, Jeannie Kim. *Cold War, Hot
    Houses: Inventing Postwar Culture, from
    Cockpit to Playboy*. New York: Princeton
    Architectural Press, 2004. Georges
    Teyssot, ed. *The American Lawn*. New
    York; Montreal: Princeton Architectural
    Press; CCA, 1999.

4   See Op. Cit., Driller, *Breuer Houses*,
    pp.180-189. Unpublished thesis by Caro-
    lyn Mae Lie, *Constructing an American
    Modernism: Marcel Breuer's House in the
    Museum Garden (1949) and the Museum
    of Modern Art of New York*. New York:
    Bard College, 2006.

5   Marcel Breuer. *Marcel Breuer: Sun and
    Shadow, The Philosophy of an Architect*.
    New York: Dodd, Mead & Company,
    1956. For a broad analysis of the publi-
    cation, see Antonio Armesto. "Quince
    casas americanas de Marcel Breuer
    (1938-1965)". *2G: Revista Internacional
    de Arquitectura*, no. 17, Marcel Breuer:
    Casas americanas = American houses,
    2001, part 3: Una arquitectura con reglas.

    Sol y sombra, teoría y práctica, forma y
    materia, pp. 9-14.

6   Henry-Russell Hitchcock and Arthur
    Drexler in *Built in USA: Post-War Archi-
    tecture*. New York: Museum of Modern
    Art, 1952.

7   See Hitchcock, Henry-Rusell; Johnson,
    Philip. *The International Style: Architec-
    ture since 1922*. New York: W. W. Norton
    & Company, 1932.

8   Op. Cit, Goodwin, "Preface" in *Built in
    USA: 1932-1944*, p. 5.

9   "A revaluation of that very dark horse
    —traditional vernacular building." Ibid., p.
    14.

10 Ibid., p. 22.

11 Ibid.

12 Op. Cit., Hitchcock, "Introduction" ed.
    Henry-Russell Hitchcock and Arthur
    Drexler in *Built in USA: Post-War Archi-
    tecture*, pp. 12-14.

13 Participants in the symposium included:
    Barr, Alfred Hamilton, Henry Russell
    Hitchcock, Walter Gropius, George
    Nelson, Ralph T. Walter, Christopher Tun-
    nard, Frederick Albert Gutheim, Marcel
    Breuer, Peter Blake, Gerhard Kallmann,
    Talbot Hamlin, and Lewis Mumford.
    Published in: "What Is Happening to
    Modern Architecture? A Symposium at
    the Museum of Modern Art". *Bulletin* 15,
    no. 4, The Museum of Modern Art, 1948.

14 Ibid., p. 4.

15 Ibid.

16 See the analysis by Antonio Armesto on
    the influence on Breuer of the English
    tradition of domestic architecture. Op.
    Cit. Armesto, 2G, pp. 16-18.

17 Marcel Breuer, "Human Architecture" in
    Bulletin 15, no. 3, The Museum of Modern
    Art, Spring 1948, p. 15.

18 Ibid.

19 Breuer probably took the idea of sun
    and shadow from his travels through
    Spain in 1931, when he visited bull rings
    (with their circular floor plans) where the
    tickets are divided into sections depend-
    ing on whether the seat is in the sunny or
    the shaded area of the arena.

20 Op. Cit. Breuer, "Human Architecture", p.
    15.

21 House in the Museum Garden, *Bulletin* 16, no. 1. The Museum of Modern Art, 1949.

22 Peter Blake, "The House in the Museum Garden." Op. Cit. *Bulletin* 16, no. 1, p. 1.

23 The notes and texts from the book *Marcel Breuer: Sun and Shadow. The Philosophy of an Architect* were edited by Peter Blake, based on the recordings of his conversations with Marcel Breuer, aiming to preserve their spontaneous and informal character, although the book was conceived and supervised by the architect. Something that stands out about the book is its horizontal format, although it is bound vertically. The introduction states that the idea was to adapt the book to the landscape format of the photographs. The design by Alexey Brodovitch is structured via a four-column grid. The axis of symmetry is used to lay out the text boxes on either side – in two colums – with the images or the drawings. The way the book is read, given its peculiar binding, leads the reader to look at the closest page first (i.e., the bottom page) since in the vertical format the right-hand (odd numbered) page also comes into view first. In consequence, the titles on the opening line of each chapter are placed on that page. As we will see later on, the book's design follows the same rules of composition as those of the architecture, both in how the pages are laid out and in the reader's movements in turning the pages. See the sections called "Backdrops and Structural Frameworks" and "Paul Klee's Balance: *Senecio*".

24 Marcel Breuer. "Architecture in the Landscape", in Op. Cit., Breuer, *Marcel Breuer: Sun and Shadow. The Philosophy of an Architect*, p. 41.

25 Marcel Breuer, "Architecture in the Landscape", Ibid, p. 40.

26 Ibid, pp. 40-41.

27 Ibid., p. 38.

28 Ibid.

29 Ibid.

30 Giulio Carlo Argan. *Walter Gropius y el Bauhaus*. Buenos Aires: Nueva Visión, 1961, p. 128.

31 It is worth recalling that the American expansion into the suburbs was possible because of the automobile. With cars, people could live outside the city, far from their places of work, in independent family units and in contact with nature.

32 Breuer used this floating veranda in several of his houses, for example, the entrance porch of the Chamberlain cottage, as well as several of the cottages in Wellfleet, in Cape Cod. It also appears in the second house he designed for himself in New Canaan, from 1947.

33 *House & Garden* 137, no. 2, 1970, p. 12, pp. 16-17.

34 The structural framework of the Caesar cottage is a three-dimensional bar-based construction. The supports are continuous from the ground up to the roof structure, and thus tectonic in nature. Later, the structure was literally wrapped in wooden boards on both sides, interior and exterior. The entire structural framework is reinforced woodwork. The house is built through dry construction except for the concrete chimney and the boiler room, on the ground floor, which is clad in stone. If we look at the first chairs that Breuer built as a student in the Bauhaus carpentry shop, we see that he uses that same structural principles to create load-bearing forms. This adds another layer to the analogy, since the seat and the back of a chair are surfaces supported by the framework so the space that is created can be occupied. In that sense, we might say that the Caesar cottage is like a chair sitting on top of the landscape.

35 There are many cases in which Breuer incorporated trees crossing through open courtyards or marking the entrance. They include, notably, the following: Harnischmacher House I, Wiesbaden, 1932. Doldertal Apartment houses, Zurich,1932-1936 (with Alfred and Emil Roth). Frank House, Pittsburg, Pennsylvania,

1938-40, (with W. Gropius). Chamberlain cottage, Wayland, Massachusetts, 1940-41, (with W. Gropius). House on the Beach, Miami, Florida, 1945. Breuer House II, New Canaan, Connecticut, 1947-48. Kniffin House, New Canaan, Connecticut, 1947-48 (with E. Noyes). House in the Museum Garden, MoMA, New York, New York, 1949. Hanson House, Lloyd Harbor, Long Island, New York, 1950-51. Gagarin House, Litchfield, Connecticut, 1953-56. Hooper House II, Baltimore County, Maryland, 1956-59. Koerfer House, Ascona, Ticino, 1963-67. Stillman House II, Litchfield, Connecticut, 1964-65. Geller House II, Lawrence, Long Island, New York, 1967-69. They also include other non-residential designs such as the Servicemen's Memorial, Cambridge, 1945; or Saint John's University and Abbey, Collegeville, Minesotta, 1953.

36 "It may, perhaps, seem paradoxical to establish a parallel between certain aspects of vernacular architecture, or national art, and the Modern Movement. All the same, it is interesting to see that these two diametrically opposed tendencies have two characteristics in common: the impersonal character of their forms; and a tendency to develop along typical, rational lines that are unaffected by passing fashions. It is probably these traits that make genuine peasant art so sympathetic to us – though the sympathy it arouses is a purely platonic one." Op. Cit, Breuer, "Where Do We Stand?" in *Architecture and Design, 1890-1939*, 1975. Craston Jones, *Marcel Breuer. Buildings and Projects 1921-1961*. New York: Frederick A. Praeger, 1962, pp. 259-261.

37 Marcel Breuer, "On Paul Klee" in Op. Cit, Jones, pp. 256-257.

38 Op. Cit. *Sun and Shadow*, pp. 10-11.

39 The argument of his *Pedagogical Sketchbook* is based on the line as a fundamental element in form. He analyzes how the line can generate planes through movement. What kind of optical reaction it produces in our eye, as well as the psychological impression. To that end, Klee divides the book into four parts: the first is dedicated to the line and its progression toward generating a plane; the second is dedicated to analyzing the third dimension and its optical and psychological effects; the third part deals with the earthly elements (land, water, air) as energy projection; and the fourth deals with the symbols of centripetal and centrifugal movement and of color. Paul Klee, *Pedagogical Sketchbook*. New York: F. A. Praeger, 1953.

40 As Josep Quetglas writes, "It is possible that every architect, wittingly or not, has always formulated an idea of the relationships between humans and nature, a definition of people's place in the world, and that it is precisely in the form of houses where that idea is expressed." Josep Quetglas, *Les Heures Claires. Proyecto y arquitectura en la Villa Savoye de Le Corbusier y Pierre Jeanneret*. Barcelona: Massilia, 2008, p. 488.

41 Op. Cit. *Sun and Shadow*, p. 32.

42 Ibid. p. 35.

43 Ibid, p. 34.

Le Corbusier and Pierre Jeanneret

Villa
LA
ROCHE

For Le Corbusier, bringing the "essential joys" into dwellings implied generating a frame for the landscape: a large picture window, an enclosure that would bring the trees into the of the house. A "room installed in front of the site".

Cohabitation between People and Nature

"Plant more trees!" With this motto, Le Corbusier (Le Chaux-de-Fonds, 1887; Cape Martin, 1965) argued that trees should be planted in every modern city. For him, trees "support our physical and moral wellbeing".[1] His inspiration was Istanbul, as can be gathered from his sketches from his travels to the east, along with notes that make it explicit: "Everywhere, trees grow around the houses: a pleasant coexistence between humanity and nature." He adopted the Turkish aphorism that says: "Wherever we build, we plant trees."[2]

In fact, whenever Le Corbusier came upon an existing tree on a design site, it was immediately incorporated into the overall design process. This was the case with his Villa La Roche-Jeanneret, as we will see later. Yet, from his first houses in La Chaux-de-Fonds to his last houses in India – as well as other designs with larger scales and varied programs, like the convent of La Tourette or the Carpenter Center, as well as the Pavilion de L'Esprit Nouveau from 1925, which helped cement his idea of *Immuebles-Villas*, where each apartment is intended to offer the benefits of a small house with a yard – Le Corbusier paid attention to his architecture's relationship with trees.[3]

And yet, how did Le Corbusier associate the trees with the design of a house? What was the goal in connecting trees to his architecture? How was that coexistence perceived by the inhabitants? We will respond to all these questions in the following pages through an analysis of the Villa La Roche and the Villa Le Lac since in both designs, trees were taken into account from the initial idea through to the later stages of development.

Three Trees at the Villa La Roche

The design for the Villa La Roche-Jeanneret was published in the first volume of the complete works of Le Corbusier and Pierre Jeanneret (1910-1929) under the title "Design for a villa in Auteuil, initial design for a double house". The site for this initial design ran lengthwise along rue Doctor Blanche, in Auteuil, Paris. In March

02

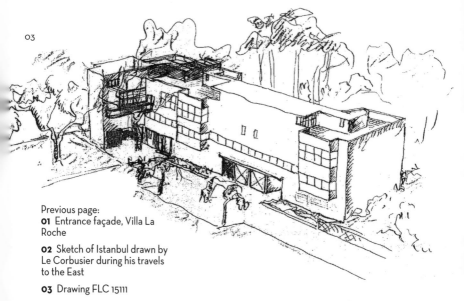

03

Previous page:
01 Entrance façade, Villa La Roche

02 Sketch of Istanbul drawn by Le Corbusier during his travels to the East

03 Drawing FLC 15111

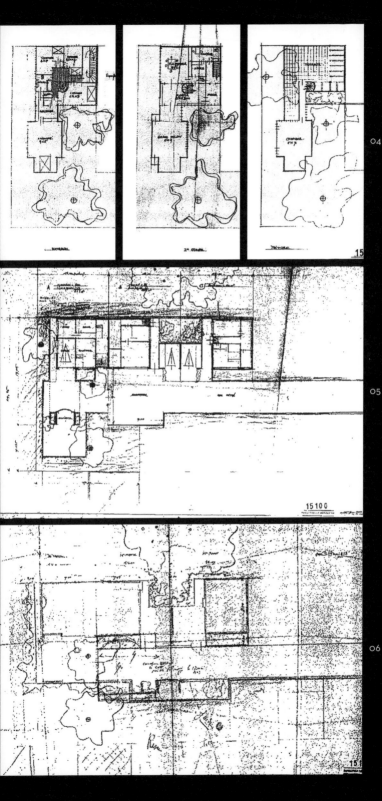

1923, Le Corbusier and Pierre Jeanneret began speculating about building a series of houses on land owned by the *Banque Inmobilière*. In their early sketches they worked on the plots facing the private interior lane, called Doctor Blanche. In late April of the same year (FLC 15108), two pre-existing trees appeared for the first time in the schematic drawings, and also in the perspectives.[4]

The trees were standing on the lots at the end of the interior lane: henceforth we will refer to them as the first tree – the one located further east, and the second tree – the one further west at the end of the street. In this early drawing, Le Corbusier proposed building four houses on the southern corner of the lane, in an "L" shape around the trees. In front of the buildings, he blocked off and widened the street to provide access to all the lots and make it possible for cars to turn around. However, he extended the axis of the street visually, asymmetrically with respect to the second tree, opening the ground floor of the house perpendicular to the lane, as can be seen in the perspective drawings. On the eastern corner, he placed a stand-alone house, at an angle with respect to the axis of the street and located just behind the first tree. The other three constructions were terraced houses, lined up to the south.

A third tree, however, was located at the edge of the lot, toward the south. In a drawing dated May 7 (FLC 15120), Le Corbusier made a hole and hollowed out the main volume of his new design, creating a void in the shape of a half cylinder, in response to the tree trunk's sharp inclination toward the building. Between May 10 and May 15, he developed the program for the building at the end of the lane, including the three trees on the lot (FLC 15100, 15099 and 15111). During this stage, the entire façade facing the third tree was set back from the plot's edge to leave space for the tree, given the aforementioned slant of its trunk.

From the earliest drawings, the ground floor remained unoccupied by the building, which made it possible for the pedestrian path to continue through on that level. However, as the volume of

04 Drawing FLC 15099   **05** Drawing FLC 15100   **06** Drawing FLC 15120

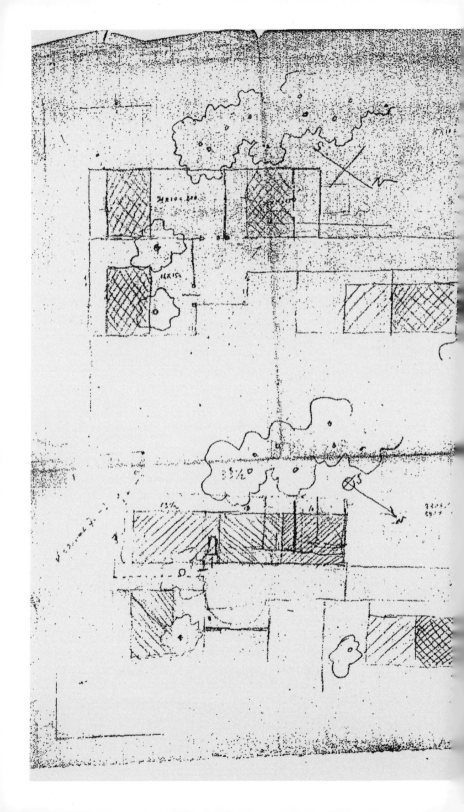

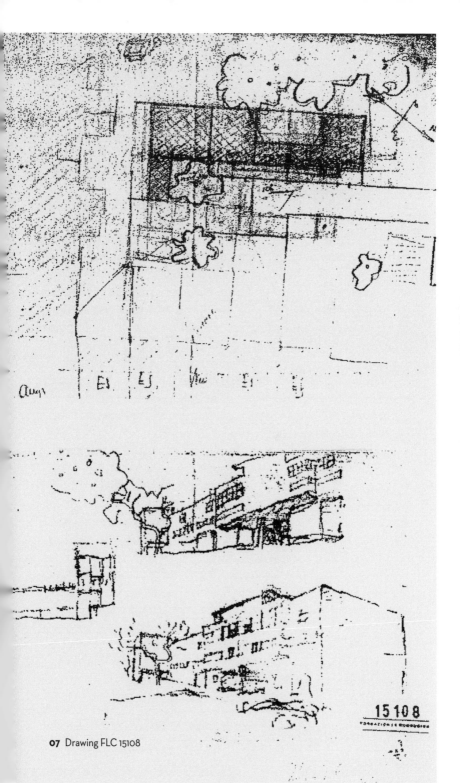

07 Drawing FLC 15108

that wing was elevated and situated symmetrically and perpendicularly with respect to the central axis of the interior street, Le Corbusier created even more distance between that axis and the second tree. In contrast, he located the entrance to the house symmetrically, in line with the trunk of the same tree. Thus, beginning with this design dated from May, the architects had already established the relationships between the second tree and the façades of the future Villa La Roche.

Similarly, the connection between the tree and the porch on the ground floor was determined as soon as the volume was lifted off the ground, framing the tree as a backdrop for the street. On the other hand, the hatched surface on the ground floor, perhaps representing a landscaped area or flower bed in front of the house, enclosed the first and third trees within a single area, connecting them on the ground level. Finally, the line that connects the trunks of both trees coincides with the diagonal of the rectangle that forms the base of the house: a parallelepiped made up of two squares which, after taking off the four corners, gives rise to the cross-shaped geometry of the volume, situated perpendicular to the axis of rue Dr. Blanche.

In late May, and due to the redistribution of the lots, the architects added a fourth house around the first tree. The tree was thus surrounded by a courtyard, open to the east, closing off the house from the square located at the end of the lane. As a result, that tree is cut off from the other two and from the corner house (FLC 15116), foreshadowing what would eventually become the built design for the Villa La Roche.

For that design, Le Corbusier drew four more perspectives. The tree appears in all of them. It even appears in one where he was apparently only interested in the interior of the library, with the trunk framed by one of the panes in the horizontal window (FLC 15113). The interior courtyard of the house was entirely determined by the presence of the tree. It could be seen from every room in the house, either through the horizontal windows or the large picture windows. Each type of opening isolated a certain

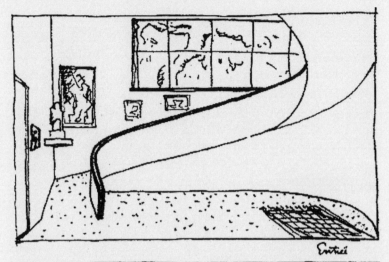

Entrée

Salle à manger

Hall d'entrée

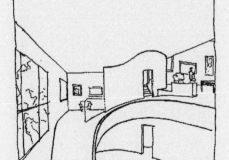

08 Three fragments of drawing FLC 15254

09

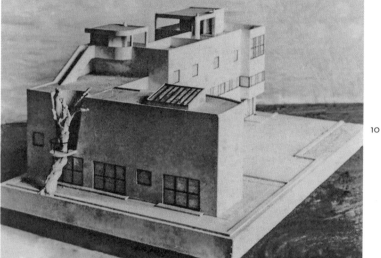

10

09, 10 Model
of the Villa La
Roche-Jeanneret
presented at the
Salon d'Automne,
Paris, 1923

11 Fragment of
drawing FLC
15254

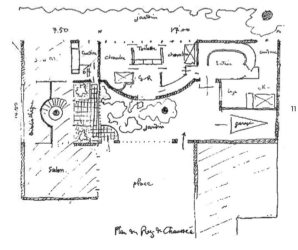

11

part of the tree: the trunk, the leaves of the crown, or fragments of both. Views of the tree were framed interchangeably from the house, and they were ultimately materialized in the final design, establishing those relationships through the sightlines.

Beginning in July of 1923, Raoul La Roche, a banker and collector of Cubist and Purist paintings, reserved the "L"-shaped lot, which closed off the lane. For the project, Le Corbusier drew three other interior perspectives of the design (FLC 15254). They feature drawings of some of the paintings from La Roche's art collection, Purist works by Le Corbusier himself and by Amédée Ozenfant (1886-1966). There are two perspective drawings of the lobby with the ramp and another from the dining room on the first floor. Le Corbusier drew the window framing the leaning trunk of the third tree. Likewise, in the perspective drawing of the dining room, he represented another large window that framed, this time, the second tree. From his very first sketches, the architect made it clear that the pre-existing trees would be visible from inside the villa.

La Roche ultimately purchased another lot on September 22 of the same year. Initially, the lot corresponded to a third house located between the lots that the two owners had already bought. With all the land purchased and the clients finalized, Le Corbusier put the final touches on a complete design for two terraced houses. He made a model of the project, to be presented at the Salon d'Automne in Paris in 1923, of which two images have been preserved. One shows the back of the La Roche house, where we see how Le Corbusier incorporated the leaning trunk of the third tree: encircled, literally, by a small balcony, and cutting into the volume of the house in the form of a truncated cone. In the other image, strangely enough, we find that he did not add the second tree to the model, the one located in front of the main door to the Villa La Roche. However, if we look at the two sketches of the façade he did during the same month, we do see the second tree represented in relation to the plane of the front door and the large picture window in the entryway.

The frontal image of the model is similar to the perspectives he drew during the design process for the two terraced houses. It is worth recalling that the first views were drawn between April and May of 1923 (FCL 15111 and 15108), and another perspective was published in the first volume of the Complete Works (pg. 61), possibly drawn in November of the same year. Now, what differences are there between those perspectives and the photographs of the model? In the drawings, the second tree always appears against an empty background, framed by the ground floor which corresponds to the wing of M. La Roche's gallery. However, in the model, the ground floor was occupied, cutting off the sightlines at the end of the street. Perhaps this was due to the fact that, if the volume had been built on the ground floor, nearly touching the tree, there would have been no choice but to cut it down. Maybe that is why Le Corbusier left the tree out of the model. Although it is only conjecture, it is still a clear indication of the relevance of the decision not to build the gallery on the ground floor.

The Villa La Roche was finished on March 13, 1925. Nearly two years had gone by since the beginning of the joint project for the Villa La Roche-Jeanneret and three years since Le Corbusier began thinking about how to occupy the lots situated at the end of rue Dr. Blanche. From the outset, he respected and included the pre-existing trees in the different designs. However, what we call the first tree fell outside the bounds of the lot that was ultimately purchased by Mr. La Roche. Nevertheless, we can confirm that he did not disregard the tree; he ended up including it in his design for the Villa.

If we look at one of the photographs of the interior of the gallery, taken during the opening, we see that the trunk of a tree is visible through the door of the small corner balcony, just before the beginning of the ramp. This view, in fact, is not coincidental. Just the opposite. We recall that the line between the first and third pre-existing trees was taken as the diagonal and geometric point of reference for the volume of one of the first designs. Indeed, the view of the trunk of the first tree coincides with that

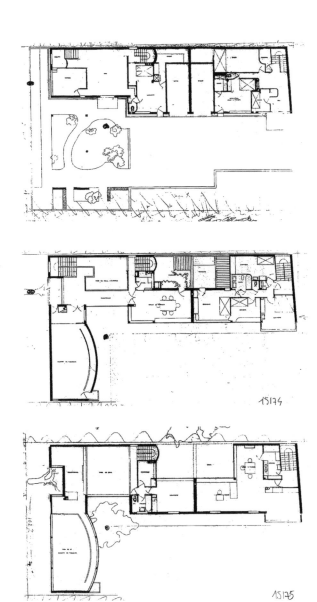

12 Ground floor of the Villa La Roche, drawing FLC 15173

13 First floor of the Villa La Roche, drawing FLC 15174

14 Second floor of the villa La Roche, drawing FLC 15175

15 Gallery of the Villa La Roche looking toward the base of the ramp

16 Vestibule

17 Façade that closes off rue du Docteur Blanche

18 Gallery of the Villa La Roche looking toward the back balcony

16

17

18

guideline and also defines the diagonal of the gallery space – the line that regulates its outline in plan. Le Corbusier determined that geometric relationship beginning in drawing FLC 15099, and it later reappears in the built version.

The trunk of this first tree can be seen through the glass door of the balcony, framed, centered and isolated from its branches, like a perfect cylinder. Again, the frame around the glass door turns the view of the tree into another of the owner's Purist paintings. It is worth recalling that Le Corbusier had already drawn one of the perspectives of the house that enclosed the first tree in its courtyard (FLC 15113), showing its trunk, framed – in this case – by a window. Therefore, each of the trees initially present on the site ended up linked with the villa that was eventually built.

Now, let's look at how the second tree maintains the relationships that Le Corbusier developed in the previous phases of the design, based on pictures taken during that period. The first was taken from the street, which shows a repetition of the symmetric relationship between the second tree and the convex, elevated plane of the gallery. The image hints at the setback plane that provides access to the Villa La Roche. In the second photograph, however, which shows the front door, we can see how the same tree now coincides with the axis of symmetry of the front façade. Le Corbusier enclosed the tree between two contrasting surfaces and made it into a virtual point of relation between the plane of the gallery and the entrance façade. It was a way of generating a series of contrasts including symmetry-asymmetry; concavity-convexity; opacity-transparency; approaching-receding; full-empty; curved-flat; and volumes resting directly on the ground versus others raised above it.

In a third photograph published in the first volume of the Complete Works (pg. 60), the same tree appears again, with the title "Entrance (Villa La Roche)". However, the image shows the interior of the entryway looking toward the outside, with the double door wide open. We can see how the tree trunk emerges from a grassy flower bed surrounded by gravel. This same section of lawn is also the support for the central cylindrical pillar that holds up the gallery. Thus, Le Corbusier used the same area to situate both "cylinders": the tree growing upward, and the pillar that directs the building loads downward to the ground. The same photograph shows the existence of a void above the wall that supports the gallery pavilion at the end. The opening recalls, perhaps, the connection with the courtyard house that enclosed the first tree, whose branches we can see behind the wall that separates the two properties.

Therefore, Le Corbusier established an inseparable relationship between the three pre-existing trees and the built villa. Additionally, the layout of the different architectural frames transformed the three trees into Purist abstractions. The front door, the entryway, the gallery, and thus the entire villa, were arranged based on the pre-existing trees.[5] The trees, in turn, were framed and incorporated as though they were pictorial figures.

A Window, a Tree

Le Corbusier identified trees with greenery in his urban designs. In the schematic designs he created to explain his ideas on the city, he would usually draw a sun (light, life), a cloud (space, the sky, the air) and a tree (the natural ground). While the dwellings were raised, separated from the ground – either on stilts or as high-rises – the trees represented contact with the ground. The windows, with large panes of glass, were given the role of relating the house with those three natural elements: the sun, the sky and the trees.

Those same elements were represented graphically in the book *Poésie sur L'Alger* and served as the foundation for his Plan Obus for the city of Algiers. Likewise, in the book *La Ville Radieuse*, Le Corbusier defined what were, for him, the "essential joys (pleasures or comforts)" to be included in urban planning:

Sun in the house,
a view of the sky through large windows,
trees he can see from his house.
I say that the materials of urban design are:
sun,
sky,
trees,
steel,
cement,
in this order of importance.[6]

What does it mean for the architect that he can see the trees from his house? As he wrote: "When the eye is five feet or so above the ground, flowers and trees have dimension: a measure relative to human activity, proportion."[7] Elevating the inhabitant's point of view with respect to the ground plane was, thus, his mission. The tree as a vertical axis emerging from the earth is responsible for determining the relative height achieved by inhabited spaces with respect to the ground, through the openings in their façades.

Consequently, the way of bringing these "essential joys" into dwellings implied generating a frame for the landscape: a large picture window, an enclosure to capture those pleasures. The window would bring the trees into the rooms of the house.[8] The window onto the landscape would offer a "room installed in front of the site". The following pages offer an analysis of a project that exemplifies those relationships: the houses for the Plan Macià in Barcelona.

Le Corbusier designed a temporary development for support workers coming into the city from rural areas. The project was intended to house the new inhabitants in such a way that "each home reconstitutes living conditions similar to those in the country".[9] To that end, he assigned a tree to each house, leaving the ground floor open facing the tree. In fact, he planned to plant a tree on the axis of symmetry of each façade so that it would be visible from the picture windows facing it.

His motto was: "ONE house: ONE tree", which he wrote on the original blueprints in 1933. Nonetheless, when he published the project in *La Ville Radieuse* in 1964, he modified it to read: "ONE WINDOW, ONE TREE". Based on this reformulation of the motto, we now understand the use and the intention behind Le Corbusier's incorporation of trees into his designs.

And so, what is a window for Le Corbusier? What are the implications of its shape and size in relation to the nearby trees? In the first volume of his complete works, he asserted that, for him "the window is one of the essential purposes of the house".[10] In this same "call to industrialists", he suggested that, thanks to the technical advances of reinforced concrete, the façade was freed from its load-bearing function; as a result, the extension of the window could be enlarged, both horizontally and vertically. The same text included a drawing that read: "the openings resulting naturally from reinforced concrete". Indeed, the slab and column structure of reinforced concrete allows for a series of large rectangular openings in the façades. For Le Corbusier, the traditional vertical window was transformed into a large pane of glass, spanning the entire length and width of the space freed up by the Dom-ino structure.

The changes in the size and proportion of the windows also entailed a transformation in the relationships between the interior and the exterior. This was the clear impact of the new options presented at the *Salon d'Automne* of 1923, which caused the well-known polemic between Auguste Perret and Le Corbusier regarding the advantages of the horizontal window versus the classic vertical or "French" window. In that sense, Le Corbusier marked a turning point in architecture with his use of the horizontal window (*fenêtre en longueur*) in his houses beginning in the 1920s.

In truth, this led to a shift in the relationships that house-dwellers could experience between the interior and exterior.[11] It is

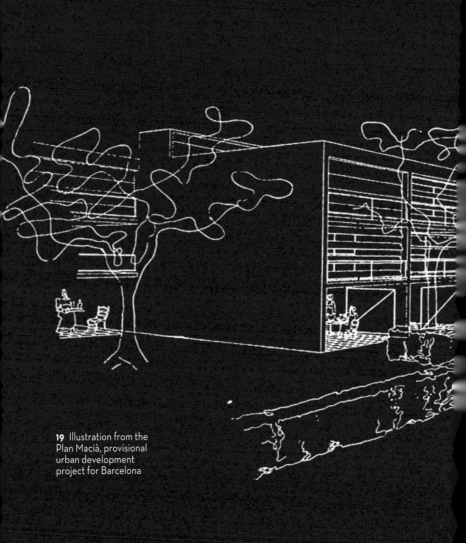

19 Illustration from the
Plan Macià, provisional
urban development
project for Barcelona

Lotissement :
« UNE FENÊTRE,
UN ARBRE ».
Lotissement pro-
visoire destiné à
la main - d'œuvre
auxiliaire venue
des campagnes.
Ce lotissement
tient compte de la
maille 400 × 400
mètres du réseau
routier. Bien que
ne prévoyant que
des immeubles à
rez-de-chaussée
surélevé et dédou-
blé, la densité est
de 900 habitants
à l'hectare.
Chaque l o g i s
reconstitue d e s
conditions d'habi-
tation semblables
à celles de la
campagne.

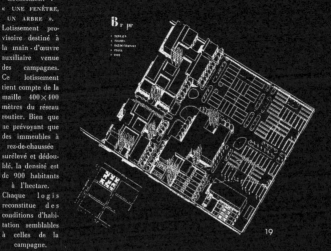

19

20

20 Perspective of the houses from the Plan Macià intended for workers coming into Barcelona from rural areas, 1933, published in the book *La Ville Radieuse: Éléments d'une doctrine d'urbanisme pour l'équipement de la civilisation machiniste*, Le Corbusier, 1964

worth recalling that Le Corbusier presented his model for the Villa La Roche-Jeanneret at the same *Salon d'Automne*. It shows the horizontal windows that stretched from one side to the other of the main volume on the first floor. The large picture windows were also included, one in each unit. All the windows were derived from a base module subject to variations according to a series of "regulating principles".

As the architect and professor Bruno Reichlin asserted, each different type of window establishes a particular type of relationship between the interior and the exterior. A vertical window acts as a frame for the exterior, forming an outlined image of the landscape: a *veduta* that can be comprehended in its entirety, since it shows a complete image that runs from floor to ceiling and is bounded on either side. The vertical window acts as a cut-out of the exterior or, as Otto F. Bollnow wrote:

> When we look through the window, the world recedes into the distance. [...] Window-frame, mullion and transom emphasize this effect, for they transport what is seen through the window, they cut a specific section out of the surrounding world and make it into an 'image'. To that extent, the window idealizes the part of the world that is cut out and isolated in this way.[12]

In contrast, the horizontal window broadens the scope of our vision in the horizontal plane on either side. As a result, the top and bottom limits disappear from the inhabitant's field of vision since the limits of the ground and sky are compressed. Consequently, the image that is cut out by the horizontal window is perceived as a fragment of the landscape or the exterior, and it loses the characteristics of a *veduta* or a framed image associated with a vertical orientation. We might say that, whereas the vertical window frames a view, the horizontal orientation transforms what we see into a sequence.

These characteristics of the horizontal window, combined with the paths and views that take place as a result of the *promenade architecturale* in the work of Le Corbusier, offer a different and valuable link to the exterior – an amplified vision of the surroundings. Although it is made up of fragments, the view defined by the horizontal window chains together the partial images seen as we move through the space, incorporating an ongoing stretch of time. In fact, the images cut out by the windows generate a new order in keeping with the sequence of our movements. The effect is similar to a film montage or a collage, since, as Walter Benjamin wrote, "both forms – montage and collage – can be distinguished from the arbitrary in that they suggest an idea of order, even if it is not apparent. Both make reference to complexity, that which contains many elements that are mutually implicated."[13]

This relationship between the inhabitants and the trees through the horizontal windows (and large picture windows) of the Villa La Roche introduces a new order between human life and natural life, which might be summed up in the following motto: ONE horizontal window, ONE tree in a sequence. To offer a clearer example of this new relationship between trees, the landscape and the interior, we will analyze the temporal sequence that Le Corbusier incorporated into his villa on Lake Geneva.

A Big *Fenêtre en Longueur* for a Small House

Le Corbusier began the design for a retirement house for his parents in 1923, at the same time he was drawing the initial versions of the Villa La Roche-Jeanneret. The jumping off point for the house was the research he had undertaken earlier for the Maison Citrohan, which began in 1920.[14] From the first sketches, Le Corbusier located the house on the shore of Lake Geneva, although it was not until May 1924 that he knew definitively that it would be situated along the lakeshore, when a narrow plot was purchased, after a long search, in the town of Corceaux-Vevey. The construction of this small villa began in August 1924, and his parents moved in just two years later.

Thirty years after the house was finished, in 1954, Le Corbusier published a book called *A Little House*. In it, he explained the whole design process, as well as the relationships and the circumstances of the trees in the garden that he situated along the open end of the narrow plot. In his description of the terrain, he highlighted the importance of the location for the construction of the house, facing the impressive landscape:

> The region – is the Lake of Geneva. [...] The Lake spreads out to the south, backed by the hills. The Lake and the Alps mirrored in it are in front, lording it from east to west. That is some sort of setting for my plan: facing south, its length is a living-room four metres in depth, but sixteen metres long. The window, by the way, is eleven metres long (one window, mind you!).[15]

The plot Le Corbusier bought for the house was, thus, located in a strategic position because of the unrivalled landscape, the south-facing orientation, and the excellent situation with respect to the major nearby cities, "at the railway station twenty minutes away trains stop which link up Milan, Zurich, Amsterdam, Paris, London, Geneva, Marseille..." However, we should observe the relevance of the horizontal window in response to the interesting location. This was the case to such an extent that he wrote: "The plan is tried out on the site and fits like a glove. Four metres from the window is the lake and four metres behind the front door the road."[16] Thus, the position of the *fenêtre en longueur* and the door determined the direct connections with the site.

The form of the plot was rectangular, and it measured 30 meters long by 12 meters wide (FLC 9380).[17] The longest side was oriented east-west, with the southern side facing Lake Geneva and the northern side running tangent to the old Chemin de la Bergère. The west side bordered with the neighbor's property, and the east side ran up against a small dock, with a breakwater perpendicular to the line of the two slopes that outlined the lake.

According to the plans, the house was a single story in height (FLC 9365). It had a rectangular base measuring four meters wide by 16 meters long, with its longest side oriented east-west, like the plot. The south-facing façade was separated from the lake shore by a distance of four meters, and the north-facing façade sat at

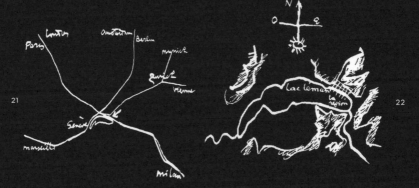

21   22

21 Relationship between Villa Le Lac and major European cities

22 Sketch of the region around Lake Geneva, published in *A Little House*, Le Corbusier, 1954

23 Virtues of the location, drawing published in *A Little House*

24 Floor plan on the site, drawing published in *A Little House*

25 Drawing in which Le Corbusier illustrated the uses and circulations in the villa:
1. The road | 2. The entrance hall | 3. The door | 4. The dressing room with the fuel oil boiler | 5. The kitchen

6. The laundry room (and stairs to the basement 7. Exit to the patio | 8. The living room | 9. The bedroom 10. The bathroom | 11. The wardrobe | 12. Small guest room (with a bed at floor level and second bed-divan stacked on top) | 13. An open porch facing the garden 14. Front and 11-meter window | 15. Stairs to the roof

23   24

25

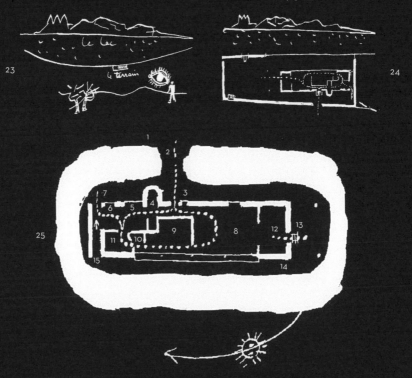

the same distance from the Chemin de Bergère. The western façade was at a distance of four meters from the party wall. The eastern side of the plot was left open for a garden and flower beds. In front of this garden and along the lake shore there was a 1.75-meter-high wall running the length of seven meters. It had a vertical window at its axis of symmetry, *veduta* style – but in the exterior. In the built volume, in contrast, he designed a horizontal opening – 11 meters wide by 1.15 meters high – in the south-facing façade, looking out onto the lake and the Alps.

The entrance to the villa is situated at almost the exact middle of the north-facing façade; whereas on the east façade, facing the garden, he added a second door, providing direct access to the garden. On this same façade, there is also a flat eave, supported by two cylindrical columns: a small porch integrated into the garden; a space facing the garden, protected from the sun and rain. The roof of the entire house is landscaped and accessible; its perimeter is protected by a low guardrail.

The house was drawn in November 1929 (FLC 9376, 9377) exactly as it was built, no doubt for the publication of the first volume of the *Complete Works 1910-1929*. However, it does not coincide fully with what we see today, since Le Corbusier carried out two further interventions. The first came in 1930 when the old Chemin de Bergère was enlarged to make way for a highway. The northern limit of the plot, initially bounded by hedges, was replaced with a stone wall. Likewise, he built an addition on the northeast corner, on top of the original volume. The second intervention dates back to 1950, when the southern façade was resurfaced in response to a series of large cracks that opened due to variations in the water level in the lake.

Despite all these changes, and its small size, Le Corbusier pursued a particular relationship between the trees and the openings in the villa, as we will see in the following pages.

The Enclosure, the Interior and the Porch Facing Lake Geneva

In the following analysis, we focus on the section built in 1924, leaving out the extension and the alterations to the north end of the plot. For our purposes, we will divide the Villa Le Lac into three archetypal elements. They are three spatial units, which are clearly identified in this compact and concise design: the enclosure around the lot, the interior space – the living space per se, and the small porch facing the garden. Likewise, we will look at the relationships that each unit establishes with the trees planted by Le Corbusier. Finally, we will study the characteristics of the openings of each unit in relation to the trees and the landscape.

The enclosure abides by the limits of the plot, forming a rectangle measuring 30 meters long by 12 meters wide;[18] the plot is unoccupied in the south-east corner, where Le Corbusier built a vertical extension of the low wall that crowned the slope of the lakeshore. This wall has a window in it that frames the landscape, as we commented earlier. The architect also installed a built-in table, perpendicular to the wall, supported by the wall itself and a cylindrical leg at the center of the far end. The table stands on a section of stone pavement (later replaced by gravel), generating a domestic space within the garden.

Here, Le Corbusier planted a paulownia tree in the grass-covered area of the garden. Following the wall along the lake to the point just where it ends, he planted a pine, and near the pine he planted a poplar. Further west along the same line, he planted a weeping willow.[19] In the northeastern corner of the enclosure, Le Corbusier laid out a stretch of ground with the same length as the low wall for use as a flower bed and vegetable garden. There, he planted an acacia at the intersection between the plot's east-west axis of symmetry and the axis of symmetry of the space allocated for the garden. The only pre-existing tree, a cherry tree, remained in the exterior south-east corner of the plot and was maintained.

The house's interior measures four meters wide by 16 meters long, following a proportion of 1:4; however, if we measure it from the western wall of the enclosure to the axis of the porch pillars, the proportion is 1:5. The interior distribution[20] is divided into three parts: the services area, situated in the west, with the kitchen, laundry room, coat closet, hot-water heater, entryway and toilet, plus the staircase down to the basement and the door leading out to the back patio; the central area, coinciding with the 11-meter window looking out over the lake, with the living room, dining room and bedroom with its bathroom and shower; and a space to the east intended for a use as a guest room or study, or even a dining room.

The program and circulations between the three interior areas are shown in a drawing from the book *A Little House* called "a circuit". The diagram shows the uninterrupted connection between the three interior spaces, since the spatial distribution makes it possible to pass through the entire house following a path that doubles back on itself. The circuit begins at the main entrance located in the north façade. As you enter, on the right there is a coat/shoe rack and the passageway into the services area. From the coat closet you can also access the bedroom, passing the bathtub and sink. Circulation between the two areas is continuous.

If you turn left from the entrance, you move directly into the living room, coming up against a cabinet used for storing sheet music, placed perpendicular to the north façade. The connection between this central space and the eastern edge is through two doors that can be hidden behind the wall/cupboard. From this guest room, a glass door opens onto the garden. It is not placed symmetrically in the façade, but off to one side, toward the lake with respect to the axis of symmetry. Because of this asymmetry or deviation from the center, when the space is open to the living room, there is a diagonal visual connection that ties the three elements of the design together: the interior, the porch and the exterior enclosure. Moreover, this visual axis is, very carefully, directed toward the trunk of the Paulownia tree. Thus, at the moment we enter the house, we see the tree trunk framed by the glass door of the bedroom: it is the same system as in the Villa La Roche. In other words, the openings in the architectural volumes are located along the axes established by the nearby trees.

The porch adjoining the eastern façade, which looks out onto the garden, measures 2.5 meters long by 4.5 meters wide. The small flat roof is supported by two free-standing thin metal pillars. Le Corbusier added curtains to make it possible to close off the porch area temporarily, which were replaced by two metal sliding doors, installed only on the north side. On the south side, he did not add any enclosing elements so as not to obstruct the view of the lake and the mountains in the distance. Based on this image of the landscape, crossed by the vertical line of the pillar and the horizontal line of the wall along the lake shore, or the horizon of the lake itself, Le Corbusier founded his principle of the "right angle". This principle was an element of formal control used by the architect in both his building designs and his urban planning. He gave it both a formal and mystical meaning: "It is a perfection that has something of the divine in it and it is, at the same time, a takeover of my universe. In the four right angles I have the two axes, support from the coordinates with which I can represent space and measure it."[21]

In the following pages, we will analyze how each of the three elements in the design – interior, enclosure and porch – establish their own framing for Lake Geneva and the Alps. The interior opens onto the landscape through the 11-meter-long widow, ge-nerating an uninterrupted panoramic view. As we commented earlier, the result is a vision of the exterior in the equivalent of a sequence shot. It creates a temporal succession as you move through the interior space. In cinematographic terms, it would be called a tracking shot, which creates a moving view, where the divisions in the window frame simulate the sequence of frames in the film. This *fenêtre en longueur* offers an unprecedented relationship with the surroundings, as Le Corbusier affirmed in the aforementioned book:

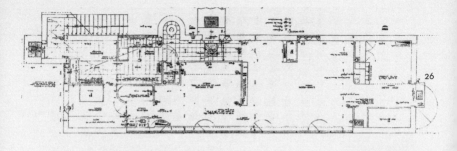

26

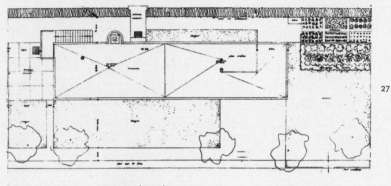

27

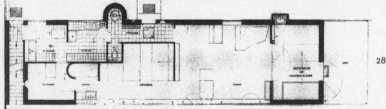

28

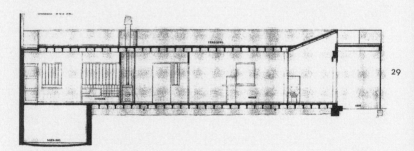

29

26 Layout plan of the Villa Le Lac, delivered for construction, 1924, drawing FLC 9365

27 Site plan of the Villa Le Lac, delivered for construction, 1924, drawing FLC 9380

28 Plan of the Villa Le Lac redrawn for the publication of the first volume of the complete works of Le Corbusier and Pierre Jeanneret, drawing FLC 9376

29 Redrawn section of the Villa Le Lac, drawing FLC 9377

The window eleven metres in length gives it style! The part played by the window is an innovation, for it becomes the main feature, the chief attraction in the house.[22]

Before then, it was quite unusual to see such a large horizontal window in a house. In contrast, the window he opened in the garden wall frames the landscape like a picture. Its situation is also a curious because it is outdoors. In this way, Le Corbusier subverted its exterior condition to make it into another interior room, as he writes:

> The walls to north, east and south enclose the small garden ten metres square like a cloister garth and convert it into a green hall.[23]

Finally, the porch, as we noted before, refers the landscape to a series of coordinates. To continue with the cinematography simile, it is like a fixed shot of the landscape. Again, in Le Corbusier's words:

> The position [the pillar] occupies at the intersection with the old lake wall produces a noteworthy feature: a right-angled cross – coordinated with the water and the mountains.[24]

Having analyzed the three constituent parts of the villa, it is worth remarking that their formal characteristics can be altered by the incorporation of the trees into the house. Specifically, we are referring to the ever-present paulownia tree. In fact, the enclosed garden also has a natural roof due to the paulownia's exceptional crown. Thus, the enclosure with a leafy roof that protects the small stretch of grass in front of the window, can be understood as an interior. And vice versa: the interior of the villa, wide open to the landscape through the horizontal window, is converted into a porch. The *fenêtre en longueur* generates another order of relationships with the nearby surroundings; and the tree does the same with the enclosure.

30

31

30 Porch in the garden   **31** Façade facing the garden with the porch

Two Temples Akin to the Villa Le Lac

The analysis of the villa on Lake Geneva, centered on the three basic spatial units – interior, enclosure and porch – has uncovered certain analogies with the classic temples Le Corbusier included in his publications predating the design of the villa. Let's look, for example at the illustration of a primitive temple published in his book *Toward an Architecture*. The chapter called "Three Reminders to Architects: Plan" includes a drawing of the temple, where we see an enclosure in which the 2:1 proportion is the same one used by Le Corbusier in his villa.

Moreover, the temple's interior is situated along the enclosure's longitudinal axis of symmetry. Its proportions, again, coincide with those of the villa's design. Likewise, we see that, at the entrance to the temple, there is an altar and a libation vessel located on the diagonals of the base squares. These two elements that welcome visitors at the entrance appear concealed and transformed in the house: in this case, they are the trees. It is worth recalling that Le Corbusier also planted the paulownia and the acacia on the diagonals of the base squares that organized the design as a whole. In that sense, we see that the role given to the trees has its parallel in the primitive temple.

It is worth noting that the entrance to the house from the north does not coincide with the conditions in the temple: i.e., along the enclosure's longitudinal access of symmetry. However, if we follow the photo layout from the book Le Corbusier published in 1954, *A Little House*, we find that upon entering the plot from the north, the following photographs do not show the interior of the house. Instead, the order of the photographs shows the path that runs around the perimeter of the plot following along the enclosure walls, passing through the garden, around the paulownia, leaning out toward the lake through the window above the shore wall, extolling the beauty of the lake and the Alps, and then approaching the house under the shelter of the porch, held up by two columns, where there are also three steps leading inside.

32

33

34

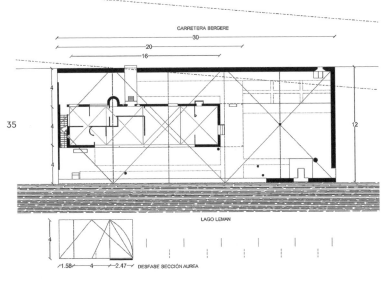

CARRETERA BERGERE

LAGO LEMAN

1.58 — 4 — 2.47 DESFASE SECCIÓN AUREA

35

32 Expansion of the Villa
Le Lac, 1930

33 Garden with the built-in
table and paulownia tree

34 View of the villa from
the lake

35 Geometric relationships
in the floor plan of the Villa
Le Lac

Accordingly, the true desired point of entry for the house would be through the bedroom – in other words, along the axis of symmetry, as Le Corbusier observed in the illustration he published of the primitive temple.

Finally, it is worth mentioning another temple that shows certain similarities with the villa. It is the Temple of Zeus at Dodona, with an oak tree inside its enclosure, again, next to the porch where the main entrance is located. Thus, there is an even stronger similarity with the relationships between the trees and the composition of the house: the enclosure, the porch and the interior.

The House is a Box in the Air, Pierced All Around, Facing Trees

The two houses analyzed here show the relevance Le Corbusier allocated to trees, as well as the connections forged through the openings in his architecture. In fact, the architect eventually defined a house as: "a box in the air, pierced all around" with doors and windows. Regarding trees, he wrote that they are "companions, friends of man. Bearers of shade and freshness inciting poetry, sources of oxygen, retreats for the singing birds."[25]

For Le Corbusier, trees helped the house take root on the site, thus generating an oriented and meaningful place. He achieved this precisely by framing trees through the windows and doors. Through the trees, he made habitation into a poetic and lyrical experience, far removed from the rationalist and mechanicist principle of the house as a machine for living in: the relationship between houses and trees can even offer a sacred experience, as we showed earlier in the analogy with the primitive temples.

For the architect, place is what we see through the windows as we travel through spaces, whether interior or exterior. So, he put the inhabitants in a situation to look out at the world stretching out before them. Through the *fenêtre en longueur* he created a sequence of views, fragments stitched together by travelling

36 The garden with the paulownia tree, photograph published in *A Little House*, 1954

37 Reconstruction of the Temple of Zeus at Dodona

38 Primitive temple published by Le Corbusier in *Vers une architecture*, 1923 (A. Entrance, B. Portico, C. Peristyle, D. Sanctuary, E. Instruments of worship, F. Vase of oblation, G. Altar)

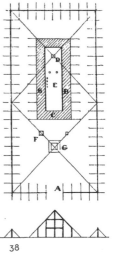

through the space. In contrast, by generating vertical openings - doors or windows - he framed trees against the backdrop of the horizon or against a fragment of the outside, where the tree situates or organizes part of the immediate surroundings. As Otto F. Bollnow wrote, "through the window the human inner space is observably and clearly positioned in the great order of horizontal and vertical",[26] words that echo the poem of the right angle.[27]

However, what idea of place can be generated from the relationships offered between Le Corbusier's villas and trees? Let's look back at the author's definition in that regard: "The architect constructs the place by controlling what we see." In other words, for him, place consists, first of all, of a space to be built. Thus, a place is not something given, on which the architect simply executes a design. On the contrary, a place is generated by an ideal arrangement of views as they are framed by the architecture.

For Le Corbusier, place requires an architectural creation, since "what should be preserved is not so much the terrain, as its conquest. The 'artificial site' that touches the ground lightly is the agent of conquest. The lighter the contact, the greater the power of control."[28] Le Corbusier refers both to the physical contact with the site as well as the visual contact that is established through the appropriate layout of the windows with respect to the elements that make up the site, such as the trees. He expressed this as follows:

> Composed of the expanse and gradations of the ground, of sheets of water and of vegetation, of rock formation and the sky, covered with stretches or with tufts of green opening to perspectives, enclosed by the horizon, the site is the nourishment offered by our eyes to our senses, to our intelligence, to our hearts. The site is the base of the architectural composition.[29]

39 South façade of the villa seen from Lake Geneva   **40** Horizontal window seen from the inside

41 View of the trunk of the paulownia from inside the villa

42 View of Lake Geneva framed by the window in the garden wall

43 Detail from a plan of the Cité ouvrière in Saint-Nicoles-d'Aliermont, 1917, drawing FLC

22408, which reads: "Point de vue dans l'axe de l'arbre"

42

Thus, the construction of place culminates with the construction of architecture. The essential qualities of the site are exalted by the architectural form – more specifically, by how that architecture arranges the openings that will frame and order the inhabitants' experience of the site.

43

44 Illustration from Le Corbusier's book, *The House of Man*, where he writes: "And the 'essential joys' have entered the dwelling. Nature is inscribed in the lease, a pact is signed with nature. The trees are present in the room of the dwelling."

Endnotes

1   Le Corbusier. "Joies Essentielles", en *La Ville Radieuse. Éléments d'une doctrine d'urbanisme pour l'équipement de la civilisation machiniste.* Paris: Vincent, Fréal, 1964, p. 86

2   Le Corbusier. *Puerta de hielo. L'Esprit Nouveau, 1920-1925.* Castellón: Ellago, 2005, p. 83.

3   Following is a list of projects in which trees played a fundamental role in the definition of the design: Villa Fallet, La Chaux-de-Fonds (1905); Villa Favre-Jacot, Le Locle (1912); Villa Berque, Paris (1921); Villa "Le Lac", Corsaux-Vevey (1923); Pavillon de L'Esprit Nouveau, Paris (1925); Maison Ternisien, Boulogne-sur-Seine (1926); Maison Guiette, Antwerp (1926); Maison Cook, Boulogne-sur-Seine (1926); Villa Mandrot, Le Pradet (1930-31); Houses for surplus workers, Pla Macià, Barcelona (1933); Villa Henfel. Maison de week-end, La-Celle-Saint-Cloud (1935); Pavillon des Temps Nouveaux, Paris (1937); Peyrissac Residence, Cherchell (1942); Maison Curutchet, La Plata (1949); Cabanon de vacances, Cap Martin (1951-52); Maisons Jaoul, Neuilly-sur-Seine (1952-56); Villa Sarabhai, Ahmedabad (1955); Sainte Marie de la Tourette Priory, Eveux-sur-Arbresle (1957-1960); and the Carpenter Center for the Visual Arts, Cambridge, Mass. (1961-64).

4   The following analysis of the design process for the Villa La Roche-Jeanneret takes into account the studies by Tim Benton, published in his book *The Villas of Le Corbusier and Pierre Jeanneret 1920-1930.* Revised and expanded edition. Basel; Boston; Berlin: Birkhäuser, 2007, pp. 47-77.

5   Here, we will borrow a quote from Josep Quetglas to extend this implication in the determination of the form of the Villa La Roche to the other trees and their spaces. The entire quote that references the villa is as follows: "Le Corbusier had taken note of the location of the trees in drawings, from the earliest sketches for the design, both in plan and in

section, and he had even published a photograph that repeats the gesture we described earlier in reference to La Tourette. From the remaining draft sketches, we know that not just this one tree, but also the two other pre-existing trees on the site, were the three co-protagonists in the design. So, in truth, we should say that the door, and with it the entryway-living room, and thus the entire Villa La Roche, derives its layout from the tree." In Josep Quetglas. "Point de vue dans l'axe de l'arbre". *Massilia,* 2004 bis. Le Corbusier y el paisaje. Barcelona: Associació d'idees, 2004, p. 149.

6   Op. cit., Le Corbusier. "Joies Essentielles", in *La Ville Radieuse,* p. 86.

7   Le Corbusier. *Aircraft.* London: Trefoil Publications, Ltd, 1987, p. 122.

8   Le Corbusier. *The Home of Man.* Oxford: Architectural Press, 1948, p. 87.

9   Op. cit., Le Corbusier. "1932. Le Plan 'Macia' de Barcelone", in *La Ville Radieuse,* p. 306.

10 Le Corbusier. *Le Corbusier et Pierre Jeanneret. V. 1, Oeuvre complète 1910-1929.* Berlin, Birkhäuser, 1995, p. 77. First published, although with slight modifications to the text, in *Almanach d'architecture moderne: documents, théorie, pronostics, histoire, petites histoires, dates, propos standarts, apologie et idéalisation du standart, organisation, industrialisation du bâtiment.* Paris: Connivences, 1987 (1925), p. 102-103.

11 For more on what happened, see Bruno Reichlin, "The Pros and Cons of the Horizontal Window: The Perret-Le Corbusier Controversy". *Daidalos* no. 13, 1984, pp. 64-78.

12 Otto Friedrich Bollnow. *Human Space.* London: Hyphen Press, 2011, p. 154.

13 Walter Benjamin. *The Work of Art in the Age of Its Technological Reproducibility, and Other Writings on Media.* Cambridge, Harvard

University Press, 2008. Cited in and translated from Juan Luis de las Rivas. *El espacio como lugar. Sobre la naturaleza de la forma urbana.* Valladolid: Universidad de Valladolid. Secretariado de Publicaciones, 1992, p. 192.

14 The Maison Citrohan consisted of a two-story volume, with a terrace supported by pillars on the front.

15 Le Corbusier. *Une petite maison: 1923.* Zurich: Girsberger, 1954. English translation, *A Little House.* Basel: Birkhäuser, 1954, p. 5.

16 Ibid., p. 9.

17 This site plan was part of the project that Le Corbusier sent to the builder, from his studio in Paris, for the construction.

18 The rectangle keeps the following proportions: the short side is a single square, with sides of 12 meters in length; the long side measures two-and-a-half squares. The long side, oriented toward the south, borders on the stone wall that forms a barrier against the waters of the lake. This wall rises approximately two meters above the water level, and 65 centimeters above the ground level of the plot, with a width of 50 centimeters.

19 Contrasting with the long side open onto the lake, the other long side, facing the north, was closed off with a hedge, although it was later replaced with a wall. The same was the case for the short side facing the east. A door was opened in the south-east corner to provide direct access to the boat dock. As for the partition along the neighboring plot, and according to the written correspondence between Le Corbusier and the owner of the property dating from September 24, 1924, both par-

ties agreed to build up the existing 1.8-meter-high wall to coincide with the new roof level along the entire width of the house. Moreover, this wall was also extended three meters toward the lake side from the edge of the house. It was built using a concrete frame, and the interior panels were made from lattice work.

20 The interior partitions are determined by the golden ratio, where 1.53 meters is the distance resulting from taking a 1:4 ratio with respect to the western party wall: in other words, the smallest measurement derived from the golden section of a 4-meter square.

21 Le Corbusier. *El espíritu nuevo en arquitectura.* Murcia: Colegio Oficial de Aparejadores y Arquitectos Técnicos, 1983, p. 21.

22 Op. cit., Le Corbusier. A Little House, p. 30.

23 Ibid., p. 24.

24 Ibid., p. 29.

25 Op. cit., Le Corbusier. *The Home of Man,* p. 94.

26 Op. cit., Bollnow. *Human Space,* p. 152.

27 See the Spanish edition edited by Juan Calatrava. *Le Corbusier y la síntesis de las artes: El poema del ángulo recto.* Madrid; Paris: Círculo de Bellas Artes; Fondation Le Corbusier, 2006. See also the diferent reflections edited by the same author in *Doblando el ángulo recto: 7 ensayos en torno a Le Corbusier.* Madrid: Círculo de Bellas Artes, 2009.

28 Mark Wigley. "On Site". *Lotus* no. 95, 1997, p. 123.

29 Le Corbusier. *Le Corbusier Talks with Students.* New York: Princeton Architectural Press, 1999, pgs. 40-41.

If the house shares and dialogues with a tree it is because it is understood as a sheaf of unending lines, something like the network of connections, dependencies and endless transformations that trees possess as natural elements.

Juan Navarro Baldeweg

Villa
PEPA

The Rural Landscape as a Foundation

Juan Navarro (Santander, 1939) built Villa Pepa (1992-1993) as a retreat and a place for contemplation, and so he could be near his artist's studio. The house has not been widely published or exhibited: it remains largely unknown due to the architect's own desires. That said, he has not been able to prevent others from talking about its existence and its importance. In fact, the villa has been published in three of the architect's books, referring to Alacant as its generic location, without specifying the town or its exact location.[1]

Despite his efforts, Villa Pepa was referenced, photographed and exhibited in the Sunday magazine *EPS*, published by *El País*, a newspaper with a large national circulation, when Juan Navarro was the guest artist for the newspaper's stand at the 2006 Arco contemporary art fair. Likewise, a number of scenes were shot at the villa, the studio and the surrounding area for the Spanish Television program *Elogio de la luz*,[2] dedicated to contemporary

02

Previous page: **01** General view of the Villa Pepa   **02** View from the south

Spanish architecture. Finally, a number of the art and architecture critics who have analyzed and written about Juan Navarro's architectural and artistic work cite its relevance for him as a place of refuge.[3]

Villa Pepa is a design to remodel and expand an old rural construction in the region of Marina Alta. In the site plan for the villa, completed like an archaeological survey, the pre-existing conditions of the site are described. The elements drawn by the architect - whether they are buildings, trees or stone walls - are thus assessed for their subsequent intervention. Likewise, a single topographic line appears, marking an elevation of 224 meters above sea level. This contour line represents the hill on which the house sits - the true zero-level elevation - as the old inhabitants who built the house dug into the terrain to adapt it to the rolling topography. Likewise, they levelled off the area in front of it toward the south for agricultural uses: a threshing floor for threshing wheat and a raisin dryer, known as a *riurau*.[4]

In the same site plan, the dry stone retaining walls typical of the area are also marked, outlining the almond orchard near the villa. Like the house, the agricultural terraces adapt to the contours of the natural terrain. Thus, rainwater can be retained but natural runoff remains unobstructed.

The site plan also shows some larger rocky areas, as well as the exact position of the trunks of the largest trees around the house and the diameter of their crowns. The different species, however, are not differentiated, despite their great variety (pines, holm oaks, almond trees, carob trees, olive trees, cypresses). In any case, the pre-existing trees are taken as determining elements in enabling the rehabilitation of the rural complex as a villa.

The walls corresponding to the existing constructions - both the house itself and the annexes (the well, the oven and the *riurau*) - are all represented. The expansions for the new villa are also outlined in the plan; and the pathway leading up to the house can be seen, which ends at another pre-existing construction (recently set up as the artist's new studio and guest house).

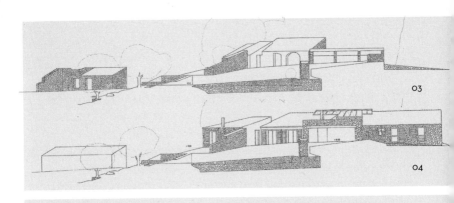

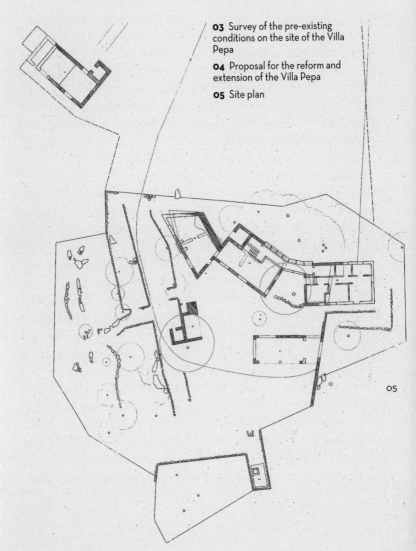

03 Survey of the pre-existing
conditions on the site of the Villa
Pepa

04 Proposal for the reform and
extension of the Villa Pepa

05 Site plan

The plot is not enclosed by fences or gates. As you travel along the path, nothing indicates that you are approaching a house. The threshold is flanked by a carob tree, an almond tree and a cypress tree, representing the main species present around the Villa Pepa. From this point, and until you reach the entrance of the house – located at the meeting point between the living room and the dining room – you pass by pines, almond trees and carob trees, ascending a dirt path between grape vines toward the small square that sits at the center of the different buildings.

The existing house was made from three volumes laid out in a fan shape open to the topography of a small hill. To the west there were two connected volumes; and to the east, separated from the others, a third independent volume. Between them was an opening. In the middle of this opening there was a carob tree and around it a low dry stone wall to retain rainwater and generate a flat area on which to collect its fruits.

Two other free-standing and pre-existing constructions were associated with the place's agricultural past: the aforementioned *riurau* and a building to house the ovens – one for cooking, baking bread and preparing preserves, and another for blanching the muscatel grapes. In front of the *riurau* there was a threshing floor that was used for threshing and for drying raisins spread in the sun atop a bed of reeds. In front of the threshing floor, there was also a well with a low stone wall built around it.

The intervention affecting these preexisting elements was minimal. Juan Navarro expanded the ends of the buildings attached to the hill, adapting them to the program of a second home. Navarro arranged the day-use areas (living room, dining room and kitchen) in the two buildings located farthest west; the eastern volume housed the bedrooms. The two were joined by a bridge to pass over the topography.[5] In the *riurau*, he eliminated the central pillar from the largest span, creating a flat lintel. He covered the back façades of the three volumes articulated by the new bridge with stone cladding using material from the site, to correspond with the existing constructions.

For the Villa Pepa, the defining elements were the trees, the dry stone walls of the terraced land, the entrance path, the surrounding rural landscape and the pre-existing constructions. In that sense, the pre-existing natural elements are as valuable as the architectural ones. In the brief for his installation *Hidráulica doméstica* for the 1985 Milan Triennial, Juan Navarro made explicit reference to the relationships between the artificial and the natural spheres:

> Architecture deals with meeting needs that are incorporated into the natural world. There is always a pact between naturality and artifice and a forced insertion of objects into natural physical coordinates. If we think of how water flows as an intrinsic coordinate and its manifestations as consequences of a natural cycle or as events in a linear argument, the house becomes a landscape, where the interior blends with the exterior.[6]

Juan Navarro understands the house as an interior space that relates to the exterior, both nearby and far away. The Villa is part of the landscape, but it also constitutes a landscape in itself, which merges with the surrounding nature. According to Juan Navarro, nature's importance for architecture is relevant in three aspects: one, in considering the "insertion of any artificial object into the natural medium"; two, in the "similarity of natural processes and creative processes"; and three, in how the "primordial and direct experiences of natural space logically have a profound effect on architectural thought".[7]

If we transfer these three considerations onto the design for the Villa Pepa, we will see how the existing rural construction, both before and after its adaptation, has ties to the vegetation and the geography of the site. We see this in its organization, which is fragmented and adapted organically to the topography of the terrain. It is also apparent in how the land has been harnessed for agricultural work, with the threshing floor in front of the *riurau*. Likewise, we observe it in how Juan Navarro's creative and artistic processes are in harmony with natural processes. And, finally, in

06

07

06 View of the carob tree behind   **07** View of the landscape framed
the *riurau* at the Villa Pepa   by the *riurau*

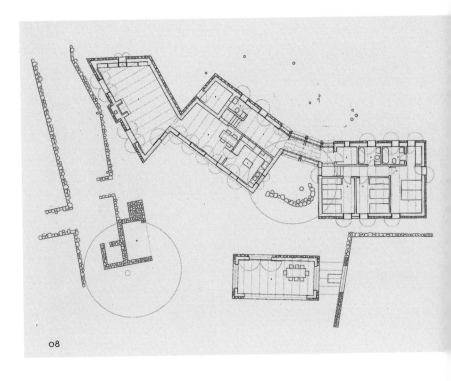

08

08 Floor plan from the construction drawings for the Villa Pepa

09, 10 Sketches of the elevation and section of the bridge-gallery

11 Elevation from the construction drawings for the Villa Pepa

09

10

11

how the artist continues to experience the natural space that surrounds the Villa in a way that affects his architectural thinking.

Relationships between the House and the Trees

Villa Pepa forges an understanding between the artificial and the natural world; specifically, its architecture generates formal and perceptual connections with the nearby trees. For Juan Navarro, a tree is more than just a beautiful object, it is "an integrated body, open to the world and to the flow of its energies." In fact, Juan Navarro has offered a very accurate definition of a tree:[8]

> When we say "tree" there is an arbitrary limit on what we are referring to. We know that the reality of the tree doesn't have an ending; it isn't enclosed within the perimeter of a figure. A tree doesn't end: its being and function are continued in the air, in the water, in the minerals in the soil, and in the sun. [...] We say "tree" and instantly the warning light of critical consciousness comes on, because it detects the mismatch between a nominal determination and an entity which, strictly speaking, overflows all its limitations.[9]

Thus, the tree is not a formal and autonomous element. It cannot be reduced to a figure. As a natural element, the tree reveals the invisible and, at the same time, the most corporeal aspects of a place: air, water, earth, and sun. Juan Navarro gives this augmented role to the trees adjacent to the Villa Pepa.

When a house is built next to a tree, it becomes "the tree"; in this case, "the carob tree", "the fig tree", "the almond tree" or "the cypress tree". The house that approaches the tree, therefore, situates it within an order – the house's own order of spatial and topological references. The tree takes on an active role in keeping with the architecture that surrounds it and defines it.

The house isolates the tree from the natural lack of order, lending it a human and architectural referential order. Its trunk, branches, leaves and fruit, as well as its colors and aromatic nuances contrast with the geometric forms of the architecture. The house next to a tree becomes a background against which the

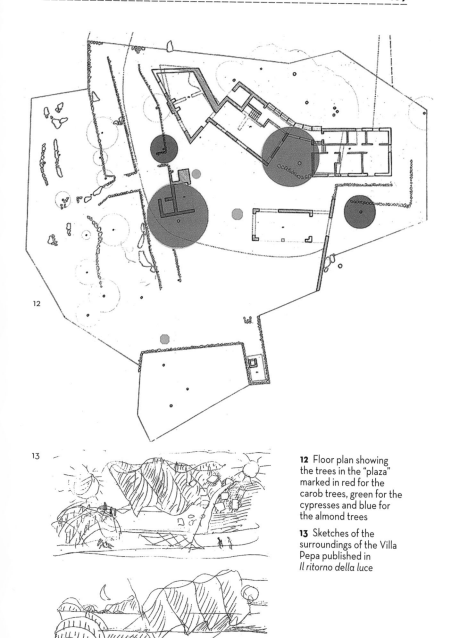

12

13

12 Floor plan showing the trees in the "plaza" marked in red for the carob trees, green for the cypresses and blue for the almond trees

13 Sketches of the surroundings of the Villa Pepa published in *Il ritorno della luce*

tree can stand out and be admired. In that sense, the distances between the tree and the house become decisive for both elements by enriching their meanings. There is no "tree" without the "house" that approaches it.

The tree, as a living and natural element, lends nuances and atmosphere to the house through its shade and the light that filters through it. It also helps to create a microclimate, improving the temperature and humidity of the surrounding environment. The tree gives off scents and aromas, it highlights the breeze, the wind, the rain and other atmospheric phenomena. Where the whitewashed walls of the house intensify the light reflected onto the tree; the tree tinges the house with colors and shadows that are, moreover, in continuous movement, undergoing constant change.[10]

Two carob trees were carefully protected during the renovation of the house. The first one is located on the south side of the oven building. The second is enclosed between the volume that houses the bedrooms, the volume occupied by the kitchen-dining room, and the new bridge that connects the two together. Between the house and the trees, "another" space is defined; an atmosphere is created, and other temporalities are invoked. There is no "house" without the "tree" next to it.

Juan Navarro captured in writing these particular relationships between trees and houses, how they complement one another and, in that sense, how the initial qualities of a house are expanded:

> The tree, the pond or the path are also parts of the domestic realm, the physicality and the imagination of daily living. When we turn toward them, when we look at them and think about them, they become intimate figures and, above all, with their quiet presence, they reveal fundamental functions of the house. That presence, at the expanded limits of the house, makes our interpretation of it more precise and intense, offering a conceptual and imaginary background for our reflection. This conjunction forces us to interpret architecture as

a crossing, as a place for the continuous passage of energies, of gazes, of life and time. The house becomes a place of transit, a mechanism for exploration and reception. It emerges as an open object and an apt tool for projecting outward in a kind of telescopic unfolding and for attracting and reeling in what lies in the distance.[11]

The house transcends its physical construction to become a continuum with the trees and other elements from the site. Juan Navarro expressed this himself in writing: "if the house shares and dialogues with a tree [...] it is because it is understood as a sheaf of unending lines, something like the network of connections, dependencies and endless transformations that tress possess as natural elements rooted in the organic continuum of the soil, the subsoil, the atmosphere, the landscape or the gaze of a passerby".[12]

The house exists in what transcends it as a finished built object. The house goes beyond the house. Its scope is not only in the construction, but in what lies around it and even far off in the distance, on the horizon. Trees are therefore an essential part of our experiences beyond the enclosures that are built to be inhabited. There can be no house without the trees that become part of its scope of action. In the same way, we cannot understand "the tree" without the house that gives it meaning through its proximity and relationships.

The Bridge-Gallery and the Carob Tree

The bridge-gallery and the gables of the volumes that it connects define a three-sided courtyard occupied by a carob tree. The preliminary sketches for the Villa Pepa show how the bridge was the focus of the architect's most careful attention: it appears outlined on the blueprints in his efforts to resolve the connection between the two volumes; it also appears in the only section he drew, specifically for the bridge, where we can see his interest in capturing the light and in passing over the uneven topography of the hill towards the threshing floor. This bridge-gallery also

14

15

14 View of the
pines and oaks on
the hill in front of
the bridge-gallery

15 View of the
carob tree in front
of the bridge-gallery

16 Floor plan of the
Casa de la Lluvia,
Liérganes, 1978-
82, Juan Navarro
Baldeweg

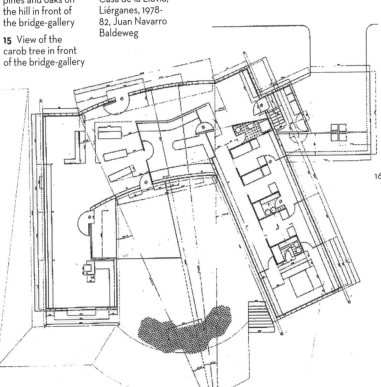

16

appears in the rear elevation, connecting the two volumes, and in the perspective drawing of the three existing buildings, linked by the bridge passing behind the carob tree. The new volume thus takes on great importance for the new house.

The relationships between the new bridge-gallery and the pre-existing constructions result in a new stability that organizes the once disjointed and free-standing volumes. This creates a different relationship between the hill and the threshing floor, the day-use area and the volume that contains the bedrooms. The carob tree becomes the center for the built volumes and the empty spaces between them.

Crossing the bridge-gallery means that the inhabitants look out, to the left and right, over the trees on either side of the house: the pine forest on the hill behind it and, in continuity, the carob tree framed against the back wall of the *riurau*. The bridge is the architectural element that, in addition to connecting the interior spaces, also offers a visual connection between the north and south sides of the terrain: it generates new axes of symmetry and a mirrored relationship. The bridge also introduces an additional, metaphorical symmetry: it emerges between the cultural and natural spheres – in other words, between the wilderness and cultivated or domesticated nature, represented by the carob tree.

All the openings that face this triangular courtyard mean that, as people move from one side of the house to the other, the carob tree is framed and present: through the horizontal frame of the bridge, through the square window of the kitchen, and through the vertical frame of the door on the landing at the top of the stairs. The carob courtyard articulates different relationships between the surroundings and the activities that take place inside the house.

Juan Navarro built a similar courtyard, open to the landscape, in the Casa de la Lluvia, where the three volumes that housed the different day-use areas and bedrooms were joined by a smaller module at the corners. He planned to put a tree there, but it ultimately had to be substituted by the construction of a pergola, to which he attached a climbing vine.

In both projects, the house surrounds, encloses and protects a tree, and the tree, in turn, provides shade, orients and presides over the different rooms of the house. It is a two-fold action where both elements interact, work together, forming a different type of space: not entirely natural, or entirely artificial, it creates a "complementary space":

> My interest is centered on what lies between things and what lies between those things and us. [...] Our job is to produce things, but I'm more interested in complementary space: what circumscribes things, surrounds them, sustains them or constitutes them.[13]

The enclosure of the Villa Pepa encircles and surrounds the carob tree; and the tree supports and founds the new domestic place.

The Square and the Cypresses

Juan Navarro has referred to the open space between the house, the *riurau* and the oven structure as the "plaza". For him, all the open-air spaces that are limited by the different volumes are the streets that enter and leave this plaza: irregular points of access that take on different angles and orientations, since "the free distribution of the volumes, not rearranged into a forced unity, articulates the open space defining more secluded areas".[14]

The first of these streets coincides with the access road to the west, limited by the volume of the living room and the oven building; the second coincides with the passage between the bedrooms and the *riurau*, facing east; the third is the path that leads to the former painting studio, between the oven and the *riurau*. The passageway that once connected the house with the hill behind, and which could well have been the fourth point of access, was closed off by the bridge-gallery.

This public space of the Villa Pepa is also suggested in the material finishes of the volumes that surround it; plastered and

17

18

19

17 View of the Villa Pepa from the west

18 View to the south in the "plaza" at the Villa Pepa

19 View of the entrance to the Villa Pepa from the north

21   22

23

20 View of the opening onto the "plaza" from the south

21 View of the west entrance to the "plaza" space in the Villa Pepa

22 View of the three cypress trees seen from the hill

23 View of the "plaza" toward the east

painted in white for the walls that are adjacent to the square and, in contrast, "stone cladding that picks up the tradition of dry stone construction"[15] around the exterior perimeter of the house (and used in the *riurau*) and the oven. The architect orients the inhabitant: within the domestic order or outside it, in the order of nature.

In all three access points there is least one tree, be it pre-existing (a carob or an almond tree), or one of the cypresses that the architect had planted. They help orient us because they give us a relative position by which to measure this exterior space. At the west entrance, there is an almond tree and a cypress. In the south opening, Juan Navarro planted a cypress next to the *riurau* which, together with the carob tree adjacent to the south side of the oven building, "helps close off the entrance and provide more privacy for the house" - according to a comment made by the architect. Finally, in the passageway between the bedroom and the *riurau*, there is the carob tree growing in front of the gallery-bridge and another almond tree on the lower terrace on the opposite side.

What takes place between all the architectural volumes and the trees listed here is a play of symmetries and a balance of forces, just as Juan Navarro wrote in one of his essays about how the symmetry between volumes produces a kind of "magnetization or general propensity that governs the arrangement of (the) parts".[16]

If we take into account the verticality of the cypresses, we see how th ey act as pivots or axes of rotation for the constellation of the different built volumes. The trees act as hinges, which let the observer imagine how the volumes built around them were shifted.

The entire space of the plaza is perceived in continuous movement, in a whirl of centripetal and centrifugal forces that the cypress trees, arranged strategically, set into motion as axes of rotation. A third cypress located outside the southern door, on the path toward the former painting studio, once again serves as a pivot around which to turn in the suggested direction.

If we look at the house from the hill behind it, from a vantage point above the roofs, we can imagine the system of hinges and markers formed by the three cypresses, planted by the architect, in relation to the built volumes. According to Juan Navarro, the connections between these "three green masts" create a visual triangulation that sparks an unexpected geometric relationship between the house's volumes, generated by the trees.

Frozen Time

The paintings that Juan Navarro has done of the house will offer us another reading, more temporal than spatial, of the relationships between the Villa Pepa and the trees. The two sketches that Juan Navarro uses to illustrate the design for the Villa in the book *Il Ritorno della luce*[17] are allegorical, rather than architectural, representations of the characteristics of the territory where the house is located. To interpret what these images represent, we will refer to Juan Navarro's idea of an artist:

> In my experience, the notion of geography or territory is associated with a visit to the Heraklion museum on the island of Crete. [...] There was a clear, skillful and precise figurative realism in the works on exhibit there. [...] There was also a broad repertoire of stylized representations inspired by botany and sea life; quick linear grids along with vivid wavy compositions, both continuous and intermittent; simple geometric forms together with other complex, organic ones. Certain techniques were attributable to a trained hand, while others were indicative of the most absolute freedom; calligraphic virtuosity coexisted with dripping.[18]

In the aforementioned sketches, we see stylized visions of the landscape of the Marina Alta: hills - in the rows of arches, groves - in the outlines of a waved surface, or terraces - in the linear grids. In the first drawing, we can make out three human figures, together with simple geometric shapes, like houses. The second drawing is a synthesis of these more abstract elements. In both, the horizon of the sea, close to the site, can be clearly distinguished. In the design brief, Juan Navarro writes that "the site is on a hill that interrupts the regular geometry of the rows of almond trees and outlines an area of wild Mediterranean-type vegetation, which suggests the nearness of the sea, invisible from this position".[19]

In both drawings, the sun and the moon appear in reference to the cyclical, experiential time of a regular day. As though he were a geographer, Juan Navarro represents the Villa Pepa site and the characteristics to take into account to connect it with the house: drawing on the geographical features of the surroundings and the daily time cycle.

Juan Navarro writes: "I think that both the empty spaces of the complex structure of the information network and frozen time are the extreme characteristics of the place we would like to live in".[20] He works with a notion of time that does not correspond to historical, evolutionary, positivist time; rather, it is one that does not evolve - archaic, perennial: a "frozen time".

How does this temporal notion translate into his architecture? We find an initial answer in its materiality: using original stones taken from the site, Monk and Nun roofing, baked clay flooring, and limestone cladding on the façade, traditional materials from the rural area around Alacant. For Juan Navarro, by using traditional construction and material systems, it is "as though the virgin landscape were condensed in them: as though the immediate contact with the materials were, through an empathetic relationship, a summing up and a deep-set memory of all the surrounding nature."[21] The materials introduce a remote layer, forming a closed loop between the new and the old, what already existed and what has been expanded.

Another way to highlight time in the Villa Pepa is through the trees, as they tether it to an organic-natural timeframe, associated with growth. Carob trees, cypresses, pines and almond trees, which surround the house, bear witness to the seasonal and cyclical weather. The two natural times characteristic of any living being are therefore inextricably linked to the Villa through the trees. The house, in proximity to trees, interrupts, fixes and freezes their natural time - seasonal and organic - as they are incorporated into a new structure of connections generated by the architect. The vital rhythms of all organic processes - birth, growth, development, decline and death - take place simultaneously in both the inhabitants and the trees. They both act as markers of time inescapably marching on.

Time is frozen at the Villa Pepa, however, additionally and especially, because it appears as a recurring motif in Juan Navarro's paintings. In some of his series, he turns to the medium of painting to represent - to present again and to imagine, to create an image of - the house in its surroundings and its everyday circumstances. He, thus, consciously imitates an ancient custom of some 11th-century Chinese painters who painted their own homes, set in the landscape amid daily activities.[22] These painters and scholars built their refuges and retreats amid mountainous landscapes, near rivers, waterfalls, caves, and trees. The landscapes were deliberately arranged to look natural, like wild gardens.

These Chinese painters also gave names to some of the characteristic elements of those sites. Sometimes they even carved those names into the rocks themselves. This act of naming a site or a construction was intended to present and represent what the site meant to the artist. In the same way, Juan Navarro has given names to some parts of the Villa Pepa:

> Although on a smaller scale, the landscape around our house (especially what we call the little mountain) has some characteristic and unique places that might recall, in miniature, places that appear in Li Gonglin's paintings. For example: the rare stone cave, the fox's shelter, the missing carob tree terrace, the big unsteady rock-balloon, the cliff balcony, the cistern-turret, the unreachable fig tree, etc.[23]

The trees in the landscape surrounding the house have been named and, at the same time, represented in the artist's paintings. In the wake of these representational actions, the trees are seen in a new way; as a result of the paintings they have been given a

24

25

26

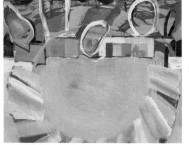

27

28

29

30

31

24 "Portrait of William Curtis", Juan Navarro Baldeweg, 1999

25 "Green landscape from the studio", Juan Navarro Baldeweg

26 "Nocturne", Juan Navarro Baldeweg, 1999

27 "August", Juan Navarro Baldeweg

28 "Landscape from the studio in grey and red", Juan Navarro Baldeweg

29 "Yellow landscape from the studio", Juan Navarro Baldeweg

30 "Green and white landscape from the studio", Juan Navarro Baldeweg

31 "Pink landscape from the studio", Juan Navarro Baldeweg

value and permanently incorporated into the house. In this way, Juan Navarro can stop the course of the trees' natural time, bringing them into a temporal relationship with the Villa.

Complementary Space

Juan Navarro's work as an artist is constructed in series: he paints the same scene over and over again; it is rehashed in different paintings until he feels that he has come to an understanding of it, more than getting at its essence or achieving a perfected final state. As he writes, "every painting can be continued in another, which is not necessarily better or more complete than the first".[24] In that sense, there is no intent of reaching an ideal final result with respect to what is laid out in the first painting, or even the first sketch. For Juan Navarro, painting is an action; as such, each step that is taken is, in itself, another action with equal interest.[25] The solutions in each series form a whole, and there can be multiple readings of the elements in it and the relationships between them.

Painting each motif multiple times, with slight variations, allows the painter to continue elaborating on the forms of the elements that he represents in each new painting. In this way, he can reformulate the relationships between them, revealing this process through the repetitions, variations, symmetries, echoes and reflections of the elements and the connections between them. He does not work with an evolving or progressive time in his series of painting, but rather with an iterative time, a suspended time.

Another consequence of working in series is that the goal is not to reach an ideal formal principle, "but working in the same seam, in the vein, the feedback loop that connects the solutions to one another, something that can't be immediately perceived."[26] This sets off an important shift in modern art: our focus moves away from the aesthetic object to center on the creation of a system of relationships. In that sense, what is interesting to observe in the series of paintings of the Villa Pepa are the relationships between the objects.

The dismemberment of the artistic object, through the use of series, thus aspires to "imagine (provide an image of) another concept of form: as a relationship, as an idea, as a desire, as a field of forces, and those fragments are its condensations, folds, sections".[27] Juan Navarro, therefore, focuses his attention on the links, the connections, the networks (whether visible or invisible) that arise between the architecture of his house and the trees – both in reality and represented in his paintings.

Juan Navarro has approached his work in relation to and in correspondence with the physical system of the environment. This has been the case since his earliest research at the Center for Advanced Visual Studies at MIT under the supervision of Gyorgy Kepes:

> Gyorgy Kepes looked at my research, and those initial designs that drew on the general idea of activating the signs of a basic physical system – an effort substantiated by certain essential coordinates, by an intersection of networks that crossed through the body. Those coordinates provide direct experiences of the nature that surrounds us and of our bodies themselves – that is, of an internal world opened up by the senses and accessible to external forces. I explored how to build projects that could define an inhabitable natural environment: a house for man.[28]

That is precisely what we deduce from looking at the two pictures of the Villa Pepa painted in 1999, both from the same point of view. We are referring to the paintings "Portrait of William Curtis" and "Nocturne". If we examine them carefully, we see that all the trees in proximity to the house are represented simultaneously (another temporal concept that we will analyze later). There is the carob tree from in front of the bridge, and we see the highest pines that grow on the hill behind; also present are the carob tree at corner of the oven building and three other trees from in front of the small threshing floor. All of them are painted using a circular shape without determining whether they are represented in plan or elevation, since there are no trunks.

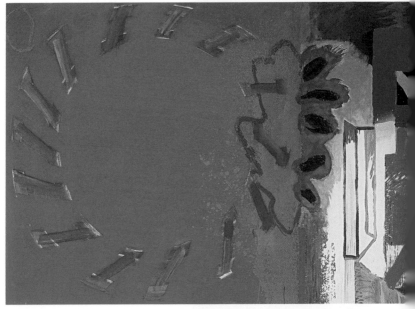

32 View of the *riurau* from the Villa Pepa

33 "House and dragon in green and silver", Juan Navarro Baldeweg

34 "House and dragon", Juan Navarro Baldeweg

35 "House and dragon in yellow and black", Juan Navarro Baldeweg

36 "Triptych of Bihzad", Juan Navarro Baldeweg

37 "House and studio", Juan Navarro Baldeweg

33

34

35

36

37

These circumferences form a constellation of objects in different orbits, a system that encircles the Villa.

The built volumes are drawn in a horizontal strip, firmly seated on the plane of the ground, and they stretch from one side of the painting to the other. The strip is seen head-on, without perspective, flattened, and divides the canvas into two parts: above and below, the sky and the ground. This strip is the *riurau*. In one of the paintings, we see a human figure inside: William Curtis; in the other, there is a splash of light. The *riurau*, as part of the inhabited house, is surrounded by the constellation of trees that conjure a domestic realm.

Another of these series in which Juan Navarro depicts the landscape show the view from the *riurau* towards his painting studio. The scene incorporates the following elements: at the top are the outlines of the distant mountains; the silhouette of the building where he has his painting studio is on the right, in the middle ground. The three trees near the pavilion are represented in the foreground (they are a cypress on the right, a prickly pear in the center and a small olive tree to the left, against a background of pine trees). The different relationships between all these elements are investigated in each painting in the series. In each "condensation, fold or section" in the series, we see the slight changes in the forms and relative positions of the elements.

The symmetries, shifts and echoes are ambiguous in their concretion; however, as Navarro himself has stated, "painters, and perhaps philosophers, have inhabited (or, at least, have wanted to inhabit) the open space of connections. Things are connected by something that is not clearly visible, and which we are barely able to define".[29] Despite the fact that the relationships are intangible, we would add that they are still representable and therefore picked up through the medium of painting.

The connections he studies encompass the trees, buildings, mountains and birds (also represented as a spiral in one of the paintings in the series). As the architect and painter has insisted, his interest lies "in what lies between things and what lies between those things and us";[30] in what he calls complementary space. These connections are part of a cycle that neither ends nor evolves; they are part of a loop, in which the different possible stages are recorded, forming a group, a series of connections that are discovered by the inhabitant or the spectator in their observations.

In the paintings "House and studio" or "Triptych of Bihzad", Juan Navarro completes the scene with the painting studio occupied by the painter himself, standing on a ladder caught in mid-activity. Here the representation is repeated in endless echoes. On the one hand, there is the house painted from the vantage point of the studio. On the other, there is the studio, where the artist is painting the view of the house. The time loop he creates in these paintings operates like telescopic time: a closed circuit generating feedback between the house represented from the studio and the studio inside the painting. Again, time is not conceived as a march forward; he stops it in a loop between the things and us, forming a complementary space.

Simultaneous Time

The temporal concept of simultaneity in Juan Navarro's pictorial work is useful in delving further into the relationship between the Villa and the trees. If we look at the paintings in the series called "Roman houses" or "Triptych of Bihzad", they depict a sequence of spaces that show different, disconnected moments in time; they are not connected by a linear narrative, but one of simultaneity. In reference to these paintings, Ángel González wrote the following:

> In the wall paintings of Pompeii, Juan Navarro saw, for his part, an interesting method for combining and connecting themes such as the female nude, the flight of swifts, or the movement of air between the trees, without the need to construct a scene or tell a "story" like the painters of illusionism.

In "Roman house with figures" we see trees swaying in the wind, a red wall with an open double door and, framed by the door, two human figures in the background. There is no progress between the two scenes or vignettes; one does not explain the other, there is no story. For there to be a story - that is, continuity over time, a narrative - "there would have to be the same spatial conditions in each vignette; but if we are aiming for spatial discontinuity between the vignettes, then time must be reduced to an instant, so they can be referred to one another. Time does not exist as a continuum, but only in the fact of its absence: in the conceptual simultaneity of the perception of all the frames. They all occur at the same time: that is the theme and the material of the piece," according to Josep Quetglas.[31]

Juan Navarro asserts that it is only in painting that we can offer simultaneously what, in reality, happens in succession. Consequently, the pictorial composition of the painting brings together, simultaneously, elements that are separated in reality both in space and in time. However, in the construction of the Villa Pepa, the aforementioned simultaneity of perception that we observe in the frames is actually achieved.

Let us analyze, for example, the analogy between the painting "La Casa" and the photograph of the corner of the kitchen and the open space that houses the carob tree, taken by the architect from the *riurau*. This square door of the *riurau* is also framed by white marble paneling on the jambs, the head and the sill. This pristine, white square frames a scene in the house, as well as another possible scene in the *riurau*, as we see in his paintings.

That helps us understand how Juan Navarro represents the physical energies of the environment in his paintings and how he relates them to the house. The artist's paintings capture not only the objects in a place, but also what surrounds them and ties them together - even if they are intangible effects. Thus, the artist shows the atmospheric shifts of the wind, the rain, or the heat in summer, or the changes brought about by the different seasons, or the variations in light throughout

38 "Gravity pieces", Juan Navarro Baldeweg   **39** "Fifth interior, light and metals", Juan Navarro Baldeweg

the day and night. All these physical factors, despite some being invisible, are decisive in his work, both pictorial and architectural. A temporal simultaneity ties all these elements together, since "it is the same material that sustains and traverses all objects, whether we call it water, wind, light, a hundred suns or a person's gaze."[32]

This perception of virtuality, of apparentness, is what Juan Navarro has captured in his art installations called "piezas de gravedad" [gravity pieces] by stopping the logical sway of an object driven by its own weight, revealing those forces or energies, making them visible. We also see this, for example, in the installation "Quinto interior, luz y metales" [Fifth interior, light and metal] (sala Vinçon), where a swing is frozen mid-air at its highest point. With this gesture, the intangible force of gravity is made evident. A similar effect is created in the same exhibition space by drawing the lines of the shadows cast on the wall near the large window. In this case, attention is drawn to the light that "pumps" through the window during the day. Juan Navarro manages to freeze the logical back and forth to which all of the "gravity pieces" would be subject, precisely by negating it.

Juan Navarro is capable of freezing the logical movements of the objects that make up his work, and that invisible force is the work itself. He stops it and traps it in each of his installations and constructions (like he did with the piece "Gold ring", for example). With a syntactic gesture, he manages to represent intangible energies through an artistic graphic representation, by giving them a form and an order. To quote his own words:

> That happens in a landscape where the grass, the trees, the surface of the water are suddenly moved by the same gust of wind. That energy that alters objects is a syntactic mechanism and a tool for cohesion. Symmetry and reflection, in my opinion, and depending on how I use them, are mechanisms of that kind.[33]

Associating things with physical energies, therefore, becomes a formal and syntactic principle in his architecture, demonstrated

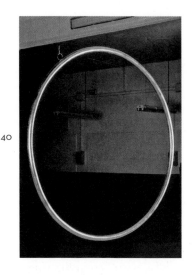

40

and made evident in his artistic representations. They are mechanisms that condition the interpretation of his architecture – in fact, that is what happens in the Casa de la Lluvia, which occupies "an aura as large as the reach of the rain", lending unity to all the heterogeneity of things that exist in the landscape.[34] The case is the same for the trees at the Villa Pepa. The house extends its aura around the entire wooded landscape and, thus, it encompasses all the atmospheric and temporal changes to which those trees are subjected: light, wind and rain.

The House: A Theater of Life
The Villa Pepa is a theater where all those forces of nature take to the stage.[35] In it, natural phenomena are invoked through the presence of trees. The house and the trees make those natural, indeterminate, intangible forces visible. The Villa is part of that landscape and, at the same time, it is a temple where those phenomena are invoked and sanctified.

From the house you can hear the sound of the wind, you can see the flight of birds and perceive changes in the sunlight. An empty space, where time can be stopped. A room from which to observe things and what surrounds them, encircles them, supports them and constitutes them.

40 "Gold ring", Juan Navarro Baldeweg

Following page:
41 "The storm", Juan Navarro Baldeweg

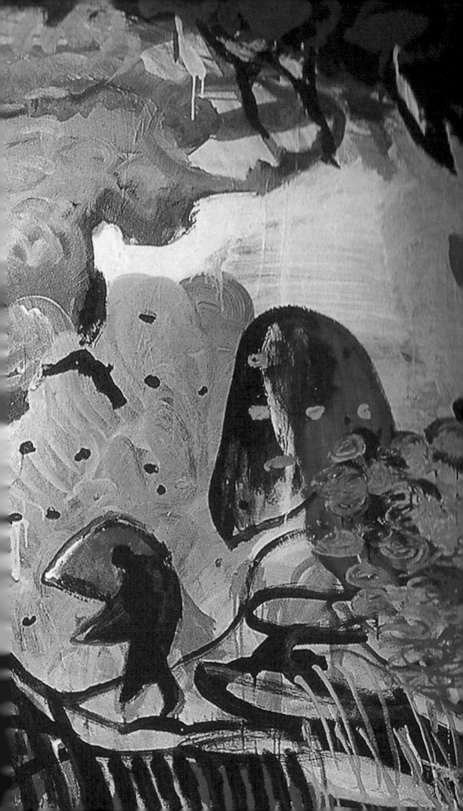

42

43

42 View of the corner of the kitchen of the   **43** Untitled (detail), 1997, Juan Navarro
Villa Pepa from the *riurau*   Baldeweg

In fact, the architect has written about architecture's role as a theatrical stage:

> I have worked on both literal and metaphorical theaters and am fully aware of the pictorial aspects of architectural space that reinforce the feeling of a theatrical distribution in a framed view or a perspective. After all, a theater is architecture brought to life by action; it is a space in which the actors perform, but where the spectators are also actors, of sorts, on their own social stage. I am obsessed with a drawing by Schinkel that shows how building lobbies can become stages set against the backdrop of the city or the landscape.[36]

Both the landscape and the villa itself serve as backdrops for daily life. All the openings in the house are frames for those scenes. They have been clearly outlined, with all their constituent elements clad in white marble: jambs, heads, sills, and thresholds. The shutters are even anchored outside the splay of the windows to avoid encroaching on the framed views of the nearby landscape.

This brings about two effects on the gaze of the inhabitant: one, the view of the outside from the inside is perfectly framed by a white halo, a frame with well-defined edges; and two, from the outside, the forms of the openings appear as clean cuts in the natural stone, revealing the domestic scenes inside.

Juan Navarro built a house in which to live, paint, think and contemplate nature. Villa Pepa is a house that is connected to the elements that surround it, especially the trees. A house where Juan Navarro, from amid the trees, contemplates the mountains, the clouds, the sky and life itself.

Endnotes

1   The first time the Villa Pepa was published was in a monograph dedicated to Navarro's work, called *Juan Navarro Baldeweg. Il ritorno della luce*, Mario Lupano, ed. Milan: Federrico Motta, 1996, pgs. 64-65. The second was in a list of works and projects in another book from 2001, released by several publishers at the same time, in different countries and different languages, called *Juan Navarro Baldeweg*. Corte Madera, CA, Gingko Press, 2001. This first edition in English was translated into German by the same publisher; into Spanish by Tanais, Seville, Madrid; and into Italian by Logos Art, Modena, (Villa Pepa was published in the Spanish edition on p. 183). The third time it was published was in *DA* magazine, vol. 56, September 2004. The last time information on the house was published was in the book *Constelaciones: Juan Navarro Baldeweg*. Pamplona: Cátedra Jorge Oteiza; Universidad Pública de Navarra, 2011, pgs. 99-105.

2   Presented by Manuel Vicent.

3   Enrique Juncosa, William Curtis, Juan González García, among others.

4   The *riurau* is a typical porch-like structure from the Marina Alta region, used to store raisins being dried in the sun when storms kicked up. The *riurau* was also used as a drying room and, eventually, as a porch or a storage area.

5   Note that this structure recalls the functional organization of a binuclear house by Marcel Breuer, although it is unfolded outward.

6   *Juan Navarro Baldeweg, obras y proyectos*. Madrid: Electa, 1993, p. 88.

7   Juan Navarro Baldeweg, interviewed by Marta Thorne. *Quaderns d'Arquitectura i Urbanisme*, vol. 163, 1984, p. 105.

8   Juan Navarro Baldeweg, "Una copa de cristal", in *Una caja de resonancia*. Margarita Navarro Baldeweg, ed. Valencia: Pre-textos, 2007, p. 12.

9   Juan Navarro Baldeweg, "Freenhofer y Lord Chandos", in Hugo von Hofmannsthal, *Una carta (De Lord Philipp Chandos a Sir Francis Bacon)*. Valencia: Pre-textos, 2008, pp. 12-28.

10 The carob tree even makes noises, as Juan Navarro told me during a visit to the Villa, in summer as its fruits fall randomly, both during the day and in the absolute silence of the night, like contemporary music.

11 Op. cit. Navarro Baldeweg, "Una casa dentro de otra", in *Una caja de resonancia*, pgs. 45-46.

12 Ibid.

13 Op. cit. Navarro Baldeweg, *La habitación vacante*, p. 37.

14 Op. cit. Navarro Baldeweg. *Il ritorno della luce*, p. 64.

15 Ibid., "con rivestimento in pietra che riprende la tradizione della muratura a secco", p. 64

16 Op. cit., Navarro Baldeweg, "Movimiento ante el ojo, movimiento del ojo", in *La habitación vacante*, p. 29.

17 Op. cit., Motta, 1996, p. 64-65.

18 Op. cit., Navarro Baldeweg, "Conversación entre Juan Navarro Baldeweg y Kevin Power", in *La habitación vacante*, p. 145.

19 In *Juan Navarro Baldeweg. Il ritorno della luce*, p. 64.

20 Op. cit., Navarro Baldeweg, "El espacio vacío, el tiempo detenido", in *La habitación vacante*, p. 55.

21 Ibid. Juan Navarro has also used local materials in other projects such as the courthouse in Maó, Menorca (1992-96), for example, or the renovation of the mills in Segura or Córdoba.

22 Of these painters, Juan Navarro holds special admiration for Li Gonglin (c. 1042-1106). The reference to Chinese painting from the 11th century was suggested to me by Juan Navarro Baldeweg himself, whose research I followed in classes taught by Professor Robert Harrist at Columbia University. By the same author, see: *Painting and Private Life in Eleventh-Century China. Mountain Villa by Li Gonglin*. Princeton: Princeton University Press, 1998. Also,

the article, "Sites Names and Their Meanings in the Garden of Solitary Enjoyment", in the *Journal of Garden History: An International Quarterly*, vol. 13, no. 4, Oct. 1993, pp. 251-257.

23 Letter from Juan Navarro addressed to the author, dated February 4, 2009.

24 Op. cit., Navarro Baldeweg, "Movimiento ante el ojo, movimiento del ojo", in *La habitación vacante*, p. 23.

25 It is worth recalling how Juan Navarro quoted Harold Rosenberg's remarks on Action Painting: "If a painting is an action the sketch is one action, the painting that follows it another. The second cannot be "better" or more complete than the first. There is just as much in what one lacks as in what the other has." Harold Rosenberg, "The American Action Painters" from *Tradition of the New*, originally in *Art News* 51/8, Dec. 1952, p. 22.

26 Josep Quetglas. "Cuatro, diez, cuatro, cinco", in *Artículos de ocasión*. Barcelona, Gustavo Gili, 2004, p. 173. Originally published in *Juan Navarro Baldeweg*, Bolzano; Antwerp: AR/GE Kunst Galerie

Museum; Singel International Kunstcentrum, 1994.

27 Ibid, p. 174.

28 Op. cit., Navarro Baldeweg, "La región flotante", in *Una caja de resonancia*, pgs. 116-117.

29 Ibid, p. 118.

30 Ibid, p. 37.

31 Josep Quetglas, "Dos notas sobre... Gerardo Delgado (Estos cuadros que ves ahora), Juan Navarro Baldeweg (Óptica doméstica)", in *Pintors Arquitectes*, eds. Pedro Azara, Manuel Arenas and Aureli Santos. Barcelona, ETSAB, 1986, pp. 12-13.

32 Ibid.

33 Op. cit., Thorne, p. 106.

34 Op. cit., Navarro Baldeweg. "Movimiento ante el ojo, movimiento del ojo", in *La habitación vacante*, p. 33.

35 In fact, Juan Navarro has suggested on occasion that the *riurau* could be used as the stage for an open-air play, where the audience could be seated on the threshing floor and the house itself could be used as a backdrop.

36 Op. cit., Curtis, p. 12.

Alison and Peter Smithson

HEXEN HAUS

Incorporating the organic matter of the trees on the architecture of porches and glass ceilings makes it possible to record the passage of cyclical time. And vice versa, the architecture of branching crosspieces that house the fallen leaves becomes a meaningful part of nature.

Making a Sheltered Enclave

Hexenhaus was how people referred to the pre-existing dwelling in Bad Karlshafen, Germany, which was renovated and enlarged over a period of 18 years by Alison Margaret Gill (Sheffield, 1928; London, 1993) and Peter Smithson (Stockton-on-Tees, 1923; London, 2003). *Hexenhaus*, or "witch's house" is a common name in the area, where the Brothers Grimm wrote their fairy tales. It got the nickname because of its location in a lush oak forest that hides the house and gives it a certain spookiness.

The base of the house is practically square. Its reduced size contrasts with the enormity of the nearby oaks. The ground floor is supported by stone walls and the gables of the first floor are bolstered by a framework of pillars and wooden beams. The top floor sits under a pitched roof, its two sides with different slopes.

02

On the north side, there are two annexes: a sauna and a storage area.

Before the Smithsons' intervention, the house was quite opaque. The interior was dark, and it hardly offered any views of the Weser River and the surrounding woods. So, the owner, Axel Bruchhäuser – founder of the furniture company Tecta, created by designers and architects – commissioned the Smithsons to develop the 22 interventions they designed and carried out from 1984 to 2002.[1] Following their work, the house is now a bright and open space, full of correspondences with the outside, connected with the trees, the seasons and the nearby landscape of the riverside. A "delicious" witch's house, in the words of its owner.

The idea behind each of the annexes that the Smithsons designed was the same: to strike up relations between the house and the forest, because "the owners of a Hansel and Gretel house – a man and his cat – felt they were not, when inside their house, appreciating enough of the quality of the wood situated on slopes above the River Weser."[2]

Alison took charge of the first extension: a small porch attached to the west façade. As Peter described it later, "The porch can be read as an exemplar of a method by which a small physical change – a layering-over of air adhered to an existing fabric – can bring about a delicate tuning of the relationship of persons with place."[3] Throughout this analysis we will see how the Smithsons achieved that "layering-over" between architecture and trees in each of their interventions; they established temporal and formal connections between the trees and the architecture; they managed to manifest the passage of time; they scattered the house across its environment, colonizing its surroundings and forming a protected enclave for its inhabitants.

Previous page:
01 View of the bedroom in the Hexenhaus (Witch's House), 1996, Peter Smithson

02 State prior to the renovations and expansions designed by Alison and Peter Smithson

Following page:
03 Southwest façade of the Hexenhaus after the Smithsons' interventions

Axel and Karlchen's Porch

From 1983 to 1985, Alison designed and constructed the first porch on the house's southwest façade. She built it using a framework of wooden slats, with a glass envelope, even for the roof. The geometry in plan is characterized by a 30-degree rotation with respect to the façade, making it coincide exactly with the north-south and east-west axes. The program consisted of a tiny room, connected to the house by an existing door.

The owner asked Alison to equip the new porch with spaces for two inhabitants: one for himself and one for his cat, Karlchen. For Axel, she imagined a wide space facing the entrance, where the geometry forms a right angle. Karlchen's space was narrower and more triangular, situated at the house's southeast corner on a cantilever over the stone wall. She placed the exterior door between these two habitats, leading onto a set of stairs that follow the geometry of the porch to connect with the level below. Alison installed another door at the back, perpendicular to the wall of the house.

The porch sits in the middle of the woods, attached to the old house and offering each of its two residents a space in direct connection with the surrounding forest. Axel's corner was initially meant to be fully mobile, including its roof, using sliding mechanisms, although during construction the owner ultimately decided against it. The floor in Karlchen's corner is also glass, so "the cat looks down from his window onto the terrace below" to hunt for mice.[4]

The porch can be accessed through two entrances, depending on whether you are coming from a lower level on the site or from above. Both of the doors were reused from the old house, taking "two halves of the original French windows and their special weather-sealing ironmongery".[5] One of them is set perpendicular to the façade, lined up with the old door jamb. It has a glass roof that protects it and a platform made from wooden slats. The other door is aligned with the four steps that connect with the lower level.

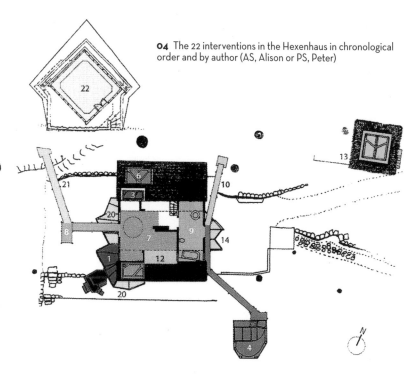

04 The 22 interventions in the Hexenhaus in chronological order and by author (AS, Alison or PS, Peter)

1. Axel's porch
1984-1986, first
intervention, AS

2. Riverbank windows
1989-1990, AS

3. Hexenhaus holes
The first holes: in the roof
above the living room on
the ground floor; and two
triangular holes in the floor
of the studio on the first
floor, 1990, AS

4. Hexenbesenraum
(The witch broom room)
1990-1996, First unbuilt
version: AS, 1991. Execution:
PS, 1996

**5. Mementos of Karlchen
(the cat)**
1993, AS

6. Sauna
1995-98, PS

7. Axel's bedroom
1996, PS

**8. Hexenhaus pier and
bridge**
1996-97 and 2000, PS

9. Bathroom
1996-97, PS

**10. Bridge to upper
walkway**
1997, PS

11. Living room bay
1997, PS

**12. Window toward the
Weser**
Window in the studio on the
first floor with views over
the river, 1997, PS

13. Tea-house
1997, PS

14. Front door porch
1997-1998, PS

15. Benches
1998, PS

16. Kitchen
1999, PS

**17. Garden store and
kitchen window**
1999, PS

18. Karlchen's flag tower
1999, PS

**19. Hole kitchen to second
bunk**
2000, PS

20. Axel's porch extension
2000, PS

**21. Bridge from pier to the
upper walkway**
2000, PS

**22. Lantern pavilion or
tree-viewing pavilion**
2000-2002, PS

Alison incorporated a series of diagonal crosspieces on the fixed glass panes, "as a built part of the wood, however one whose branches cannot move with the seasons".[6] The zigzagging profiles of the four crosspieces in the corner – two at the bottom and two at the top – evoke the forms of a tree branch. As a result, when you look out at the woods from inside, the crosspieces blend together with the real branches of the trees near the house. Both Alison and Peter used this formal pattern in almost all the other interventions in the Hexenhaus.

In the first version of the porch, the seat/box for Axel could be slid toward the exterior on a track. It could break away from the volume, since "at first they thought they wanted the porch to open fully and, like their existing French windows, still be able to give them a wide opening into the woods."[7] Part of the porch was designed as a piece of furniture that could be used outdoors, leaving the space entirely open.

The braces Alison drew for the two panels in the corner occupied by the seat took the outer support as their access of symmetry. The top diagonal crosspieces formed a structure consisting of two slats coming together at an angle with respect to the rectangular frame (similar to the frames designed for the doors of St. Hilda's College at Oxford). The overall effect of the piece was like branches sprouting from a tree trunk.

Ultimately, incorporating mobile elements into the porch was ruled out because "they remembered they never left anything open in summer because of the flies. [...] Someone has added the loose corner seat [...] in place of the corner storage box/seat base that was in the construction design but not built."[8] The top elements in the frame were replaced by crosspieces similar to the ones below, although more pronounced. This changed the shape of the corner, which butted up against the hinge of the back door. A small panel was added to connect it with the second door.

In 1992, seven years after the porch for the Hexenhaus was built, Alison was commissioned to design a porch for the canteen at the Tecta furniture factory, which Axel owned. Drawing on pre-

05

vious experience, the seating area against the exterior wall was built with frames and crosspieces resembling the ones at the Hexenhaus. It was also topped with a glass roof.

There are similar relationships between the interior and exterior in both porches: the doors can be opened or closed alternately depending on the weather, allowing for the outside to be occupied (the garden in the Tecta factory, or the woods in the Hexenhaus). However, in the factory porch, the crosspieces run at an angle on all the panes, creating a structure of diagonals that surrounds the entire space. This generates an analogy with the structure of a tree, which overlaps with the views of existing trees in the yard; it is the same formal assonance used in the porch for the Hexenhaus.

The glazed roof collects fallen leaves from nearby trees, emphasizing the building's relationship to the forest; as Alison put it:

> Extending outwards the pattern of their lives so it might adhere to the pattern of the seasons in their woods: much as envisaged... trees and porch bare of leaves or trees and porch patterned with leaves... in snow, in sun, in rain, in wind.[9]

Alison was able to reveal changes in the weather, atmospheric changes, in the environment through this small intervention. At the end of the design brief, she wrote that the porch was "one answer for the late 'eighties that I spoke about first in Barcelona, 1985-1986; the calm cell in nature".[10]

A Calm Cell in Nature

In a Tecta advertising brochure for the 1991 Milan fair, Alison wrote an essay called "Saint Jerome: The Desert... The Study".[11] The text was based on a lecture she gave in Barcelona in 1985 and another she gave a year later in Stockholm. At the time, she had been commissioned to carry out the first intervention for

Previous page: **05** St. Hilda's College, interior doors

06 Axel's porch after its construction

07

08

09

the Hexenhaus; in the brief for Axel's porch, she writes that the design was a built response to those lectures.

The text begins by presenting different pictorial representations of Saint Jerome's habitats, from 1400 to the end of the Renaissance. Its main thesis outlines the contrast between living in the middle of nature or in "the energising cell supported by urban order".[12] Alison affirms that, in either environment, "the alternative ideals might be thought to exist in the same *fragment* of the easily defensible *enclave*."[13] The goal for the design of Axel's porch was similar: to create a fragment of the house located in an enclave, the woods.

Alison expresses her concern for the future of the planet and proposes looking at Saint Jerome's habitats as a model for a change in behavior: "Projecting this foresight of a society becoming more climate, nature, and energy resource responsive." In that sense, she proposes that "a merging of the old reciprocity will allow us to begin to think of a new form of restorative habitat for a future *light touch* inhabitation of the earth".[14] We see this in the porch with the reuse of the existing doors and timber construction.

Alison describes, analyzes and categorizes the two types of representations of Saint Jerome, depending on whether he is depicted outdoors or indoors. For her, representing Saint Jerome in the desert:

> Expresses a human desire for the freedom that seems to be in nature; the undiminishable freshness in nature's cycle of renewal of its complex order and balance. As the century turns, for any one of the many we now are to be able to enjoy sublime ascetic pleasures of a place in nature will rely on a 'green consciousness' becoming effective.[15]

07 Axel's porch seen from the living room
08 Axel's porch overlooking the River Weser
09 Porch of the canteen at the Tecta factory, Lauenförde, 1990, Alison Smithson

The image of the saint in the desert shows a way of dwelling in correlation with the order and balance of the environment. In contrast, the representations of Jerome in his study, common in the Renaissance, represent a mode of dwelling with all the comforts. Those images liken his study to the "machine for living in", which was upheld "in those writings of the Heroic Period of the Modern Movement in Architecture concerned with again raising the minimal *cell* to an art".[16]

Drawing on these two epitomes of habitation, for Alison, "The Jerome Study is an allegory for perfection of thought; for the creation of the perfected object; for deliberated choice."[17] In contrast, she posits his representation in an idyllic grotto as a common reading of the two aforementioned types of spaces. Let's read it in her words:

> The overlay of Desert on Study in the idea of grotto is not unreasonable: Jerome probably took to the cave as Study because of his knowledge gained in the Desert. [...] If in the immediate future we begin to create fragments of enclaves that protect our inhabitation, we may come to live closer to the idyll represented in the Renaissance by Saint Jerome's two habitats.[18]

10

These two ideas were reflected in the porch of the Hexenhaus, as well as in nearly all the other interventions carried out over the years. The porch sits lightly on top of the existing structures; its precarious construction takes shape as a *fragment of an enclave* that offers its inhabitants the same

11

10 Saint Jerome beside a Pollard   **11** Saint Jerome in His Study,
Willow, 1648, Rembrandt   1456-60, Antonello della Messina

idyll represented in the Renaissance by the two habitats of Saint
Jerome: a space for contemplation, a quiet cell in nature.

The Witch's Broom Room (Hexenbesenraum)

The *Hexenbesenraum* (in English, the witch's broom room) was
another of the interventions Alison designed in 1991. That said,
it was not built until 1996, under Peter's direction, with the help
of Hermann Koch and based on drawings Alison had left. The

commission was for a space where Axel could slip away to rest; a free-standing pavilion but located near the house and the entrance: a room elevated off the ground atop a structure of wooden pillars, on the slope overlooking the River Weser.

Alison laid out the basic characteristics of the room where Axel could go "to find peace and to re-energise himself".[19] She had studied different options for the project in a series of sketches. She designed a centripetal upward movement from the eastern corner of the house at ground level, rising to a height of four meters where the room/overlook was located. At the top of the page, she drew a circular layout in plan, and at the bottom she sketched out square and trapezoidal configurations. In the center of the page, all the figures are merged together, hinting at the solution that Peter eventually built.

Alison chose to locate the entrance to the north, and that is how it was built later on. This location was ideal because it put visitors in a position "to have good views of the river, to be able to make out the house from behind, to be able to look down and see the forest floor, and look up and see foliage, trees and sky".[20]

In the sketches, Alison marked the sightlines using arrows like rays emerging from a point, which marks the occupant's position in the witch's broom room. At the location of this point, she drew a bench, facing the half-moon divan or bed, a feature that Peter maintained, tucked against the interior wooden wall. As she did with Axel's porch and the Tecta canteen, she proposed two ways of occupying the space: sitting or lying down. The divan and the bench define the spatial limits of this elevated cell.

The two pieces of furniture are connected by a small rectangular entryway. In the section drawn at the bottom center of the page of her sketches, the different heights of these three interior areas are clear. The entryway is at the base level, while the bench and the couch are one step higher. A man is represented sitting on the bench, looking through the window above the riser that separates the bed from the entryway. He can see the sloping terrain of the ground, at his feet, running toward the river. In the

12

12 Interior of the Hexenbesenraum

other three sections that appear on the page, the arrows are directed toward the sky and, therefore, toward the branches of the surrounding trees, since they stretch above the height of the room.

Alison designed the northeast side to be opaque – that is, with no openings facing toward the entrance to the house. However, during construction, Peter added two tiny rectangular windows following the slope of the roof; one located at the head of the divan and the other at its foot. The room was left fully glazed in the west corner, with views towards the Hexenhaus.

The roof of the pavilion, the basics of which are also laid out in Alison's sketch sheet, consisted of a diagonal ridge following the

13 Northeast view of the Hexenbesenraum

14 Southwest view of the Hexenbesenraum

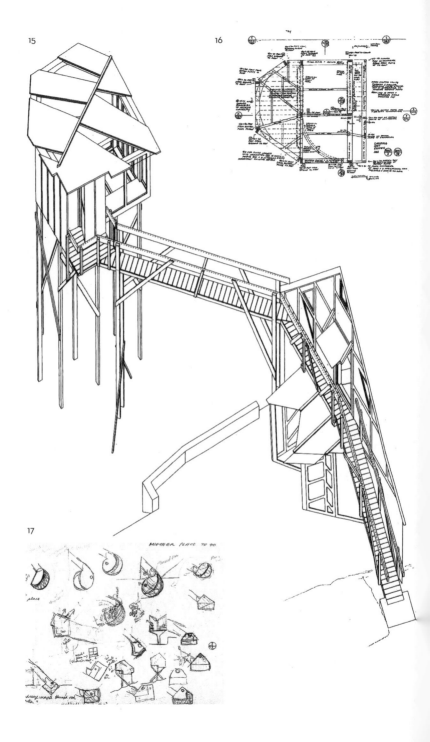

15

16

17

ANOTHER PLACE TO GO

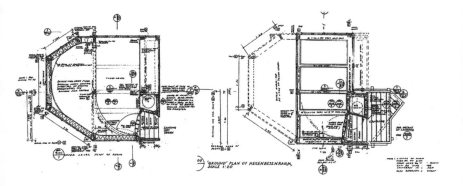

15 Perspective of the Hexenbesenraum, 1996

16 Floor plans from the construction drawings for the Hexenbesenraum, 1996

17 Early studies for the Hexenbesenraum, 1991, Alison Smithson

18 Access to the Hexenbesenraum from the ground

19 Elevations from the construction drawings for the Hexenbesenraum, 1996, Peter Smithson and Hermann Koch

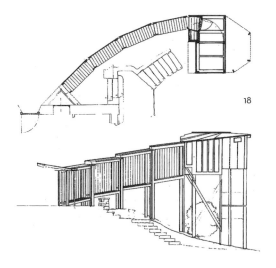

18

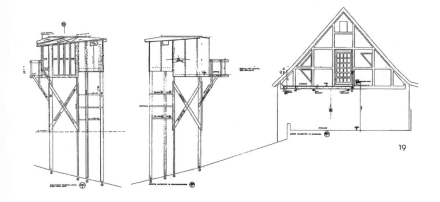

19

north-south axis, supporting trapezoidal glass and wooden surfaces on either side: three opaque panes and three transparent,
all wedge-shaped and alternating from one side to the other of
the ridgecap, forming a checkerboard pattern. The panes all have
different shapes, because the center does not coincide with the
axis of symmetry between the two gables. The effect of the roof
panes is a metaphor, again, for the leaves of the trees, imitating
the play of light and shadow.

Peter wrote that "the roof is one more façade", documenting
their goals with the different sightlines:

> In the Hexenhaus [...], the load that the in-between space trans-
> fers to the sky comes from the confinement of the tangle of tree
> branches that surrounds and completely covers the house. From
> above: in the variable density of the leafy covering. From below: in
> the view, through the building and the less dense sections of the
> foliage, of the sky.[21]

From inside the pavilion, you have the feeling of being up in a
tree, despite not being literally built on one. You can even feel a
slight rocking in the room, as a result of the height and size of the
wooden pillars. In fact, the Hexenbesenraum could be the answer
to El Lissitsky's wish – judging from a statement by its owner: "The
static architecture of the Egyptian pyramids has been overcome:
our architecture rolls, swims, flies. It will sway and float in the air."[22]

The roof of the pavilion acts as a mediator between the interior,
the trees, the sky and the inhabitants. Similarly, the façades open
onto the trees, the ground of the hillside and the River Weser.
Here too, the Smithsons emulated trees in the shape, feel and
perception of this room for the witch to store her broom.

The Lantern Pavilion

The Lantern Pavilion was the last thing to be built at the Hexenhaus. It was entirely designed by Peter between 2000 and 2002.
Initially, he called it the Tree Viewing Pavilion, since his idea was to
build a place where he could contemplate the huge, centuries-old

oak trees that encircle the house. He wanted the lush forest to surround anyone inside the pavilion, although because of its spatial configuration, like a glass lighthouse, he ultimately decided it call it the Lantern Pavilion.

Peter outlined the floor plan, roof, elevations, construction details and a section that accounted for the slope of the terrain all on a single page. He also drew the top floor of the house and included all the other interventions that had taken place at the Hexenhaus over the years.

The floor plan of the Lantern Pavilion is a square, measuring five meters on each side, supported by nine wooden posts on each side, with their corresponding glass panels. Its situation on the plot is rotated 45 degrees with respect to the axes of the house and the nearby retaining walls, which were pre-existing, to generate a platform. This rotation left two triangular spaces between the south and east façades and the stone wall. Peter placed the entrance to the pavilion on the central axis of the east façade, placing two panes of glass in two of the panel modules.

The drawings show the trunks of the trees near the old house, and their sections are filled in with concentric rings, simulating a dendrochronological study of their age.[23] Peter drew two more trunks, in the upper left corner, this time without filling in their areas. On one of the trunks, surrounding it, he wrote the words "old oak". Nearby, he outlined another trunk with a smaller diameter, which he labelled "beech". He drew a line from the center of Axel's bedroom to the trunk of the old oak, writing the following: "sighting line to old oak". In other words, Peter established a visual relationship connecting the house with the oak, passing through the pavilion.

Looking at the section, we see that Peter represented a part of the old oak's trunk in elevation. Inside the pavilion, he also drew two eyes. On the left side it reads "Standing/Eyes/Sitting" – indicating the position of someone both standing and sitting. There are two dotted lines emerging from both eyes parallel to the slope of the terrain – and the slope of the roof – that stretch out beyond the limits of the pavilion. A visual beam that is evoked, at its intersection with the walls of the pavilion, by two half-circle openings in each façade: one in the south façade – facing downhill; and another in the west façade – facing uphill – towards the old oak. The diameter of this second hole is twice the size of the one facing the river, as though leaving a record of that visual cone.

Although the four sides outlined by the vertical wooden posts offer a view of the entire surroundings, Peter accentuated the view through these semicircular frames – a view that stretches from the high point of the site down to the River Weser, taking the trunk of the old oak as its point of origin. This connection between the oak, the beech, the pavilion, the house and the river is perfectly clear in the photograph taken from just in front of the entrance to the pavilion.

The fifth façade of the Lantern Pavilion, its roof, is also made from wooden slats with separations that follow the same pattern as the posts in the vertical enclosures, with glass panels in between. Its slope, as can be seen in the section, coincides with the slope of the terrain. However, we note that the incline of the roof plane is rotated 45 degrees with respect to the perpendicular axes of the square floor plan. In other words, while the slope runs from northwest to southeast, the wooden beams are oriented north-south.

Peter deliberately added this shift in the slopes corresponding to rainwater drainage and the alignment of the beams so that the leaves falling from the surrounding trees would be caught, under their own weight, by the protruding edges of the beams. As a result, the leaves accumulate, at least for a time, on the glass roof, covering over the pavilion and transforming its roof from transparent to opaque.

The perimeter of the Lantern Pavilion's roof does not coincide with the square outline of the floor plan; it extends beyond the edges on three sides. On the east and west façades, it overhangs a regular distance. To the south, however, the cantilever forms a triangular area above the terrace, also in the shape of a trian-

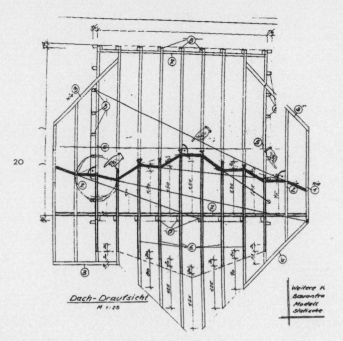

Dach-Draufsicht
M 1:25

Weitere H.
Bauanfra
Modell
Statische

20 Plan of the
roof of the Lantern
Pavilion

21 Perspective of the
Lantern Pavilion

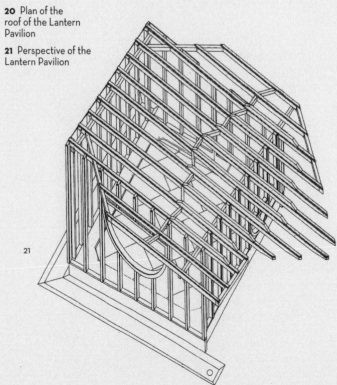

21

22 Preliminary studies for
the Lantern Pavilion, 2000,
Peter Smithson

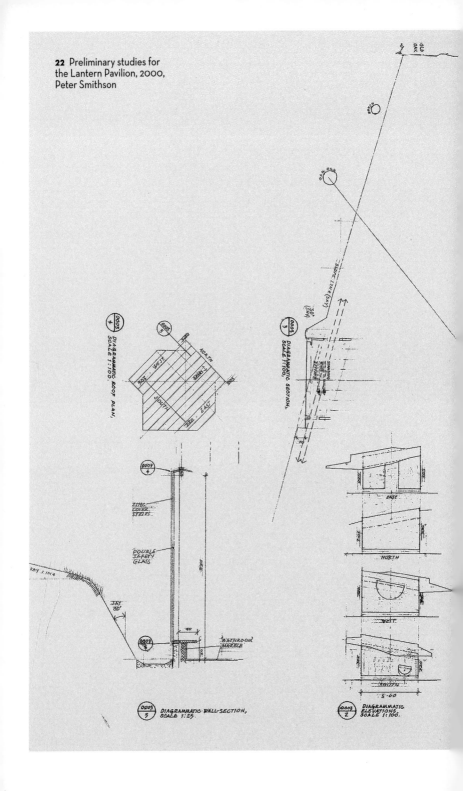

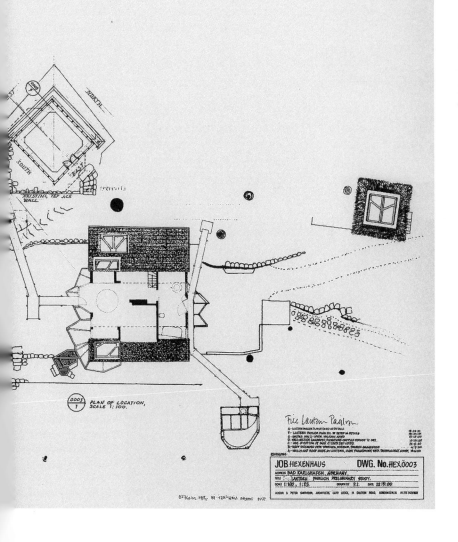

North

South

East

EXISTING TERRACE WALL

File Lantern Pavilyn

⌀0003
1
PLAN OF LOCATION,
SCALE 1: 100.

REVISIONS:

JOB HEXENHAUS   **DWG. No.** HEX0003

ADDRESS BAD KARLSHAFEN, GERMANY.
TITLE LANTERN PAVILION PRELIMINARY STUDY.
SCALE 1:100, 1:25   DRAWN BY P.S.   DATE 22:5:00

ALISON & PETER SMITHSON, ARCHITECTS, GATE LODGE, 24 GILSTON ROAD, LONDON S.W.10

gle. To compensate for these roof overhangs, Peter installed an irregular rafter that runs through the entire pavilion from east to west. Depending on the length of the projecting beams, which are supported by the south façade, they are compensated with a crossbeam at the appropriate distance. That is, he introduced a piece that, attached at an angle, accounted for the different weights of the structure. As a result of this counterbalancing, a zigzagging strut runs through the roof.

This tree-like figure in the roof of the Lantern Pavilion is clearly inspired by the first crosspieces that Alison designed years earlier for Axel's porch.[24] Peter talked about the relationship he wanted to create between the trees and the Lantern Pavilion, a justification that could well be extended to the other interventions for both the Hexenhaus and the Tecta factory:

> If you think about the Philip Johnson glass-wall house, in the evening, the architecture's space is defined by the floodlighting on the trees, and this house of Axel's is completely covered by really old trees. They are huge. Therefore there is a possibility, as it were, of making a pavilion in which the inside light goes out of all the walls and the roof. The Johnson house is a type of sandwich. The Lantern Pavilion is a kind of basket out of which light comes. It serves no function. [...] Its prime intention is formal; it is exploring a possibility of the trees to be the enclosure.[25]

The pavilion's spatial condition is transformed through the glass ceilings arranged to collect the fallen leaves. The leaves offer shade and add effects of color and texture to the strictly architectural elements. It is a recording of the passage of cyclical time seen in the deciduous trees on the site. As a result of the layout of the porches and pavilions, the trees become an integral part of the Hexenhaus as a whole. And vice versa: the architecture of branching crosspieces and glazed roofs that catch the fallen leaves becomes a meaningful part of the forest trees, a testimonial to the passage of seasonal time.

23 Interior of the Lantern Pavilion with views over the Hexenhaus and the River Weser

24

25

24 View of the Lantern Pavilion from the highest level of the site

25 Detail of the north corner of the Lantern Pavilion, with the oak and beech trees in the background

26 Interior view of the Lantern Pavilion looking toward the oak and beech trees

Bringing Trees into the House

Alison and Peter Smithson perforated Axel's house in different places and in different forms - rectangular, circular and triangular - over the course of no less than 16 interventions. Looking at all these openings, we will carefully examine the ones that fostered concrete relationships with the existing trees.

The first of the skylights was created by Alison in 1990. Located in the north gable, it also crosses through the structure of the first floor to bring natural light down to the ground floor. It offers views of the branches of the old oak located on the north slope:

> Branches of trees grow over the Hexenhaus: holes were made in
> the roof to let that branchy outside into the inside. The geometric
> language of these holes is of the same order as that of the earlier
> Axel's Porch and the Riverbank Window.[26]

In fact, the intent behind these holes was to be able to look at the surrounding trees from inside the house. Plus, the crosspieces in the opening were, again, reminiscent of the branches of the trees. Their silhouettes blend in with the branches of the oak seen from the window. Fallen leaves, snow or rain also collect on the glass. Alison thus succeeded in bringing "the branchy outside into the inside."

It is worth remarking that Alison drew the sightlines for both Axel and Karlchen, his cat. This detail confirms that, for her, both the man and his pet were treated equally as inhabitants of the house from the beginning. The letters Axel and Alison wrote to one another were always signed by their respective cats.

The other openings in the house were designed by Peter, who carried on with the same formal pattern and the same strategy with respect to the nearby trees. The one located in the less slanted section of the north gable of the roof establishes a direct link with the same oak tree. This rectangular hole - the same size as the one Alison designed - brings light into the entryway in front of the sauna.

Peter placed three crosspieces in this window, dividing the frame into four triangles. A similar design was used for the roof of the Tea Pavilion and for the new skylights in Axel's bedroom. That is how Alison and Peter brought the nearby trees into the house. In the same way, their architecture was also integrated into the surrounding forest.

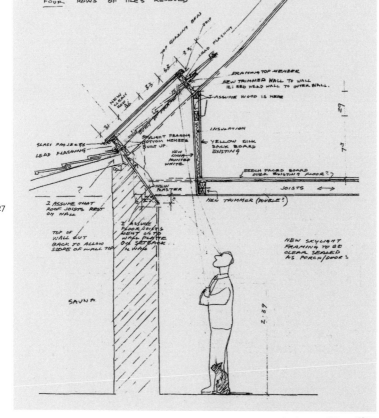

27

27 Section of the first hole in the roof of the Hexenhaus above the living room, 1990, Alison Smithson

28

29

30

31

The Tree as a Formal, Structural and Vital Pattern

Trees played a decisive role in many of the Smithsons' designs.[27] One indication of this is that the Smithsons always drew trees with care and detail, going so far as to affirm that: "When we draw a tree, it is a tree that is there... otherwise it is the tree we would plant."[28] The designs with clear ties to trees include the Wokingham Primary School (1958), the Garden Building at St. Hilda's College (1967-1970), the Joseph Lucas Limited Headquarters in Birmingham (1973-1974) and the Yellow House (1976).

The first project where existing trees took a decisive role was the Wokingham Infants School competition. In this proposal, they adapted the floor plan to the terrain "holding the line of trees which were remembrances of a previous pattern of use, as a hand would a pencil".[29] The entrance hall opened toward two of the largest oaks on the site. Furthermore, the six classroom-pavilions were connected by a "walled street-activity-space with an entirely glazed roof".[30] Something similar to the Wokingham layout was also proposed for the Lucas Headquarters (1973), since "the site was a green strip, and the building took advantage of the existence of old trees".[31]

In the sketch of the corridors designed for the school in Wokingham, we see that the occupants' gazes are directed towards the sky, taking in changes in light, passing clouds, birds and airplanes, rain or falling snow, and the leaves of the surrounding trees. Similarly, Alison drew sightlines above the garden walls that defined the space for outdoor activities adjacent to the existing trees. As seen in the sketch, the arrows beginning from the

28 View of the roof of the Hexenhaus with the different holes designed by Alison and Peter Smithson

29 View of the oak tree from inside the living room, through the first hole Alison designed in the roof

30 Hole in the gable of the roof of the sauna, 1998, Peter Smithson

31 Axel's bedroom with the holes in the opposite gable of the roof, 1996, Peter Smithson

center, and at the top of the hill, stretch up above the two walls to point at the branches of the nearby trees. Consequently, and from very early on, Alison and Peter Smithson established clear relationships between their architecture and trees, and between the trees and the occupants of the spaces they designed.

The first time the Smithsons used these formal tree-like patterns was for St. Hilda's College. Shortly afterwards they were also applied in the designs for the Lucas Headquarters and the Yellow House. In St. Hilda's for example, they considered "a majestic beech tree" when it came to drawing the façades reinforced with a branching lattice.[32] In the Birmingham offices, on the other hand, "the building steps forward, steps back, performs as it were a stately dance with the trees that lace the site [...]; thus the building form utilizes that sense of connection to place which the interpretations of existing trees can transmit".[33]

In the Yellow House, "The trees in the private garden are acacia whose light leafage filters the sun in summer and blows away as golden pennies in winter." For this design, the tree located in the corner was decisive, "a horse chestnut, into the scent and sight of whose flower candles the occupiers of the house would ascend up their staircase behind the wall in spring, and for whose rustling dry leaves, fallen flowers of intricate spotting, windfall green mace-like fruitlets and 'conkers' children would scuffle on the mound in front of the wall in winter, spring, summer and autumn."[34] For the Smithsons, the trees were a source of formal inspiration and, above all, elements through which the inhabitant managed to empathize with and relate to the environment.

Peter justified the use of irregular structures in his designs as something "deliberately *optical*" and as a way of "making a place for the art of inhabitation".[35] Indeed, the frameworks used

32 Detail of the façade of the Garden Building, St. Hilda's College, Oxford, 1967-70, Alison and Peter Smithson

33 Perspective, Lucas headquarters, Shirley, 1973-74, Alison and Peter Smithson

32

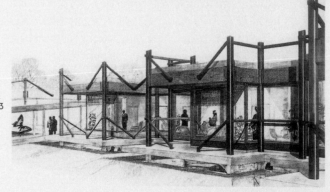

33

34 Façade of the Garden Building, St. Hilda's College

in façades, doors, windows, partitions – and even in some furniture – offered "one way to achieve a receptive architecture [...] through layering; for between the layers there is room for illusion and for activity".[36]

The movement of the inhabitants past these frames, and the angles of the crosspieces "create the effect of identifying and intensifying the fragments you glimpse through the lattice". As a consequence, these structures, or braces, condition "what you see in a way similar to the sense of space achieved by a picture frame."[37] This attitude on the part of the Smithsons, in fact, shows a certain affinity with the qualities they defended in Brutalism.

Indeed, according to Peter, Brutalism "begins when you are trying to uncover the brick-ness of brick". Or, as he would assert later, referring to an image of a courtyard in an old house with a

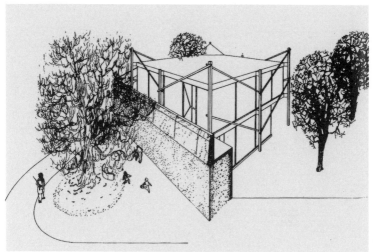

35 Perspective, Yellow House, 1976, Peter Smithson

tree, brutalism was "trying to show the tree-ness of the tree".[38] This "treeness" was the formal, spatial and perceptual concept that the Smithsons extracted from trees for their architecture.

There are figurative takeaways, but also perceptual and even structural influences, as exemplified in the branching distribution of the different pavilions that make up the Hexenhaus, a tree-like spatial composition, realized with platforms, ramps and aerial walkways extending like branches that stretch out over the site, connecting the pavilions with the house.

In the Hexenhaus, as the architects expressed it: "there is an unconscious insistence on the interaction between 'temporary' and 'permanent'." Just as they did for the *Patio & Pavilion* exhibition – where they placed a series of objects on top of the translucent plastic roof as a sign of human culture – they also

36

36 Sketch of the roof of the street-space for the Wokingham Elementary School

37 Patio & Pavillion installation for the exhibition *This is Tomorrow*, London, 1956, Alison and Peter Smithson

37

let branches, leaves and other bits of trees collect on top of the Hexenhaus. It was a way of highlighting the interactions between what is temporary and what is permanent, between natural and artificial. The glass ceilings of the Hexenhaus are windows that record the ongoing changes in nature and the evolution of life.

Endnotes

1 For more on how, by whom and when the different interventions took place in the Hexenhaus, and on the Smithsons' relationship with the owner, Axel Bruchhäuser, see: Maddalena Scimemi, "Un'opera aperta degli Smithson a Bad Karlshafen", *Cassabella*, vol. 726, 2004, pp. 6-20; Max Risselada, "Conglomerate Ordering: Growing Houses" in *Alison and Peter Smithson: From the House of the Future to a House of Today*. Rotterdam: 010 Publishers, 2004, p. 180 ff; and Andrew Mead, "Putting down roots," in *Architects' Journal*, vol. 214, no. 6, August 2001, pgs. 251-257.

2 Marco Vidotto, ed. *Alison + Peter Smithson. Obras y proyectos*. Barcelona: Gustavo Gili, 1997, p. 204.

3 Ibid.

4 Ibid.

5 Ibid.

6 Ibid.

7 Ibid.

8 Ibid.

9 Ibid.

10 Ibid.

11 Alison Smithson, "Saint Jerome. The Desert... The Study", in op. cit., van den Heuvel and Risselada, pp. 225-230.

12 Ibid, p. 298.

13 Ibid.

14 Ibid.

15 Ibid, p. 226.

16 Ibid.

17 Ibid, p. 227.

18 Ibid, p. 228.

19 Max Risselada, "Conglomerate Ordering: Growing Houses", op. cit., p. 194.

20 Alison and Peter Smithson, "El Hexenbesenraum en la Hexenhaus", *Bau*, vol. 15, 1997, p. 113.

21 Peter Smithson, "Desde arriba y hacia arriba", in *St. Hilda's College, Oxford: la arquitectura del entramado*, Marco Vidotto y Aquil·les González, eds. Madrid: Colegio Oficial de Arquitectos de Madrid, 2001, p. 40.

22 In Peter Smithson, Karl Unglaub, *Flying Furniture*. Cologne: Verlag der Buchhandlung Walther König, 1999, p. 97.

23 Dendrochronology, from the Greek δένδρον (tree), χρονος (time) and λογότυπα (study) is the science that deals with the dating of the growth rings of trees and shrubs. Based on growth rings, dendrochronology analyzes the spatial and temporal patterns of biological, physical or cultural processes.

24 We also find similar tree-like forms in the crosspieces of the Canteen Porch (AS, 1992) and the Weaving room (PS, 1997), which were later developments to Axel's porch, as well as the other windows added to the Hexenhaus. This was also the case, for example, in the Hexenbesenraum, although the forms were tested first at Tecta in the Yellow Lookout (A + PS, 1992) and in the Stair Tower, (PS, 1995). In all these interventions, Alison and Peter Smithson established formal and perceptual – and even metaphorical – links and connections with the nearby trees.

25 Peter Smithson. *Peter Smithson: Conversations with Students*. New York: Princeton Architectural Press, 2005, p. 86.

26 Alison and Peter Smithson, *The Charged Void. Architecture*. New York: Monacelli Press, 2000, p. 573.

27 The following list compiles all of Alison and Peter Smithson's projects in which trees played an active role in the design: Conventry Cathedral. Oct 1950-July 1951. Limerston street, Chelsea. 1953-1961. Golden Lane. 1952. 'Parallel of Life and Art' Exhibition, I.C.A. Dover Street, London. 11 Sep-18 Oct. 1953. Rumble Villa, St. Albans. 1954. House of the Future, Ideal Home Exhibition, Olympia, London. Aug. 1955-March 1956. Patio and Pavilion, 'This Is Tomorrow' Exhibition, Whitechapel Art Gallery, London. Aug.-Sep 1956. Wokingham Infants School. 1958. Paolozzi Studio House. Lawson's Land, Hawkhurst, Kent. 1959. Wayland Young Pavilion, Bayswater. 1959-1982. (tree in the middle of the expansion). Folly ...A 'Solar' Pavilion. Upper Lawn, Fonthill. 1959-1982. Losey House, Snowdonia. May 1959-Oct. 1961. Occupational Health

Clinic, Park Royal. 1962-1964. 'Extensions of Man' Exhibition (or N.M.A. Exhibition). Oct. 1962. Burleigh Lane Houses, Street. 1965-1966. Garden Building St. Hilda's College, Oxford. 1967-1970. Wedding in the City, Fourteenth Triennale, Milan. May-July 1968. Lucas Headquarters, Shirley. Nov. 1973-January 1974. 'A Line of Trees...A Steel Structure'. 1975-1976. Magdalen College, Oxford. June-Oct. 1974. The Yellow House at an Intersection. July 1976. Landscape into Art: Swinging Elland; Kingsbury Lookouts; (Formal relationship with the Hexenhaus pavilions. Relationship with John Hedjuk) Tees Pudding, Middlesborough; The Slaggie Elfeven of the Spenymoor Slag Heaps; Skateboard Junction, Stockton on Tees; Kelvingrove Art Gallery and Museum Approach, Glasgow. All from 1977 by AS, except the last one. Leafy Arbours over the Verbindungskanal, Berlin. 1977. Walk in the Dry Passages and New West End to Worcester Cathedral, Worcester. 1977-1978. Colleges' Gate, Colleges' Path and Distance Stones, Urbino. 1979-1983. Amenity Building, University of Bath. Phase 1: 1978-1980. Phase 2: 1984-1985. 'Twenty-Four Doors to Christmas' Exhibition, Kettle's Yard, Cambridge. 1979. Der Berlinerbaum. 1980. Arts Barn, University of Bath. 1980-1990. Lützowstrasse Youth Centre, Berlin. 1980. Parc de la Villete,

Paris. 1982. Deodar Road, Putney. 1991-1999. Porter House, Rousset-les-Vignes, Drôme.1993-1995.

28 Op. cit., Vidotto, *Alison y Peter Smithson. Obras y proyectos*, p. 10.
29 Ibid, p. 74.
30 Ibid.
31 Alison and Peter Smithson, *The Charged Void: Urbanism*. New York. Monacelli Press, 2005, p. 229.
32 Ibid., p. 128.
33 Ibid., p. 144.
34 Ibid., p. 150.
35 Peter Smithson, "La arquitectura del entramado", in *St. Hilda's College, Oxford: la arquitectura del entramado*, Op. cit. Vidotto and González, p. 37.
36 Ibid.
37 Ibid., p. 38.
38 Op. cit., Smithson, *Peter Smithson: Conversations with Students*, p. 24.

Theoretical Contributions
Ricardo Devesa

Houses with Trees

This chapter offers three theoretical contributions to architectural design to be derived from the analysis of the five case studies presented here. They are three theoretical reflections on how places are shaped by trees, how trees affect the incorporation of time into architectural space, and how domesticity can be expanded through the inclusion of trees in inhabited spaces. Before laying out the parameters of these contributions to domestic architecture, we will briefly review the five cases and their qualitative values in terms of the house's relationships with the existing trees.

The first is La Casa by Bernard Rudofsky. As we described it in the corresponding chapter, the design incorporates the existing trees into its overall composition. The house in itself is a compilation of architectural archetypes: garden walls, pergolas, porches and patios. All these spaces are associated with domestic life outdoors. The house generates intimacy beyond its interior spaces by bringing in trees to complete the conditioning of those outdoor spaces. The design revises and updates the meaning of the domestic program through the incorporation of trees.

Second, is Marcel Breuer's Caesar cottage. Although the house intercepts an existing tree, that tree is not integrated into the design's system of geometric or compositional relationships. The tree, unconcernedly, crosses through the space of the (floor-less) patio located in front of the lake. Here, the relationships take place on a different level: dispositions related to the dialectics of figure-ground, inside-outside, far-near and in front-behind. The trees orient the inhabitants, whereas the house organizes its sur-

01 Caesar Cottage, Lakeville, Marcel Breuer   **02** La Casa, Frigiliana, Bernard Rudofsky   **03** Villa La Roche, París, Le Corbusier and P. Jeanneret

roundings. There are two contrasting orders that complement one another, as Breuer highlights with the title of his book *Sun and Shadow*, precisely because they stand in opposition.

In the Villa La Roche and the Villa Le Lac by Le Corbusier and Pierre Jeanneret, the third case study in the sequence, we see how openings and thresholds – doors, windows, bays or hallways – are used to forge connections with the trees. In the Paris villa, the openings in the façades are aligned with the axis determined by the acacia at the entrance. This layout means that the tree is always present throughout the entire *promenade architecturale*. Moreover, the "learned game of forms assembled in the light" takes place around the tree. In the same way, in the Villa Le Lac, the enormous crown of the paulownia covers the space enclosed by the walls that surround the plot, providing a roof for the exterior space, which is related, once again, to a window that frames the landscape of the lake.

The final two houses, the Villa Pepa by Juan Navarro and the Hexenhaus by Alison and Peter Smithson, share an affinity for trees: they expand and reinforce perceptual and sensory effects, as opposed to formal or geometric links as in the three previous cases. Because Juan Navarro is both an architect and a painter, and because Villa Pepa is his second residence, adjacent to his painting studio, he notices everything in the trees that helps us perceive intangible phenomena, like gravity and the energies of the *genius loci*. The carob trees, cypresses and pines that surround his villa are used as natural elements that reveal the phenomenological and temporal aspects of man in his abode.

Likewise, Alison and Peter Smithson, in the extensions and pavilions added to the Hexenhaus, hidden in the dense growth of the adjacent woods, manage to emphasize cyclical-temporal occurrences: falling leaves, rain, dew. All this is highlighted by the pavilions' glazed ceilings. Additionally, formal analogies with the branches of the trees underlie some of the constructive elements in their enclosures: crossbars and beams that are inspired by arboreal geometries. In clear contrast to the previous cases, a

04

05

04 Hexenhaus, Bad Karlshafen, Alison and
Peter Smithson

05 Portrait, 1999, Juan Navarro Baldeweg

Following page:
06 Villa Le Lac, Corceaux-Vevey,
Le Corbusier and Pierre Jeanneret

formal mimesis occurs between the architecture and the vegetation, between the artificial and the natural, an approach that has expanded broadly into contemporary architecture.

After analyzing these houses in relation to their trees, we are in a position to infer a series of contributions to the theory of architectural design. Specifically, they will be presented with respect to three notions involved with the concepts of place, time and domesticity.

Making a Place with a Tree

In Paul Klee's painting *Tree Culture*, four trees are shown arranged around a construction made up of planes and ordered geometric lines. Near the bottom of the canvas are two staircases - or train tracks depending on your interpretation - leading up to the rectangular planes, which seem to represent walls or partitions. In the center, there are a series of parallel lines - simulating enclosures represented in plan - surrounding the trees. It is an abstract construction of planes and lines, which accommodate and surround the trees. It is the inhabitants who decide to incorporate trees into their domestic habitat, into their symbolic and referential space. This happens when the house is built close enough to the trees so that the two entities together - architecture and vegetation - form a meaningful place.

The trees that are growing in a specific place are incorporated into a house at the moment when someone decides to settle around them, near them, appropriating them. A place, therefore, is an anthropomorphized site, endowed with meaning, order: in other words, a site that has been transformed by people through construction. That is how a site is readied for human action. That is what happens when people cultivate, inhabit, contemplate or even worship a tree, thereby making it sacred. Ultimately, a site becomes a place when is granted or attributed a human form, when it is subjected to a cultural action on the part of a human being.[1]

07 *Tree Culture*, 1924, Paul Klee

A tree, however, can constitute a place on its own, without any architectural element built near it, because its inherent morphology offers a spatial quality that is potentially inhabitable by man. In fact, Christopher Alexander took the concept of tree-places as one of the models for his pattern language:

> Trees have the potential to create various kinds of social places: an umbrella – where a single, low-sprawling tree like an oak defines an outdoor room; a pair – where two trees form a gateway; a grove – where several trees cluster together; a square – where they enclose an open space; and an avenue – where a doble row of trees, their crowns touching, line a path or street. It is only when a tree's potential to form places is realized that the real presence and meaning of the tree is felt.[2]

People, then, make it possible for trees to be redefined as places in and of themselves, regardless of any built elements around them, precisely because they can be occupied and used as real architectural spaces. It comes as no surprise that, throughout human history, trees have been used as places to take shelter, as a refuge, as a place of safety.[3]

Trees have served as a source of food and sustenance for people; that is why they are desirable in proximity to the built environment, to houses. Plus, trees can been used as a geographic point of reference. They provide orientation. For all these reasons, architects have used them as clear elements in generating relationships with building sites: to shape and found a place, like in Klee's painting, building the architectural elements that form habitable spaces near them and around them.

In these five case studies, we have analyzed how each architect establishes his own ideas of place by creating certain links between houses and trees. Each deploys a particular notion of place in keeping with the relationships that are created with trees. Some of those connections take place in the purely formal, abstract, geometric sphere, for example, where place is understood as a geometric space that needs to be organized. Other houses relate to trees based on their symbolic or even mythological meanings, where place is the result of the meanings that are generated through narratives.

Some architects set up specific visual relationships between the house and the tree, through doors, windows or overlooks, and place is created by organizing a site to frame the outside from the inside. Still others, on the other hand, establish phenomenological links with the trees, and their idea of place is determined by the relationship with sensory and atmospheric changes on the site. In other cases, the trees are used to design clear boundaries, producing domestic rooms in the outdoors; consequently, place is an exterior that is inhabited and integrated into the house.

The "logic of place always coincides, in general terms, with man's paradigm at each moment regarding the relationships between himself and his environment."[4] Now we would add: between himself, his environment and the built environment. In truth, man relates to what is nearby, at hand, in a particular place, whether that is trees or other natural and material resources.[5] It is therefore through architecture that man establishes the relationships between himself and the nearby environment, based on "a spatial proximity according to the plan of a discernible inner order.[...] Any place planted with trees, any room in which seating is placed in order, is understandable to us...because human...ordering...has assigned its place."[6]

Beginning with modernity, as seen in the examples gathered in this book, is when architects have been most aware of designing their houses in relation to the preexisting conditions of the site. Norberg-Schulz states: "The modern house opens up to its surroundings, demanding interaction and response."[7] The architect of modernity thus sets the trees from the site into an order relative to the built volumes, with respect to their habitable spaces. This new interest, on the other hand, has been present across the oldest and most diverse cultures, as Bollnow shows us: "Everything by which we are surrounded is understood by us as a manifestation of life and intellect. The bench in front of the door, the shady

08 Upper Lawn Pavilion, Wiltshire, 1959-1962, Alison and Peter Smithson

09 Image to illustrate Christopher Alexander's "tree-places" pattern

09

tree, house and garden, have their nature and their significance in this manifestation."[8] Lending an objective character to the tree, through the house, is what makes any site into a place: a specific, concrete place, signified by the architecture and its inhabitants.

The five case studies span the 20th century. Through them, we can explain some of the paradigms of modern man's interrelationships with site. The trees, along with other considerations such as orientation, views, topography or program, were the starting point for these houses. All of them pursued certain relationships with the trees, rearranging the original site. We might even say that the trees were moved from their natural positions without being transplanted, only through the relative layouts of the architectural elements.

The architectural design is what creates a possible place for practically any site. The trees and other existing elements on the site serve, therefore, as an excuse, through their relationship with the design, for proposing an idea of place that is already settled in the architect's mind. In fact, every design constructs a new place, and the architect achieves this by limiting the site – by separating it from what already exists using architectural elements and resources – because the house creates an order for the pre-existing elements, like the trees. This order may be geometric, spatial, topological, but it may also be symbolic, perceptual and temporal. The house thus lends order to specific pre-existing things, according to a meaningful idea of place on the part of the architect.

Thus, the first contribution to a theory of design starts with the construction of place based on how the architecture is connected with the conditions and elements of the site. Place is not understood from a static notion. Place is never stable, nor is it pre-established a priori before the design. Rather, it is defined through the architectural design, based on the relationships it establishes with the elements on the site (the trees, in the projects we have analyzed).

Likewise, place changes over time. Not only in terms of its physical condition, but also culturally speaking.[9] As Kevin Lynch wrote: "The idea of place, founded on the stability of human artifice, does not impose a static or conservative image but rather the possibility of describing its identity and understanding its character. The tradition of a place includes the awareness of being the result of continuous modification."[10] There is no place without a design, without artifice, and it can be reinterpreted over time.

It is through design that place is created. The design constructs the identity of the place, through a narrative, a series of relationships that are shaped by the architect. Place is designed; as opposed to designing for a place. The specificities of the site – in our study, offered by the trees – are cemented by the form of the architecture. Therefore, preserving the trees on a site does not mean that they remain as natural elements; rather, they are also transformed by the design into artificial elements, into compositional and, therefore, spatial elements, and consequently into cultural entities. Place is defined as an artificial construction of the site based on an architectural design.

By virtue of the design, the trees are metaphorically uprooted from their site. They do not move, but their relationships are modified through the construction of the project in proximity to them, which takes them into account in the different ways we have seen here. As Mark Wigley asserts: "Far from the resource of the pre-existing order, place is an artifact to be reordered and admired from the visual station of the house surveying its 'visual empire'".[11] Josep Quetglas offers a similar interpretation in a reflection on the architecture of Alvaro Siza: "Before the house there was no plot; we were unaware of its form. The house is the vestige of the gaze that comprehends."[12]

Incorporating a tree into a house gives the site a significance and a meaning of its own. Building a house in consonance with a tree is tantamount to founding a place and, at the same time, taking on the identity of that place.[13] In reality, every architect draws the same place on different sites. In other words, most architects represent the same idea of place in the different locations where they work. For example, Le Corbusier always designed with the same idea of place, whether it was in Ahmedabad, Algiers, Paris or La Plata. Wigley expresses it as follows: "Whereas each site allegedly says something different to the architect, the architect always hears the same thing."[14]

Houses that take existing trees into consideration turn those trees into a design material, an element to build their idea of place. In some houses – such as Breuer's Caesar Cottage or Rudofsky's La Casa – this takes place through a unitary and autonomous organization, intercepting the trees, ordering them in keeping with the house's composition. Others – like the Hexenhaus by Alison and Peter Smithson – on the other hand, use an unstructured and fragmentary configuration to generate phenomenological and, also, figurative relationships. Some houses create immaterial and, therefore, symbolic links, like Juan Navarro's Villa Pepa. And there are also houses – Le Corbusier's Villa Le Lac, for example – which, with the help of trees, orient themselves and position themselves on the site, transforming it into a new place.

The houses that incorporate the pre-existing trees from the site create a place and, consequently, a home for man in the world.

The Vector of Time in Architecture

Trees take root, sprout, grow and die. They change according to the seasons and react to the atmospheric conditions of the environment. In fact, an approximate life span can be determined for each tree species, given favorable conditions. Trees are at the mercy of the passage of time, of the seasons, depending on a natural cycle.

Architecture, on the other hand, is governed by the time-frame characteristic of things that are built by man.[15] It is not a natural element, but an artificial object. Architecture is grounded in the construct imagined and built by man precisely to resist the passage of time, the harshness of the elements. Architecture is, therefore, part of culture. Its time is rooted in the comings and goings between the past and the future: between the experience and the expectation involved in every work of architecture.[16]

While trees are destined to disappear, the purpose of architecture is to persist over time, although, for that to happen it must be maintained and transformed: into another program, into a ruin or, even, upon demolition, into recyclable waste or a memory.

Human lives are transient, like trees. That is why people sometimes plant a tree when a baby is born, as a witness to the life cycle and the natural cycle that both organisms experience.[17] A tree in proximity to a house. The tree thus contributes a natural time to the cultural historical time of architecture. The trees show the passage of time to the people living in the house. The architect's interest in trees lies in the fact that they mark chronological time; they bear witness to the inhabitant's experience of time: cultural time comes into conjunction with natural time.

Architecture, however, should not mimic the natural time of trees; it has its own temporal logics. Whereas the tree is inexorably tied to its life cycle, architecture is designed to survive over time. To understand the temporality inherent in architecture, we will echo the image of the seed evoked by Josep Quetglas in reference to the architecture of Rafael Moneo:

> Walter Benjamin, another attentive reader of Nietzsche, used, almost at the same time as Kiesler, the same image of the seed, a plant prophet that holds all of time within it, in both directions – the past, in that it sums up generations of previous plants, and the future, in that it is already, potentially, all its future developments. [...] Things shut up time inside themselves again, curl up tight, come to a standstill. [...] Architecture does not take place in time. Time takes place in architecture.[18]

The metaphor of the seed is relevant to understanding the cultural and historical, as well as prophetic, time characteristic of architecture. As Quetglas asserts, it is through architecture that time is revealed to us. However, buildings are also subject to natural time as they are built to shelter and support the lives of their inhabitants or users. For this reason, the modifications, adaptations, reforms and rehabilitations of architecture are consubstantial with it. Paradoxically, architects strive to maintain their projects in the ideal state in which they were designed and built. However, from the moment a building is conceived, and even after it has been built and inhabited, it is subject to constant changes and modifications, to an entropic effect.

Architecture, inhabited or not, is always subject to alterations; they are a part of its evolution and, therefore, inherent to it.[19] The time of architecture does not end with its construction; it is a complete journey through time, one that is borne by its characteristic and intrinsic formal features. Time takes place in architecture.

In that sense, what kind of temporal relationships exist between houses and trees? Fernando Espuelas offered the best instrumentalization of the Greek philosophers' concepts of time, as they apply to architecture. These are *Chronos*, *Aion* and *Kairos*.[20] For classical thinkers, the temporal concept of *Aion* was based on an understanding of time as past and future. Only those temporalities persist or subsist over time, since the present looks toward the past as it moves into the future. According to Deleuze, it is "something that has just happened and something that is going to happen, always flying in both directions at once."[21] According to Espuelas, *Aion* refers, on the one hand, to architectural design (which ventures into the future) and, on the other, to the work of historians and critics (which is based on reading the past).[22]

However, to quote Josep Quetglas, design "comes from behind, it comes up from the depths, it is an emissary from the past."[23] To project is to cast forward; but the thrower and the projectile remain behind. During the design, memory is the baggage of the past that lets us think about the future: in other words, *Aion*.

In contrast, *Chronos* was understood as "a more vast present which absorbs the past and the future."[24] While *Chronos* enthrones the present (the "now"), *Aion* dissolves the present between the past and the future (the "instant"). According to Espuelas, *Chronos* is a valid concept for the object that has been materialized, for the built work. A work where the passage of time is recorded in a continuous present. *Chronos* records evolution in matter, the more corporeal aspects, whereas *Aion* "is the locus of incorporeal events."[25]

Finally, *Kairos*, the third of the temporal concepts from classical philosophy, was used to refer to the time of opportunity: "The Greeks have a word to designate the coincidence of human action and time, which makes the time appropriate and the action good: it is *Kairos*, the auspicious moment, the opportune time."[26] This concept was not used by Espuelas. In architecture, it could be translated as the human action that takes place when a building is inhabited. *Kairos* is experienced when there is a conscious inhabitation of spaces on the part of users,[27] since "Kairos is no longer the time of decisive divine action, but that of possible human action."

The presence of trees near the house helps to condense these three temporal vectors into its architecture. If the trees are close the house, they will be a reminder of the users' life experiences, their memories, their future hopes and their "nows", in consonance with the temporality of the architecture.[28]

Time as the passing of hours and seasons – a cyclical and perennial time. The eternal present defined as *Chronos*. Time as the continuous and irreversible growth of every living being – a time that is opportune, good, to be remembered – formulated as *Kairos*. An outdoor room conditioned by trees, which affirms the temporal concept of *Aion*, invoking the past and proposing a future.

Consequently, in response to the question about what temporal notions arise in architecture due to the interaction with natural elements, specifically in the relationship between houses and trees, we would reply: both trees and houses are changeable entities that have their own measures of time enclosed within them. When the architect decides to incorporate a tree into an architectural design, both elements are temporally correlated and enriched, as we saw in our five case studies.[29]

The trees enrich the architecture by providing all their natural conditions to it, through growth, with their formal and sensory changes due to the seasons – flowering, leaves, colors, fruit, and in their adaptation to climatic changes and atmospheric agents. Trees make it possible, therefore, to incorporate into the architectural project those attributes that go beyond the stable, immutable and imperishable qualities it is normally expected to have. The trees incorporated into the design will increase awareness of the ephemeral nature of any constructive action.

Synchronizing the house with the trees also involves attuning the inhabitants' lives to this natural marker of time. It implies putting down roots, to a certain extent, with the memory of the site, making it into a place. However, through the act of building near a natural, living element that grows, changes and disappears with the passage of time, that memory is also subject to the same transformation. The enduring environment of the house combines with the changeable environment of the tree and vice versa: the perennial changes of the tree benefit from the permanent character desired for the house.

Yet, it is worth asking whether a house should only last as long as the life of a tree. As Nathaniel Hawthorne wrote: "But we shall live to see the day, I trust [...] when no man shall build his house for posterity."[30]

Architectural design in relation to trees is offered as a theater of memory, as well as a theater of prophecy and, at the same time, as a setting for the continuous present that is life. Houses and trees are permanently joined in a formal, sensitive and significant whole for the inhabitant who experiences them in harmony.

Outdoor Domesticity

To live, among other things, means to inhabit or dwell in a place. Architecture deals with setting apart or separating a site in order to constitute a place, which can be inhabited. A space that, in general, forms an interior and, therefore, is covered over and isolated from the exterior. That being said, the spaces apt for dwelling – in keeping with its definition: "to remain for a time or to live as a resident" – are not limited to interiors; they also include exteriors, spaces in the open air. The main task of architecture is therefore to build a dwelling by defining and relating living spaces, whether they are interior or exterior.

A house is more than a series of interior spaces isolated from the outside. It is true that one of its primary purposes is to protect us from changes in temperature, humidity, exposure to the sun, rain, wind and a host of inclemencies or instabilities in our environment. A house helps us maintain a homeostatic balance with our surroundings.[31] Inhabiting implies both the occupation of covered spaces and dwelling in the other, adjacent, rooms that are left open to the air. Rooms without a roof. Sometimes they are enclosed rooms, like in the case of the *hortus conclusus*.[32] All of them are habitable parts of the domestic body.

Trees can allow for those open spaces to be considered inhabited rooms. Trees create a microclimate around themselves, bringing about a balance of temperature and humidity. Trees orient us; they stand out and mark off limits. Trees offer protection, rootedness and identity, since they are part of the memories of the inhabitants of a place. Trees, through their characteristic spatiality, constitute a place in and of themselves.[33]

A tree is enough to make a place inhabitable, as long as it is associated with certain architectural elements, through a limitation or a relationship consciously established with the inhabitant. Thus, we are truly able to turn an outdoor area into another room that belongs to the house. Therefore, an architecture that embraces plant life and trees is one that helps condition those outdoor spaces for habitation, as it imprints its formal, spatial and experiential order onto the tree. An order that in turn incorporates the formal and physiological characteristics of the tree itself.

It is worth recalling Bernard Rudofsky's reflections in this regard, when he stated that the presence of trees contributes to making a house feel inhabited, lived in. Some of the cases we have analyzed here offer good examples: the pergolas, patios and walls that organize the olive and carob trees in La Casa by Bernard Rudofsky; the garden under the paulownia at the Villa Le Lac by Le Corbusier and Pierre Jeanneret; the carob tree enclosed within the Villa Pepa by Juan Navarro; and the different pavilions covered in the fallen leaves from nearby trees in Alison and Peter Smithson's Hexenhaus.[34]

Le Corbusier had in mind how trees help to create inhabitable open-air spaces when he wrote the following about the palm grove of Ghardaïa, in M'zab: "Whereas everything seemed to go against man: desert, stoniness, sun's infernal blaze, suddenly the most lilting melody is heard: architecture and paradisiacal verdure, streaming waters, coolness, flowers and fruit: palm trees, orange groves, apricot and pomegranate trees, green shadow and starry nights to worship, filtered through the date palms."[35] He goes on:

> Family life was lived in security, inside the home, under the open sky of the atriums, and in courtyards that were also partly gardens. Each family had its trees, its flowers, its trickling fountain. The women and children were in the gynaeceum, in safety. Strangers were never permitted to enter it. Noble, charming, and worthy human habitations.[36]

Alison and Peter Smithson also reflected on the incorporation of exteriors into domestic spaces in some of the essays from their book *Changing the Art of Inhabitation*. The photograph used for the book's cover was taken during the reconstruction of the "Patio and Pavilion" exhibition at the ICA in London in 1990.[37] Let's read Peter's text that accompanies the image:

In the group exhibit 'Patio and Pavilion' we worked on a kind of symbolic habitat in which are found responses, in some form or other, to the basic human needs – a view of the sky, a piece of ground, privacy, the presence of nature and of animals when we need them – to the basic human urges – to extend and control, to move.[38]

For Peter Smithson there were two elements that defined inhabitation: the frame or spatial structure and the symbolic object, both of which appear in the image of the pavilion's translucent ceiling and the bike wheel.[39]

The house as such needs a relationship with the outside. Sometimes this link can stretch beyond the immediate surroundings and extend into the far-off landscape which the house also makes it its own, despite the distance. This is how Juan Navarro Baldeweg puts it:

> Architecture is the focal point for those lines that cross through diagonally and pierce material productions, until they draw us in. Ultimately, what the works reveal is what defines them from the outside: something that doesn't have a beginning or an end and that escapes the exterior-interior distinction. The artist's eye is focused on something that is nearby and far off at the same time.[40]

In that sense, the distinction between exterior and interior, which has been used to define the concept of a dwelling, should be put aside, since both spaces are an indisputable part of inhabitation.

Consequently, a house is a collection of interior spaces that are interrelated and, in turn, related with exterior spaces, whether they are enclosed or not, nearby or far away. It is an expanded concept of domesticity that, in addition to the interior, legitimizes

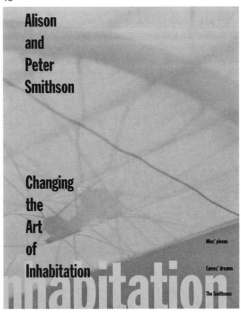

10 Cover of *Changing the Art of Inhabitation*, 1994, Alison and Peter Smithson

11 Patio covered with grape vines in Granada, photograph by Bernard Rudofsky for his article "The Importance of Trivia", published in *The Prodigious Builders*

12 Sketch of the Patio & Pavilion installation for the exhibition *This is Tomorrow*, 1956, Alison and Peter Smithson

13 Engraving of the Garden of Eden imagined by 17th-century British colonizers, included in Bernard Rudofsky's article "The Conditioned Outdoor Room", published in his book *Behind the Picture Window*

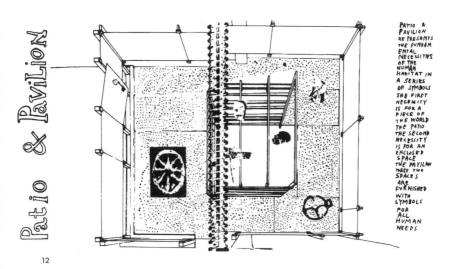

Patio & Pavilion

PATIO &
PAVILION
RE PRESENTS
THE FUNDAM
ENTAL
NECESSITIES
OF THE
HUMAN
HABITAT IN
A SERIES
OF SYMBOLS
THE FIRST
NECESSITY
IS FOR A
PIECE OF
THE WORLD
THE PATIO
THE SECOND
NECESSITY
IS FOR AN
ENCLOSED
SPACE
THE PAVILION
THESE TWO
SPACES
ARE
FURNISHED
WITH
SYMBOLS
FOR
ALL
HUMAN
NEEDS

14

the exterior spaces conditioned by the vegetation, by the trees and the architectural elements in relation to the trees.

Ultimately, the house is a meaningful construction derived from the relationships between the built volume and its surroundings - especially trees - as domesticity is expanded into the outdoors.

Previous page:
14 An old Prussian *Rundling*, a circular village with the sanctuary, idols and sacred fire located in the center (according to Hartknoch). Illustration from the article "Brute Architecture" by Bernard Rudofsky, published in his book *The Prodigious Builders*

Endnotes

1   According to the *Oxford English Dictionary*, one of the meanings of "culture" is the ideas, customs, and social behaviour of a particular people or society.
2   Pattern no. 171, in Christopher Alexander. *A Pattern Language: Towns, Buildings, Constructions*. Oxford: Oxford University Press, 2018, p. 799.
3   Although they do not offer protection from the rain, solid walls or a stable floor, like caves do, trees were also used by primitive cultures for temporary shelter.
4   Josep Muntañola. *La arquitectura como lugar*. Barcelona: Edicions UPC, 1996, p. 31.
5   Otto F. Bollnow. *Human Space*. London: Hyphen Press, 2011, p. 188. Cited in Juan Luis de las Rivas. *El espacio como lugar. Sobre la naturaleza de la forma urbana*. Valladolid: Universidad de Valladolid. Secretariado de Publicaciones, 1992.
6   Op. cit., Bollnow, p. 190.
7   Christian Norberg-Schulz. *Principles of Modern Architecture*. London: Papadakis Publisher, 2000, p. 49.
8   Op. cit., Bollnow, p. 190.
9   For an extensive bibliography categorized according to the sciences that have dealt with the notion of place, see: Josep Muntañola. *La arquitectura como lugar*. Barcelona, Edicions UPC, 1996, pp. 195-223.
10 On Kevin Lynch's ideas about how an ideal environmental image affords emotional security through stable content values. In Juan Luis de las Rivas. *El espacio como lugar. Sobre la naturaleza de la forma urbana*. Valladolid, Universidad de Valladolid. Secretariado de Publicaciones, 1992, p. 197.
11 Mark Wigley. "On Site". *Lotus* no. 95, 1997, p. 123.
12 Josep Quetglas. "Respiración de la mirada". En *Artículos de ocasión*. Barcelona, Gustavo Gili, 2004, p. 186.
13 For more on this, see the text by Eugenio Trías "El templo" en *Pensar, Construir, Habitar. Aproximación a la arquitectura contemporánea*, edited and coordinated by Piedad Solans, (Mallorca: Fundación Pilar i Joan Miró, 2000), p. 201.
14 Mark Wigley. "On Site". *Lotus* no. 95, 1997, p. 129.
15 For a number of approaches to time in architecture, see: Fernando Espuelas. "Tiempo", in *Madre materia*. Madrid: Lampreave, 2009, pp. 93-105. See also: Juan Ignacio Linazasoro. "El tiempo y la arquitectura", in *Escrito en el tiempo. Pensar la arquitectura*. Buenos Aires: Universidad de Palermo, Facultad de arquitectura, 2003, pp. 81-88.
16 See Reinhart Koselleck. *Futures Past: On the Semantics of Historical Time*. New York: Columbia University Press, 2004, pgs. 13-18.
17 Planting a tree when a person is born, forging a mutual association, or relating someone's life to a significant tree, is something many people have done. It is a narrative device that has often been used in novels and films, for example: Betty Smith, *A Tree Grows in Brooklyn*. New York: Harper & Brothers, 1943; *The Sacrifice* (Andrei Tarkovsky, 2000); *The Color of Paradise* (Majid Majidi, 1999).
18 Quetglas, Josep. "La danza y la procesión. [Sobre la forma del tiempo en la arquitectura de Rafael Moneo]", in *El Croquis*, Rafael Moneo monographic, 1967-2004, p. 544.
19 Rafael Moneo warned us that "whether we like it or not, change, continuous intervention, is the fate of architecture", when he explained the different extensions to the Mosque of Córdoba. Although, for Moneo, the life of buildings is manifested through "the permanence over time of their most characteristic formal features and which, consequently, does not lie so much in the design process as in the autonomy a building acquires after it has been built". The transformations, therefore, whether predictable or unpredictable, are inherent in all architecture, and also possible at each and every one of its stages or phases. See Rafael Moneo. "La vida de los edificios. Las ampliaciones de la Mezquita de Córdoba". *Arquitectura*, no. 256, September-November 1985, p. 26. As an example, it is worth remembering how Alison and Peter Smithson were able to alter and modify the Hexenhaus over a period of more than 18 years in continuous dialogue with the requirements of the owner, Axel. Or the rehabilitation Juan Navarro Baldeweg

carried out on the pre-existing rural house to make his villa. These two case studies are examples of how the houses' historical time also incorporates the experiential time of their inhabitants and the natural time of the areas' trees.

20 These concepts were studied by Gilles Deleuze in his book *The Logic of Sense*. New York: Columbia University Press, 1990.

21 Op. cit., Deleuze, p. 63.

22 Op. cit., Espuelas, p. 95.

23 Josep Quetglas. *Imágenes del pabellón de Alemania. Der Gläserne Schrecken*. Montreal, Section b, 1991, p. 32.

24 Op. cit., Deleuze, p. 162.

25 Ibid., p. 165.

26 Pierre Aubenque. *La prudencia en Aristóteles*. Con un apéndice sobre la prudencia en Kant. Barcelona: Crítica, 1999, p. 113. Cited by Espuelas, Op. cit. p. 96.

27 Ibid., p. 117.

28 This opportune time, in which human action coincides with a favorable occasion, can also be understood in the way some non-fictional narratives are told in relation to that trees that have been significant in people's lives, precisely because they are near to their homes. This can be seen, for example, in the film *The River* (Jean Renoir, 1951), based on real events, in which sacred trees are at the center of human action. All the stories of love, heartbreak, death, prayer, play, etc. take place under the giant tree between the house and the Ganges River. The trees on the banks of the river are the visible part, the barometer of the life of its inhabitants.

29 In La Casa, Bernard Rudofsky offers a time in relation to the past, through an updated take on tradition; in the Caesar Cottage, Marcel Breuer proposes a contrast between the time of architecture and that of nature; Le Corbusier, on the other hand, as we saw in the Villa La Roche and in the Villa Le Lac, uses a sequential, successive, fragmented time, the product of the spatial itineraries between the interior and the exterior; Juan Navarro Baldeweg, in his Villa Pepa, creates a frozen, suspended time, as

explained through his paintings of the villa; and, finally, Alison & Peter Smithson, in the different pavilions of the Hexenhaus, work with a cyclical, seasonal time, in harmony with the seasonal changes of the hundred-year-old forest where it is located.

30 Nathaniel Hawthorne. *The House of the Seven Gables*. London: G. Routledge and Co., 1852, p. 139.

31 Homeostasis is the ability of certain systems to maintain a relatively constant internal state despite changes in external conditions.

32 Juan Eduardo Cirlot. *Diccionario de Símbolos*. Barcelona: Ediciones Siruela, 1996, p. 127-128.

33 Think back, for example, to *The Poor Man's House*, an engraving from the first volume of Ledoux's *L'Architecture*, where a naked man takes shelter under the branches of a solitary tree by the sea, a scene that reminds us of Robinson Crusoe's shelter during his first night on the deserted island.

34 The relationship between houses and trees has been central to the plot of many films. For an analysis of this question, see an article by the author published in *Palimpsesto* magazine, no. 4, titled "Five film scenes, five ways of inhabiting domestic spaces associated with trees."

35 Le Corbusier. "Witnesses: The Melody of the Oasis", in *The Radiant City: Elements of a Doctrine of Urbanism to be Used as the Basis of Our Machine-age Civilization*, New York, Orion Press, 1967, p. 232.

36 Ibid., p. 186

37 Alison and Peter Smithson, *Changing the Art of Inhabitation*. London: Academy Editions Ltd, 1994.

38 Ibid., p. 109.

39 For more on the vertical relationship in Smithson's domestic architecture, see Beatriz Colomina, "Unbreathed Air 1956", *Grey Room*, vol. 15, 2004, pgs. 28-59.

40 Juan Navarro Baldeweg, "La geometría complementaria", in *La habitación vacante*. Valencia and Girona, Pre-textos and Demarcación de Girona, Col·legi d'Arquitectes de Catalunya, 1999, p. 38.

Afterword
Iñaki Ábalos

On the Subject-House-Tree Relationship

Invited by Ricardo to write a closing note for this admirable and subtle book, I agreed to offer a slightly edited version of my closing remarks as a member of the committee that evaluated his PhD dissertation of the same name, defended on November 26, 2012. Fortunately, the remarks were recorded and were, therefore, easy to transcribe.

I would just like to point out that the work of a dissertation committee requires rigor and a critical perspective even when – as was the case here – the candidate's research is unanimously assessed in positive terms by the committee. Researchers who have focused on a particular topic for years and who aspire to a career in academia as holders of a PhD are not expecting a pat on the back after years of work, although they do, of course, hope for some enthusiasm on the part of the committee. They know that the defense has, above all, a critical purpose: to reveal how much more could have gone into the investigation, while highlighting the value of the work that has been done. Without those components there is no contribution, just the suspicion of a lack of rigor on the part of both the candidate and the members of the committee. I say all this because Ricardo's agreement to include a transcript of the defense has the potential to mislead a distracted reader who might find this epilogue somewhat stilted by traditional stand-ards. It is, however, the product of an academic reading, as was befitting of the event, and a document that, in my opinion, con-tributes more to the book in reaching the readers' hands with as few changes as possible. This is what was said:

I must admit that, at first, this topic seemed a bit lightweight, romantic even, although my impression changed as I began reading. First, because of the quality of the writing, and the precision and rigor of the research. Second, because of the surprises it holds in the analysis of the contributions to architectural design associated with how trees expand our notions of place, time and habitability.

The selection of the five case studies seemed very courageous to me from the outset, since they do not include the supposed canonical examples (perhaps less fertile, despite their transcendence in historiography), which would have been the safer bet. The houses were selected in keeping with the author's experience and his first-hand knowledge. Therefore, the research is not so much focused on the house-tree relationship as on the subject-house-tree relationship. The subject in this case is the author himself, and his presence is very important during the analysis of the houses.

The author laid out clear restrictions for his analyses, focusing his work mainly on the logical-formal relationships between houses and trees, which acts, undoubtedly, as a significant constraint since it limits some of the possibilities, although it gives the work the consistency required from a doctoral dissertation. However, my critical assessment does not focus on that aspect, but rather on how the two elements are approached. I would say that, while the houses the author analyzes are seen from a 20th-century perspective, the trees, on the other hand, seem to be looked at from the 19th century. I mention this because the trees are not given a voice or memory. They are passive objects. There is an unbalanced relationship, in which the architecture is a hyperactive object and the trees, in contrast, are passive (things are done to them). What is initially proposed as a dialogue between houses and trees sometimes turns into a monologue.

The author recognizes this imbalance, and that is why he opens up a series of cracks in the final analyses and contributions, in which he offers alternative space-time readings connecting the two elements, aligning with my comment from before. The self-imposed constraints – both a strength and a weakness of all research – bring about results, however, since the author imposes them in order to isolate a topic and to achieve a systematicity that allows for reaching conclusions. And those conclusions offer interesting contributions, there can be no doubt. However, I do believe that the trees should have a voice and memory in the Latourian sense of nature. They shouldn't be just another object, in order to avoid that dichotomous approach to nature as an entity that is separate from society.

How do architects think about trees? The author seems to think we all look at them the same way, and that is not true. 19th-century architects didn't see them the same way as architects from the 16th or 21st centuries. How they speak to us, and how we incorporate them into architectural design, is very different for each of us and throughout the history of the discipline.

Trees do have memory. In that sense, I should point out that I would like to see a more extensive reflection on the narratives surrounding trees and nature, which began gaining a strong presence with the rise of the aesthetic of the Picturesque in the late 18th century. In general, the hegemony of the architect's vision of nature is based on granting privilege to the trees and the mountains, as though lettuce and tomatoes were somehow of lesser importance. However, even before the Picturesque, many painters of still lifes had already shown how rich a relationship there can be with less heroic natural elements, more everyday objects, rather than trees or sunsets. The work of the great Sánchez Cotán is an example that needs no further elaboration. This anthropization of nature, at least for the majority of Western architects, as something erect, that stands upright like we do, that has an elevation, is what most of us have unconsciously prioritized.

I would have liked to see an indication that the author had considered the visions of John Ruskin, Uvedale Price, Richard Payne Knight. For example, Ruskin's contributions were extremely important for architects with regard to the care of materials and details in architecture, ornamental aspects, proportion, color, light and shadow (aspects that go beyond the relevant values of architecture such as tectonics and space) – and also when it comes to trees and nature. In fact, we still see trees through Ruskin's eyes (and this research owes a lot to him) since his formal-visual-temporal analyses have penetrated deep into architecture schools and been absorbed into their genetics. In this idea of the tree as a subject, with its own vitality, the horizon is present as well, since it is the part that relates the three elements in this research (subject-tree-house) – something that is evident, for example, in the work of Juan Navarro Baldeweg.

That's why I feel confident saying (more as a product of the interest derived from the reading than a critique) that perhaps there should be a second, symmetrical volume about trees and houses, developed from the perspective and sensibilities of a gardener, if you will. Another book to address this re-construction or re-elaboration of the cultural construct of the idea of nature. Drawing not exclusively on the tendencies fascinated by the formal mimicry of nature, but on the new ability to understand nature by studying it and seeing it based on the series of equations and algorithms that focus, not on form, but on evolution – on life. To understand and model how life occurs in the plant kingdom and to what extent the house's existence, architecture's existence, "out there" as part of that world of life can be understood and integrated into our designs. Our architecture may breathe and adapt to the seasons and daily cycles, but it still does so based on the culture of regulations, coefficients by areas, the systematic drive that is so typical of positivism, of a very 20th-century culture.

This other perspective talks about generative processes. Aside from the experiments we've seen in architecture over the last two decades (with relative success), I would say that the scientific toolkit, the cultural toolkit, contemporary design and its implicit idea of nature all still require further reflection and future development. Perhaps that could have been tackled incipiently in this dissertation. That would help us, as architects, to understand what it is we're doing when we do what we do, so often impelled by a need or a mimetic intuition that drives us, even without an argument behind it. That is also the purpose of research and books, to understand both why we make things and to help us understand the language those things use to communicate with us - sometimes contented, sometimes complaining - a language that it is often hard for us to hear. Obviously, this comment is not pertinent as a criticism of the work but as an accolade. There is no more valuable conclusion than one that appears to the reader without being explicit in the text: one that derives from the interest the work incites in its readers' imaginations. The research we have the honor of assessing today makes a great contribution, showing us a path that will continue to shed more and more light on this incredible duality of the dialogue between houses and trees.

Bibliography

La Casa, Bernard Rudofsky

Books

Armesto, Antonio. "Cosenza, Rudofsky, Coderch: la tradizione come oggetivitá". En *Luigi Cosenza. Il Territorio abitabile*, edited by María Pia di Fontana y Miguel Mayrga, pp. 141-147. Florencia: Alinea, 2007. Spanish version provided by the author.

Ashton, Dore. *Constantino Nivola: Biografia per immagini*. Nuoro: Ilisso Edizioni, 2001.

Bocco Guarneri, Andrea. *Bernard Rudofsky. A Humane Designer*. Viena, New York: Springer, 2003.

Cosenza, Gianni; Francesco Domenico Moccia; Giulio Carlo Argan; Giovanni Astengo; Salvatore Bisogni; Cesare De Seta; Gabriele Mucchi; Luigi Cosenza. *Luigi Cosenza. L'opera completa*. Napoli: Electa, 1987.

Crespi, Alberto; Fred Licht; Salvatore Naitza; Ugo Collu; Giorgio Dettori. *Nivola: Dipinti e grafica*. Milán: Jaca Book SpA, 1995.

Gordon, Alastair. *Weekend Utopia: Modern Living in the Hamptons*. New York: Princeton Architectural Press, 2001.

Hendreich, Evelyn; Gisela Schmidt-Krayer; Inken Baller. *Villa Oro: Luigi Cosenza, Bernard Rudofsky, 1937, Neapel*. Berlin: Westkreuz, 2008.

Kenko, Yoshida. *Tsurezuregusa. Ocurrencias de un Ocioso*. Madrid: Hiperión, 1986.

Lejeune, Jean-François; Sabatino, Michelangelo, edts. *Modern Architecture and the Mediterranean: Vernacular Dialogues and Contested Identities*. London: Routledge, 2010.

Martegani, Micaela; Alastair Gordon. *Constantino Nivola in Springs*. Southampton, NY; Nuoro: Parrish Art Museum; Ilisso, 2003.

Nivola, Constantino. *Nivola: Scultore*. Milán: Electa, 2003.

Caramel, Luciano; Carlo Pirovano, edts. *Costantino Nivola: sculture, dipinti, disegni*. Milán: Electa, 2003.

Rudofksy, Bernard. *Are Clothes Modern? An Essay on Contemporary Apparel*. Chicago: P. Theobald, 1947.

– *Behind the Picture Window. An Unconventional Book on the Conventional Modern House and the Inscrutable Ways of its Inmates*. New York: Oxford University Press, 1955.

– *Architecture without Architects: An Introduction to Nonpedigreed Architecture*. New York: Museum of Moderm Art, 1964. Spanish translation, *Arquitectura sin arquitectos. Breve introducción a la arquitectura sin genealogía*. Buenos Aires: Museum of Modern Editorial Universitaria de Buenos Aires, 1973.

– *Streets for People; A Primer for Americans*. Garden City, NY: Boubleday, 1966.

– *The Kimono Mind. An informal Guide to Japan and the Japanese*. London: V. Gollancz, 1966.

– *The Unfashionable Huma Body*. Garden City, NY: Boubleday, 1971.

– *The Prodigious Builders. Notes Toward a Natural History of Architecture with Special Regard to Those Species That Are Traditionally Neglected or Downright Ignored*. New York: Harcourt Brace Jovanovich, 1977. Spanish translation, *Constructores prodigiosos: Apuntes sobre una historia natural de la arquitectura*. México: Pax México, 2008.

– *Now I Lay Me Down to Eat. Notes and Footnotes on the Lost Art of Living*. Garden City, NY: Anchor Press/Doubleday, 1980.

– *Sparta/Sybaris: keine neue Bauweise, eine neue Lebensweise tut not*. Salzburgo: Residenz, 1987.

Magazines

Abercrombie, Stanley. "With Summer in View: the Spanish Retreat of Architect-Author Bernard Rudofsky". *Interior Design* vol. 55 nº8 (1984, August), pp. 138- [145].

Anelli, Renato. "Mediterraneo ai tropici. Patii e giardini. Transformazioni del patio mediterraneo nell'architettura moderna brasiliana". *Cassabella* 708 (2003, February), pp. 86-95.

Ashton, Dore. "Constantino Nivola". *Arts and Architecture* vol. 76, nº3 (1959, March), pp. 10-11.

Fernández Galiano, Luis, "Esparta y Síbaris. Bernard Rudofsky, disciplina y hedonismo". *Arquitectura Viva* 114 (2007), pp. 72-73.

Gravagnuolo, Benedetto. "Movimento Moderno in Neapel". *Bauwelt* Vol. 82, nº7-8 (1991, February), pp. 276-282.

Harnden, Peter G. "Una Casa a Malaga". *Domus* 385 (1961, December), pp. 21-30.

Llecha, Joan. "La arquitectura que nos viste". *Quaderns d'Arquitectura i Urbanisme* 255 (2007, otoño), pp. 120-133.

Martegani Luini, Micaela. "Nivola, Le Corbusier". *Abitare* 372 (1998), pp. 198-[203], 231.

Nivola, Constantino. "The Pergola-Village, Vined Orani". *Contract Interiors* 112 (1953, January), pp. 80-85.

Nivola, Constantino; Le Corbusier. "Nivola Between Sculpture and Architecture". *Zodiac* 4 (1959), pp. 180-189.

Pia Fontana, María. "Manifiesto de intenciones: proyecto ideal de una casa en el mar". *DPA, Documents de Projectes d'Arquitectura* 20 (2004, June), pp. 14-19.

Ponti, Gio. "Turismo mediterraneo italianao e turismo ideale nella dalmazia". *Lo Stile nella casa e nell arredamento* 8 (1941, August), pp. 10-22.

Rudofksy, Bernard. "Quattro esempi di giardini". *Domus* 122 (1938, February), pp. 12-13.

— "La scoperta d'un'isola". *Domus* 123 (1938, March), pp. 2-5.

— "Non ci vuole un nuovo modo di costruire ci vuole un nuovo modo di vivere". *Domus* 123 (1938, March), pp. 2-5.

— "La moda: Abito disumano". *Domus* 124 (1938, April), pp. 10-13.

— "Variazioni". *Domus* 124 (1938, April), pp. 14-15.

— "Origine dell'Abitazione". *Domus* 124 (1938, April), pp. 16-19.

— "Outdoor Living Rooms". *Interiors* 52 (1943, May), pp. 19-23.

— "House at Sao Pablo". *Architectural Review* 95 (1944, June), pp. 167-162.

— "Patio at Sao Paulo, Brazil". *Architects' journal* 106 (1947, July), pp. 59-61.

— "Le piu desiderabili ville del mondo". *Domus* 234 (1949), pp. 1-9.

— "An Outdoor House on Long Island". *Architectural Review* 664 (1952, April), pp. 268-270.

— "Giardino stanza all'aperto. A proposito della 'Casa giardino a Long Island', NY". *Domus* 272 (1952, July), pp. 1-5.

— "Stairways". *Arts and Architecture* vol. 79 nº2 (1962, February), pp. 24-25.

— "Vivienda en Nerja". *Arquitectura* 206-207 (1977, 2º cuaquarter), pp. 96-99.

Scott, Felicity. "Underneath Aesthetics and Utility. The Untransposable Fetish of Bernard Rudofsky". *Assemblage* 38 (1999, April), pp. [58]-89.

— "Architecture Without Architects: A Short Introduction to Non-Pedigreed Architecture by Bernard Rudofsky". *Harvard Design Magazine* 4 (1998), pp. 69-72.

— " 'Primitive Wisdom' and Modern Architecture". *Journal of Architecture* vol. 3 nº3 (1998, August), pp. 241-261.

Segawa, Hugo. "Le belle Americhe = America the Beautiful". *Spazio e Società* vol.19, nº80 (1997, October), pp. 86-89.

Caesar Cottage, Marcel Breuer

Books

Alonso, Eusebio; Jesús Aparicio; Juan Carlos Arnuncio. *4 centenarios: Luis Barragán, Marcel Breuer, Ärne Jacobsen, José Luis Sert. José Luis Sert.* Valladolid: Universidad de Valladolid, Secretariado de Publicaciones e Intercambio Editorial, 2002.

Argan, Giancarlo. *Marcel Breuer, disegno industriale e architettura.* Milán: Görlich, 1957.

— *Walter Gropius y el Bauhaus.* Buenos Aires: Nueva visión, 1961.

Armesto, Antonio. "La villa y el cottage de Marcel Breuer", in Cycle of lectures "Professors. Architects": School of Architecture of San Sebastián, directed by Juan José Segú y Asier Acuriola. Donostia: Erein, 2006.

Balena Arista, Francesca. *Le Corbusier e il razionalismo: Adolf Loos, Walter Gropius, Theo van Doesburg, Mies van der Rohe, Erich Mendelsohn, Gerrit Thomas Rietveld, Jacobus Johannes Pieter Oud, Marcel Breuer, Giuseppe Terragni.* Milano: Il sole 24 ore, 2008.

Bjone, Christian; Robert Walker. *First House: The Grid, the Figure and the Void.* Chichester: Willey-Academy, 2002.

Breuer, Marcel; Bunji Murotani. *The Legacy of Marcel Breuer: Marcel Breuer Associates, architects and planners.* Edited by Katsuhiko Ichinowatari. Tokuo: Process Architecture, 1982.

Breuer, Marcel. *Marcel Breuer: Architect and Designer.* Edited by Peter Blake. New York: Architectural Record, MoMA, 1949.

— *Marcel Breuer. Sun and Shadow. The Philosophy of an Architect.* Edited by Peter Blake. New York: Dodd, Mead & Company, 1956.

Cobbers, Arnt. *Marcel Breuer, 1902-1981: definidor formal del siglo XX.* Köln: Taschen, 2007.

Cranston, Jones. *Marcel Breuer. Buildings and projects 1921-1962.* London: Thames & Hudson, 1962. Spanish translation, *Marcel Breuer: construcciones y proyectos: 1921-1961.* Barcelona: Gustavo Gili, 1963

— *Architecture Today and Tomorrow.* New York; London; Toronto: McGraw-Hill, 1961.

Driller, Joachim. *Breuer Houses.* London: Phaidon, 2000.

Droste, Magdalena; Manfred Ludewig. *Marcel Breuer, designer.* Kölh: Taschen, 1992.

Earls, William D. *The Harvard five in New Canaan. Mid century modern houses by Marcel Breuer, Landis Gores, John Johansen, Philip Johnson, Eliot Noyes and others.* New York: Norton, 2006.

Ford, Edward R. *The Details of Modern Architecture. Volume II. 1928 to 1988.* Cambridge, Mass.; London: MIT Press, 1996.

Gatje, Robert F.; I.M. Pei. *Marcel Breuer: a memoir.* New York: The Monacelli, 2000.

Hitchcock, Henry Russell. *Exhibition by Marcel Breuer.* Cambridge: Harvard University, 1938.

— *Built in USA: post-war architecture.* New York: Museum of Modern Art, 1952.

Hyman, Isabelle. *Marcel Breuer, Architect: The Career and the Buildings.* New York: Harry N. Abrams, 2001.

Masello, David. *The Architecture without Rules: The Houses of Marcel Breuer and Herbert Beckhard.* New York; London: W. W. Norton & Company, 1993.

Mock, Elizabeth. *Built in USA: 1932-1944.* New York: Museum of Modern Art, 1944.

Papachristou, Tician. *Marcel Breuer. New Buildings and Projects.* New York; Washington: Praeger, 1960. Spanish translation, *Marcel Breuer. Nuevas construcciones y proyectos.* Barcelona: Gustavo Gili, 1970.

Remmele, Mathias; Pioch, Alexandra. *Marcel Breuer: diseño y arquitectura.* Edited by Alexander von Vegesack, Mathias Remmele. Weil am Rhein: Vitra Design Museum, 2003.

Zevi, Bruno. *Historia de la arquitectura moderna.* Barcelona: Poseidón, 1980.

Wilk, Christopher. *Marcel Breuer: Furniture and Interiors*. New York: Museum of Modern Art, 1981

Magazines

Abercrombie, Stanley; Marcel Breuer. "Koerfer house, with Herbert beckhard; Moscia, Tessin, Switzerland 1963-67; Stillman house III, with Tician Papachristou; Litchfield, Connecticut 1972-74". *Global architecture. Detail* 5 (1977).

Armesto, Antonio. "Quince casas americanas de Marcel Breuer (1938-1965)". *2G: Revista Internacional de Arquitectura* 17, *Marcel Breuer: casas americanas = American houses* (2001/1), pp. 4-25.

Breuer, Marcel. "¿Noi pietra, essi legno: la casa di Marcel Breuer nel Connecticut". *Domus* 233 (1949), pp. 2-7.

— "A cantilivered house". *House and Garden* (1947, August), pp. 59-65.

— "House for the growing family: Marcel Breuer, architect". *Architectural Forum* (1949, May), pp. 96-101.

— "The case of the aging house". *House and Garden* (1951, April), pp. 96-103.

— "Traveaux recent de Marcel Breuer". *Architecture d'Aujourd'Hui* 44 (1952, September), pp. 1-16.

— ""House in Pennsylvania". *Architectural Review* 675 (1953, March), pp. 152-155.

— "Marcel Breuer: architectural details". *Architectural Record* 2 (1964, February), pp. 121-136.

Colomina, Beatriz. "DDU at MoMA". *Any* 17 (1997), pp. 48-53.

— "La casa suburbana, espejo y escaparate". *AV Monografías* 102 (2003, July), pp. 10-15.

Frampton, Kenneth. "40 years of Breuer, 1924-64". *Architectural Design, AD* vol. 34, nº9 (1964, September), pp. 468-470.

Martí, Carlos. "La casa binuclear según Marcel Breuer. El patio recobrado". *DPA, Documents de Projectes d'Arquitectura* 13 (1997, December), pp. 46-51.

Mori,Toshiko. "Marcel Breuer's own house in New Canaan, built in 1951". *Architectural Record* vol. 198, nº 4 (2010, April).

Mumford, Lewis. "What is happening to Modern Architecture?: A symposium at Museum of Modern Art". New York: *Museum of Moder Art Bulletin* Vol. XV, nº 3, (1948, primavera).

Portoghesi, Paolo. "Marcel Breuer in America". *Zodiac* 8 (1961, June), pp. 54-57.

Scott, W. Hylton. "Trabajos de Marcel Breuer II". *Nuestra Arquitetura* 11 (1947, November).

Villa La Roche, Le Corbusier and Pierre Jeanneret

Books

Ábalos, Iñaki. "Le Corbusier, naturaleza y paisaje", in *Doblando el ángulo recto: 7 ensayos en torno a Le Corbusier*. Edited by Juan Calatrava. Madrid: Círculo de Bellas Artes, 2009.

Aglieri Rinella, Tiziano; Bruno Reichlin. *Le case La Roche-Jeanneret di Le Corbusier. Riflessioni per un progetto di restauro*. Roma: Officina, 2008.

Baker, Geoffrey H. *Le Corbusier. The Creative Search: The Formative Years of Charles-Edouard Jeanneret*. New York; London: Van Nostrand Reinhold, 1996.

Benton, Tim. "The 'petit maison de weekend' and the Parisian suburbs", in *Le Corbusier & the Architecture of Reinvention*. London: AA Publications, 2003.

— *The Villas of Le Corbusier et Pierre Jeanneret, 1920-1930*. Edición revisada y expandida. Basel; Boston; Berlin: Birkhäuser, 2007.

Benton, Tim; Robert Vigouroux; François de Franclieu; Giuliano Gresleri; Georgios Simeoforidis; Georgios Tzirtzilakis; Jon Bosman; Dario Matteoni; Bruno Reichlin; Jacques Sbriglio; Jean-Lucien Bonillo; Stanislaus von Moos. *Le Corbusier et la Méditerranée*. Marsella: Parenthèses; Musées de Marseille, 1987.

Bonaiti, Maria; Varlerio Casali; Carlos Ferreira; Jean-Pierre Girodani; Giuliano Gresleri; Thilo Hilpert; Mogens Krustrup; Mary McLeod; Fernando Perez Marzá; Jacques Sbriglio; Cyrille Siimonnet; Harris Sobin; Marida Talamona; Jürgen Ulpts; Stanislaus von Moos. *Le Corbusier et la nature*. Paris: Fondation Le Corbusier, 2004.

Colomina, Beatriz. *Privacidad y publicidad. Arquitectura moderna como medio de comunicación de masas*. Murcia: CENDEAC, 2011.

Cortés, Juan Antonio. "La caja y el parasol, dos modelos recurrentes en la obra de Le Corbusier", in *Le Corbusier*. Madrid: Ministerio de Cultura, Dirección General de Bellas Artes y Archivos, Centro Nacional de Exposiciones; Centro de Arte Reina Sofia, 1987.

Granell, Enrique. "UNA casa: UN árbol", in *Le Corbusier y España*. Edited by Juan José Lahuerta. Barcelona: Centre de Cultura Contemporània de Barcelona, 1997.

Le Corbusier; François de Pierrefeu. *La casa del hombre*. Barcelona: Apóstrofe, 1999.

Le Corbusier. *Album La Roche. Ch.-E. Jeanneret, Le Corbusier*. Edited by Stanislaus von Moos. Milan: Electa, 1996.

— *A propósito del urbanismo*. Barcelona: Poseidón, 1980.

— *Almanach d'architecture moderne: Documents, théorie, pronostics, histoire, petites histoires, dates, propos standarts, apologie et idéalisation du standart, organisation, industrialisation du bâtiment*. Paris: Connivences, 1987.

— *Buildings and projects, 1933-1937*. Colección Le Corbusier archive, 12. Edited by H. Allen Brooks. New York; London; Paris: Garland; Fondation Le Corbusier, 1983.

— *Cuando las catedrales eran blancas: Viaje al país de los tímidos*. Barcelona; Buenos Aires: Poseidón, 1977.

— *Hacia una arquitectura*. Buenos Aires; Barcelona: Poseidón, 1978.

— *Le Corbusier et Pierre Jeanneret. V. 1, Oeuvre complète 1910-1929*. Edited by W. Boesiger, O. Stonorov, M. Bill. Berlin: Birkhäuser, 1995.

— *Los tres establecimientos humanos*. Barcelona: Poseidón, 1981.

— *Poesía en Argel*. Murcia: Colegio Oficial de Arquitectos de Murcia, 1991.

— *Une Petite Maison: 1923*. Zurich: Girsberger, 1954. Al castellano, *Una pequeña casa*, translated by Estela Ponce de León. Buenos Aires: Infinito, 2005.

May Sekler, Mary Patricia. "Le Corbusier, Ruskin, the Tree, and the Open Hand", in Paul Turner; Maurive Favre; Russel Walden; Brian Brace Taylor; Charles Jenks; Anthony Sutcliffe; Robert Fishman; Martin Purdy; John Winter; Maxwell Fry; Jane B. Drew; Stanislaus von Moos. *The Open hand. Essays on Le Corbusier*. Edited by Rusell Walden. Cambridge, Mass.; London: MIT Press, 1977.

Monteys, Xavier. *Le Corbusier: Obras y proyectos = obras e projectos*. Barcelona: Gustavo Gili, 2005.

Ozenfant, Amaédée; Ch. E. Jeanneret. *Acerca del purismo: escritos, 1918-1926*. Edited by Antonio Pizza. Madrid: *El Croquis*, 2004.

Quetglas, Josep. "El taller y el santuario", in *Doblando el ángulo recto: 7 ensayos en torno a Le Corbusier*. Edited by Juan Calatrava. Madrid: Círculo de Bellas Artes, 2009.

— "La línea vertical", in *Le Corbusier y la síntesis de las artes: El poema del ángulo recto*. Edited by Juan Calatrava. Madrid; París: Círculo de Bellas Artes; Fondation Le Corbusier, 2006.

Sancho Osinaga, Juan Carlos. *El sentido cubista de Le Corbusier*. Madrid: Munilla-Lería, 2000.

Sbriglio, Jacques. Le Corbusier. *Habiter: de la villa Savoye à l'Unité d'Habitation de Marseille*. Paris; Arles: Cité de l'architecture et du patrimoine; Aristeas: Actes sud, 2009.

— *Le Corbusier. Les Villas La Roche-Jeanneret* = *Le Corbusier: The Villas La Roche-Jeanneret*. Paris; Basel; Boston; Berlin: Fondation Le Corbusier; Birkhäuser, 1997.

Vaudou, François. *Le Corbusier: Villa le lac à Corseaux-Vevey*. Genève: Carré d'art, 1991.

Vogt, Adolf Max. *Le Corbusier, the Noble Savage: Toward an Archaeology of Modernism*. Cambridge, Mass.; London: MIT Press, 1998.

Magazines

Benton, Tim. "Le Corbusier y la promenade architecturale". *Arquitectura* 264-265 (1987, January), pp. 36-47.

Foster, Kurt W. "Antiquity and Modernity in the La Roche-Jeanneret Houses of 1923". *Oppositions* 15-16 (1979, invierno), pp. 130-153.

Krauss, Rosalind. "Lèger, Le Corbusier, and Purism". *Art Forum* vol. 10, n. 8 (1972), pp. 50-53.

Le Corbusier; Pierre Jeanneret. "Estudio de viviendas mínimas para Barcelona". *AC* 13 (1934), pp. 29-31. Consultado en *AC Publicación del GATEPAC*. Barcelona: Fundación Caja de Arquitectos, 2005.

— "Ville La Roche". *Architecture Vivante*, nº especial (1927, October).

— "Ville La Roche". *L'Architecture d'aujourd'hui* 10 (1933).

Nacenta, Antonio. "Una Visita a la 'Petite Maison' de Le Corbusier". *Cuadernos de Arquitectura* 56 (1964, 2º trimestre), pp. 34-35.

Quetglas, Josep. "Algo sobre el color en la arquitectura de Le Corbusier". *Arquitectura COAM* 358 (1009, 4º trimestre), pp. 92-97.

Reichlin, Bruno. " 'Une Petite Maison' sul lago Lemano: la controversia Perret-Le Corbusier = 'Une Petite Maison' on Lake Leman: the Perret-Le Corbusier controversy". *Lotus* 60 (1988), pp. 58-83.

— "Stories of Windows". *A&U* 3 (2000, March), pp. 80-93.

— "The pros and cons of the horizontal window: the Perret - Le Corbusier controversy". *Daidalos* 13 (1984), pp. 67-78.

Tarragó, Salvador. "Plan Macià, síntesis del trabajo del GATCPAC para Barcelona". *2C Construcción de la ciudad* 15-16 (1980, May), pp. 68-85.

Wigley, Marc. "On Site". *Lotus* 95 (1997, December), pp. 118-131.

Villa Pepa, Juan Navarro Baldeweg

Books

Arnheim, Rudolph. *Hacia una psicología del arte; Arte y entropía. Ensayo sobre el desorden y el orden*. Madrid: Alianza, 1980.

Cappellato, Gabriele. *Clorindo Testa, Juan Navarro Baldeweg: Esperienze di architettura: generazioni a confronto*. Milan: Skira, 1998.

Curtis, William J. R.; Enrique Juncosa. *Juan Navarro Baldeweg*. Santiago de Compostela: Centro Galego de Arte Contemporanea, 2002.

Español, Joaquín. *Invitación a la arquitectura: Diálogos con Oriol Bohigas, Juan Navarro Baldeweg, Oscar Tusquets, Albert Viaplana y Peter G. Rowe. [Cinco reflexiones sobre la arquitectura que nos rodea]*. Barcelona: RBA, 2002.

González García, Ángel. Juan José Lahuerta, Juan Navarro Baldeweg. *Juan Navarro Baldeweg. Obras y proyectos*. Edited by Mirko Zardini. Madrid: Electa España, 1993.

González García, Ángel. "Una conversación: Juan Navarro Baldeweg y Ángel González García", in *Irving Penn, Arroyo, O'Keeffe, Navarro Baldeweg, Eva Lootz*. Santander: Arte y parte, 2002, pp. 36-55.

Harrist, Jr. Robert E. *Painting and Private Life in Eleventh Century China: Mountain Villa by Li Gonglin*. Princeton: Princeton University Press, 1998.

Juncosa, Enrique. "Ideas de orden en la obra de Juan Navarro Baldeweg", in *Las adic-*

ciones. *Ensayos sobre arte contemporáneo.* Madrid: Editorial Síntesis, 2006, pp. 127-137.

Lahuerta, Juan José; Guido Beltramini; Pierre-Alain Croset. *Juan Navarro Baldeweg risonanze di Soane.* Vicenza: Centro internazionale di studi di architettura Andrea Palladio, 2000.

Lupano, Mario. *Juan Navarro Baldeweg. Il ritorno della luce.* Milan: Federico Motta Editrice, 1996.

Navarro Baldeweg, Juan. "El horizonte habitable", in ¿Qué es la escultura moderna? *Del objeto a la arquitectura.* Madrid: Fundación Mapfre, 2003, pp. 173-203.

— *Constelaciones. Juan Navarro Baldeweg.* Pamplona: Universidad Pública de Navarra, 2011.

— *Juan Navarro Baldeweg.* Edited by Erica Witschey; Raúl Rispa. Corte de Madera, Calif.: Gingko Press, 2001. En castellano: Tanais Ediciones, Sevilla-Madrid. En alemán: Gingko Press, Hamburgo. En Italiano: Logos Art, Modena.

— *Juan Navarro Baldeweg, Conversaciones con estudiantes.* Edited by Guillermo Zuaznabar. Barcelona: Gustavo Gili, 2011.

— *L'antico e il nuovo: il rapporto tra città antica e architettura contemporanea: metodi, pratiche e strumenti.* Edited by Cristina Franco, Alessandro Massarente, Marco Trisciuoglio. Torino: UTET libreria, 2002.

— *La habitación vacante.* Edited by José Muñoz Millanes. Valencia: Pre-textos; Demarcación de Girona, Col·legi d'Arquitectes de Catalunya, 1999.

— *Una caja de resonancia.* Edited by Margarita Navarro Baldeweg. Valencia; Girona: Pre-textos; Demarcació de Girona, Col·legi d'Arquitectes de Catalunya, 2007.

Quetglas, Josep. "La cámara clara de Salamanca. (Sobre algunos temas de Baldeweg)" y "Paysage au miroir", in *Artículos de ocasión.* Barcelona: Gustavo Gili, 2004, pp. 125-131 y pp. 105-111.

Rosenberg, Arnold. *La tradición de lo nuevo.* Caracas: Monte Avila, 1969.

Wagner, Marsha L. *Wang Wei.* Boston: Twayne Publishers, 1981.

Magazines

Armenteras, Celia. "Entrevista con Juan Navarro Baldeweg". *Arquitectura COAM* 352 (2008, 2º trimester), pp. 26-33.

Capitel, Antón. "Juan Navarro Baldeweg. Diverso y contínuo". *Arquitectura COAM* 337 (2004), pp. 11-13.

Curtis, William J.R. "La arquitectura como una intervención en un campo de energías [una conversación con Juan Navarro Baldeweg]. *El Croquis* 133 (2006), pp. 6-21.

— "Teatros de luz: la arquitectura de Juan Navarro Baldeweg". *El Croquis* 133 (2006), pp. 22-38.

Espuelas, Fernando. "Mostrar el envés". *El Croquis* 133 (2006), pp. 226-231.

Feduchi, Pedro. "Navarro Baldeweg : un universo lleno de referencias". *Diseño Interior* 38 (1994), pp. 62-67.

Mata, Sara de la; Fuensanta Nieto; Enrique Sobejano. "Entrevista Juan Navarro Baldeweg". *Arquitectura COAM* 274 (1988, September), pp. 114-131.

Navarro Baldeweg, Juan. "El autómata residencial". *Nueva Forma* 78/79 (1972, August), pp. 32-35.

— "Juan Navarro Baldeweg" [Conversación con Beatriz Beeckmans]. *Miradas al exterior. Revista de información diplomática del Ministerio de Asuntos Exteriores y de Cooperación* 12 (2009, October), pp. 68-74.

— "Tribute to Gyorgy Kepes". *Lotus* 125 (2005, September), pp. 27-35.

— "Un objeto es una sección". *Circo MTM* 25 (1995).

Pallasmaa, Juhani. "Luz esculpida, materia pintada y significado construido. La alquimia arquitectónica de Juan Navarro Baldeweg". *Arquitectura COAM* 337 (2004), pp. 2-3.

Quetglas, Josep. "Sobre Juan Navarro Baldeweg". *Arquitectura COAM* 271-272 (1998), pp. 82-85.

Sánchez Lampreave, Ricardo. "Transparencias interpuestas". *Arquitectura COAM* 349 (2007), pp. 66-73.

Solà-Morales, Ignasi de. "La casa della pioggia: un progetto di Juan Navarro Baldeweg = The House of Rain: a Design by Juan Navarro Baldeweg". *Lotus 44* (1984), pp. 100-108.

Thorne, Marta. "Juan Navarro Baldeweg". *Quaderns d'Arquitectura i Urbanisme 163* (1984, October), pp. 102-121.

Hexenhaus, Alison and Peter Smithson

Books

Colomina, Beatriz. "Media as Modern Architecture", in *Architecture between spectacle and use*. Edited by Anthony Vidler. Williamstown, Mass.; New Haven: Sterling and Francine Clark Art Institute; Yale University Press, 2008, pp. 58-73.

— "Amigos del futuro: una conversación con Peter Smithson", in *Doble exposición. Arquitectura a través del arte*. Madrid: Akal, 2006, pp. 88-108.

Curtis, Penelope. *Patio and Pavillion. The Place of Sculpture in Modern Architecture*. Los Angeles, London: P. Getty Museum, Ridinghouse, 2008.

Heuvel, Dirk van den; Max Risselada; Beatriz Colomina. *Alison and Peter Smithson: From the House of the Future to a House of Today*. Rotterdam: 010 Publishers, 2004. Spanish edition: *Alison and Peter Smithson: De la Casa del Futuro a la casa de hoy*. Barcelona: COAC; Ediciones Polígrafa, 2007.

Krucker, Bruno. *Complex Ordinariness*. Zurich: GTA Verlag, 2002.

Mostafavi, Monsen; Louisa Hutton. *Architecture Is Not Made with the Brain: The Labour of Alison and Peter Smithson*. Edited by Pamela Johnston; Rosa Ainley; Clare Barrett. London: Architectural Association, 2005.

Obrist, Hans Ulrich. *Smithson Time: A Dialogue*. Kölh: Verlag der Buchhandlung Wather König, 2004

Schregenberger, Thomas; Claude Lichtenstein. *As Found: The Discovery of the Ordinary*. Baden; Zurich: Lars Müller; Museum für Gestaltung Zürich, 2001.

Smithson, Alison; Peter Smithson; Marco Vidotto; Aquil·les González. *St. Hilda's College, Oxford: la arquitectura del entramado*. Madrid: Colegio Oficial de Arquitectos de Madrid, 2001.

Smithson, Alison; Peter Smithson. *Uppercase 3: [Alison & Peter Smithson]*. Edited by Theo Crosby. London: Whitefriars, 1960.

— "30 Years of Thoughts on the House and Housing", in *Architecture Theory since 1968 in the Age of Scepticism*. Edited by Denis Lasdum. New York: Oxford University Press, 1984.

— *Alison + Peter Smithson. The Shift*. Edited by David Dunster. London: Academy Edition, 1982.

— "Where to walk and where to ride in our bouncy new clothes and in our shiny new cars, cluster city", in *Architectural Positions: Architecture, Modernity and the Public Sphere*. Edited by Tom Avermaete, Klaske Havik; Hans Teerds; Chris Woltjes. Amsterdam: SUN, 2009.

— *Changing the Art of Inhabitation*. London: Artemis, 1994. Spanish edition: *Cambiando el arte de habitar*. Translation by Moisés Puente. Barcelona: Gustavo Gili, 2001.

— *Italian thoughts*. Sweden: S.I: s.n., 1993. Edición en alemán: *Italienische Gedanken, weitergedacht*. Basel, Boston: Birkhäuser, Gütersloh: Bertelsmann Fachzeitschriften, 2001.

— *Modern Dreams: The Rise and Fall of Pop*. Cambridge, Mass.: MIT Press, 1988.

— *Modernism Without Rhetoric. Essays on the Work of Alison and Peter Smithson*. London: Academy Edition, 1997.

— *Ordinariness and Light; Urban Theories 1952-1960 and Their Application in a Building Project 1963-1970*. Cambridge, Mass.: MIT Press, 1970.

— *The 1930's*. Berlin: Alexander, 1985.

— *The Charged Void: Architecture*. New York: Monacelli Press, 2000.

— *The Charged Void: Urbanism*. New York: Monacelli Press, 2005.

— *Upper Lawn: Folly Solar Pavilion*. Barcelona: Edicions de la Universitat Politècnica de Catalunya, D.L., 1986.

Smithson, Alison. *AS in DS: An Eye on the Road*. Baden: Lars Müller, 2001.

— *Imprint of India*. London: Architectural Association, 1994.

— *Places Worth Inheriting*. London: Association of Consultant Architects, 1978.

— *Saint Jerome. The Dessert, The Study. The Restorative Place in Nature. The Energising Cell. [Hieronymus. Die Wüste. Das Studierzimmer. Die natur als belebender ort. Die energiequelle]*. Lauenförde: Tecta, 1990.

— *Team 10 Meetings 1953-1984*. Delft, New York: Rizzoli International Publications, 1991.

— *The Heroic Period of Modern Architecture*. New York: Rizzoli, 1981.

Smithson, Peter; Karl Unglaub. *Flying Furniture*. Köhl: Verlag der Buchhandlung Walther Köning, 1999.

Smithson, Peter. *Peter Smithson: conversations with students: a space for our generation*. Edited by Catherine Spellman y Karl Unglaub. New York: Princeton Architectural Press, 2005. Spanish edition: *Peter Smithson: Conversaciones con estudiantes*. Barcelona: Gustavo Gili, 2004.

Tafuri, Manfredo. "Símbolo e ideología en la arquitectura de la Ilustración", in *Arte, arquitectura y estética en el siglo XVIII*. Edited by Juan Calatrava. Madrid: Akal, 1987.

Vidotto, Marco. Augusto Mazzini; Annalaura Spalla. *A+P Smithson. Pensieri, progetti e frammenti fino al 1990*. Genoa: Sagep Editrice, 1991.

Vidotto, Marco. Alison and Peter Smithson. *Obras y proyectos. Works and projects*. Barcelona: Gustavo Gili, 1997.

Wong, Lorenzo. *Climate Register: Four Works by Alison & Peter Smithson*. London: Architectural Association, 1994.

Magazines

Allen, Isabel; Deborah Singmaster. "Interiors and fit-outs". *Architects' Journal* 205 (1997, June), pp. 39-40,42,45-46,48,50,52.

Banham, Reyner. "A Clip-on Architecture". *Architectural Design* 35 (1965, November), pp. 534-535.

Dawson, Susan. "Working Details. The Yellow Lookout, a Timber Viewing Platform in Lauenförde, West Germany, Designed by Alison and Peter Smithson". *Architect's Journal* 199 (1994, June), pp. 33-35.

Elvira, Juan. "Los lugares de la duración". *Bau* 17 (1999), pp. 106-109.

Frampton, Kenneth. "Memorias del subdesarrollo: los Smithsons, entre la era industrial y la sociedad del consumo". *Arquitectura Viva* 89-90 (2003, March-June), pp. 126-129.

González de Canales Ruiz, Francisco. "Una estancia en el exterior. Estampas de Puck y arquitecturas análogos". *DC, revista de crítica arquitectònica* 9/10 (2003, October), pp. 82-101.

Halbe, Roland. "Bad Karlshafen, Allemagne, 1984-2001. Maison Bruchhäuser"; "Lauenförde, Allemagne, 1990-2000. Usine Tecta". *Architecture D'aujourd'hui* 344 (2003, January), pp. 54-59; pp. 60-65.

Hutton, Louisa. "Méditations sur les bords de la Weser = Reflections by the Weser". *Architecture D'aujourd'hui* 344 (2003, January), pp. 66-69.

Mead, Andrew. "A Smithson House Evolves Over Decades". *Architectural record* 192 (2004, April), pp. [102]-106.

— "Putting Down Roots". *Architects' Journal* 214 (2011, August), pp. 26-34.

Morelli, Marta. "El arte de habitar. Aproximación a la arquitectura desde el pensamiento de Alison y Peter Smithson". *DC, revista de crítica arquitectònica* 17/18 (2009, February), pp. 253-264.

Sicmemi, Maddalena. "Un'opera aperta degli Smithson a Bad Karlshafen". *Cassabella* 726 (2004), pp. 6-20.

Sergison, Jonathan; Stephen Bates. "Six leçons apprises d'Alison et Peter Smithson = Six Lessons learnt from Alison and Peter Smithson". *Architecture D'aujourd'hui* 344 (2003, January), pp. 74-81.

Smithson, Alison. "And now Dhamas are dying out in Japan". *Architectural design* 36 (1996, September), pp. 447.

— "La Sensació de lloc en el pavelló". *Quaderns d'Arquitectura i Urbanisme* 163 (1984), pp. 30-31.

Smithson, Alison; Peter Smithson. "El hexenbesenraum en la Hexenhaus". *Bau* 15 (1997), pp. 112-115.

— "Aujord'hui, c'est les pubs que l'on collectionne = But Today We Collect Ads". *Architecture D'aujourd'hui* 344 (2003, January), pp. 40-45.

Smithson, Peter. "Fotografías". *Bau* 13 (1995), p. 92.

Szita, Jane. "Bewitched". *Dwell* 110 (2005, April), pp. 110-112.

Making a Place with a Tree

Books

Abram, David. *La magia de los sentidos*. Barcelona: Kairós, 2000.

Aguiló Alonso, Miguel. *El paisaje construido. Una aproximación a la idea de lugar*. Madrid: Colegio de Ingenieros de Caminos, Canales y Puertos, 1999.

Aristóteles. *Física*. Madrid: Gredos, 2007.

Aravena, Alejandro. *El lugar de la arquitectura*. Santiago de Chile: Arq ediciones 2002.

Azara, Pedro. *Castillos en el aire. Mito y arquitectura en Occidente*. Barcelona: Gustavo Gili, 2005.

Bacon, Francis. *El espíritu del lugar: jardín y paisaje en la Inglaterra moderna*. Madrid: Adaba, 2006.

Bollnow, Otto Friedrich. *Hombre y espacio*. Barcelona: Labor, 1969.

Bru, Eduard. *Tres en el lugar = Three on the site*. Barcelona: Actar, 1997.

Cacciari, Massimo. "Adolf Loos y su ángel", in *Adolf Loos*. Edited by Antonio Pizza. Barcelona: Editorial Sytlos, 1989, pp. 89-137.

Casey, Edward S. *The Fate of Place: A Philosophical History*. Berkeley: University of California Press, 1997.

Como, Alessandra. "The Voyage and the House: Bernard Rudofsky's Search for Place", in *Topophilia and topophobia : reflections on twentieth-century human habitat*. Edited by Xing Ruan; Paul Hogben. London: Routledge, 2007.

Delgado, Manuel. *Memoria y lugar. El espacio público como crisis de significado*. Valencia: Ediciones Generales de la Construcción, 2001.

Espuela, Fernando. *Madre materia*. Madrid: Lampreave, 2009.

Fernández Alba, Antonio. *Sobre la naturaleza del espacio que construye la arquitectura: geometría del recuerdo y proyecto del lugar*. Madrid: Real Academia de Bellas Artes de San Fernando, 1989.

Gallego, Moisés. *La construcción del lugar: memoria pedagógica*. Barcelona: ETSAB-UPC, 1995.

Gastón, Cristina. *Mies: el proyecto como revelación del lugar*. Barcelona: Fundación Caja Arquitectos, 2005.

Hipócrates. *Tratados hipocráticos*. Madrid: Gredos, 2000.

Iñiguez, Manuel. *Tiempo y lugar: en la obra e K.F. Schinkel y A. Aalto = Denbora eta lekua: K.F. Schinkelen eta A. Aaltoren obran*. Bilbao: Servicio Editorial, Universidad del

País Vasco = Argitalpen Zerbitzua, Euskal Herriko Unibertsitatea, 1997.

Kepes, Gyorgy. *El arte del ambiente*. Buenos Aires: Víctor Lerú, 1978.

Leroi-Gourhan, André. *El gesto y la palabra*. Caracas: Universidad Central de Venezuela, 1971.

Lynch, Kevin. *Planificación del sitio*. Barcelona: Gustavo Gili, 1980.

Marot, Sébastien. *Suburbanismo y el arte de la memoria*. Barcelona: Gustavo Gili, 2006.

Muntañola, Josep. *La arquitectura como lugar*. Barcelona: UPC, 1996.

Norberg-Schulz, Christian. *Existencia, espacio y arquitectura*. Barcelona: Blume, 1975.

— *Genius Loci: Towards a Phenomenology of Architecture*. London: Academy editions, 1980.

— *Architecture: Meaning and Place: Selected Essays*. Milan; New York: Electa; Rizzoli, 1988.

— *Los principios de la arquitectura moderna. Sobre la nueva tradición del siglo XX*. Barcelona: Reverté, 2005.

Quetglas, Josep. "Respiración de la mirada", in *Artículos de Ocasión*. Barcelona: Gustavo Gili, 2004, pp. 177-187.

Rivas Sanz, Juan Luis de las. *El espacio como lugar. Sobre la naturaleza de la forma urbana*. Valladolid: Universidad de Valladolid. Secretariado de Publicaciones, 1992.

Sheldrake, Rupert. *La presencia del pasado: Resonanacia mórfica y hábitos de la naturaleza*. Barcelona: Kairós, 1990.

Solà-Morales, Ignasi de. "Place: Permanence or Production", in Anywhere. Edited by Cynthia C. Davidson. New York: Rizzoli, 1992, pp. 112-115. Spanish edition: "Lugar: permanencia o producción", in *Diferencias. Topografía de la arquitectura contemporánea*. Barcelona: Gustavo Gili, 1995, pp. 109-126.

Yi-Fu, Tuan. *Space and Place: The Perspective of Experience*. London: Edward Arnold, 1977.

Magazines

Armesto, Antonio. "Arquitectura y naturaleza. Tres sospechas sobre el próximo milenio". *DPA, Documents de Projectes d'Arquitectura* 16 (2000, June), pp. 34-43.

Domínguez, Luis Ángel. "De la necesidad del contexto en el proyecto de arquitectura". *Arquitectonics* (Arquitectura y Contexto) 9 (2004, February), pp. 15-30.

Llecha, Joan. "El paisaje bajo la casa". *DPA, Documents de Projectes d'Arquitectura* 21 (2005), pp. 32-41.

Moneo, Rafael. "[Inmovilidad substancial] El murmullo del lugar". *El Croquis*, 20 + 64 + 98= Omnibus (2004), pp. 634-640.

Norberg-Schulz, Christian. "Kahn, Heidegger. El lenguaje de la arquitectura". *Arquitectura COAM* 223 (1980, March-April), pp. 51-61.

Van Eyck, Aldo. "En su cara hay un jardín". *Diagonal* 23 (2010, Winter), pp. 30-31.

Wigley, Marc. "On Site". *Lotus* 95 (1997, December), pp. 118-131.

The Vector of Time in Architecture

Books

Argan, Carlo. *El pasado en el presente. El revival en las artes plásticas, la arquitectura, el cine y el teatro*. Barcelona: Gustavo Gili, 1977.

Aubenque, Pierre. *La Prudencia en Aristóteles: con un apéndice sobre la prudencia en Kant*. Barcelona: Crítica, 1999.

Bachelard, Gaston. *La dialéctica de la duración*. Madrid: Editorial Villalar, 1978.

— *La intuición del instante*. México D.F.: Fondo de Cultura Económica de España, 1999.

Camón Aznar, José. *El tiempo en el arte*. Madrid: Sociedad de Estudios y Publicaciones, 1958.

Colquhoun, Alan. *Modernidad y tradición clásica*. Madrid: Jucar Universidad, 1991.

Deleuze, Gilles. *Lógica del sentido*. Barcelona: Paidós Ibérica, 1989.

Díaz, Tony. *Tiempo y arquitectura*. Buenos Aires: Infinito, 2009.

Didi-Huberman, Georges. *Ante el tiempo: Historia del arte y anacronismo de las imágenes*. Buenos Aires: Adriana Hidalgo, 2008.

Dorfles, Gillo. *El intervalo perdido*. Barcelona: Lumen, 1984.

Espuela Cid, Fernando. *Madre materia*. Madrid: Lampreave, 2009.

González-Quijano, Álvaro Fernando. *El Alma, el tiempo, las cosas: Reflexiones entorno a la modernidad*. Rimac: Universidad Nacional de Ingeniería, Facultad de Arquitectura, Urbanismo y Artes, 1998.

Grahame, Clark. *Space, Time, and Man: A Prehistorian's View*. Cambridge; New York: Cambridge University Press, 1992.

Heidegger, Martin. *El concepto de tiempo: (tratado de 1924)*. Barcelona: Editorial Herder, 2008.

— *El ser y el tiempo*. México D.F.: Fondo Cultura Económica Mexico, 2001.

Hejduk, John. *Víctimas*. Murcia: Colegio Oficial de Aparejadores y Arquitectos Técnicos; Librería Yerba; Caja Murcia, 1993.

Kern, Stephen. *The Culture of Time and Space, 1880-1918*. London: Weidenfeld and Nicolson, 1983.

Koselleck, Reinhart. *Futuro pasado: para una semántica de los tiempos históricos*. Barcelona: Paidós, 1993.

Kubler, Geoerge. *La configuración del tiempo. Observaciones sobre la historia de las cosas*. Madrid: Nerea, 1988.

Kwinter, Sandford. *Architectures of Time. Toward a Theory of Event in Modernist Culture*. Cambridge, Mass.: MIT Press, 2001.

Le Goff, Jacques. *El orden de la memoria: El tiempo como imaginario*. Barcelona: Paidós, 1991.

Leroi-Gourhan, André. *El gesto y la palabra*. Caracas: Universidad Central de Venezuela, 1971.

Lledó, Emilio. *El surco del tiempo. Meditaciones sobre el mito platónico de la escritura y la memoria*. Barcelona: Crítica, 2000.

Loos, Adolf. *Ornamento y delito y otros escritos*. Barcelona: Gustavo Gili, 1972.

Lynch, Kevin. *¿De qué tiempo es este lugar? Para una nueva definición del ambiente*. Barcelona: Gustavo Gili, 1975.

Martínez García-Posada, Ángel. *Sueños y polvo: Cuentos de tiempo sobre arte y arquitectura*. Madrid: Lampreave, 2009.

Missac, Pierre. *Walter Benjamin: de un siglo al otro. Sus reflexiones sobre el tiempo y la historia, el cine, la arquitectura: una mirada diferente sobre ese extraño mosaico denominado modernidad*. Barcelona: Gedisa, 1988.

Molero Cruz, José. *Tiempo y temporalidad*. Córdoba: Publicaciones del Monte de Piedad y Caja de Ahorros de Córdoba, 1979.

Moles, Abraham A. *Teoría de los objetos*. Barcelona: Gustavo Gili, 1974.

Mostafavi, Mohsen; David Leatherbarrow. *La superficie de la arquitectura*. Tres Cantos, Madrid: Akal, 2007.

Pardo, José Luis. *Sobre los espacios: Pintar, escribir, pensar*. Barcelona: Serbal, 1991.

Platón. *Ión. Timeo. Critias*. Madrid: Alianza, 2004.

Richardson, Vicky. *Vanguardia y tradición. La reinterpretación de la arquitectura*. Barcelona: Blume, 2001.

Ruiz de la Puerta, Félix. *Arquitecturas de la memoria*. Madrid: Akal, 2009.

Sennet, Richard. *La conciencia del ojo*. Barcelona: Versal, 1991.

Tarkovski, Andrei. *Esculpir en el tiempo. Reflexiones sobre el arte, la estética y la poética del cine*. Madrid: Rialp, 2000.

Virno, Paolo. *El Recuerdo del presente: ensayo sobre el tiempo histórico*. Buenos Aires: Paidós, 2004.

Xirau, Ramón. *El tiempo vivido. Acerca de "estar"*. México D.F.: Siglo XXI, 1985.

Yourcenar, Marguerite. *El tiempo, gran escultor.* Madrid: Altea, Taurus, Alfaguara, 1989.

Magazines

Ábalos, Iñaki. "Las formas del tiempo". *Circo, Injertos,* no 2, 1997. Santander: Universidad Internacional Menéndez Pelayo.

Martí, Carlos. "Naturaleza y tradición: un comentario sobre la obra de Cesar Portela". *El Croquis* 43 (1990, June), pp. 132-137.

Moneo, Rafael. "La vida de los edificios. Las ampliaciones de la Mezquita de Córdoba". *Arquitectura COAM* 256 (1985, September), pp. 26-36.

Pallasmaa, Juhani. "Hapticidad y tiempo: notas acerca de la arquitectura frágil". Pasajes de Arquitectura y Critica 30 (2001, October), pp. 13.

Quetglas, Josep. "La Danza y la Procesión. Sobre la forma del tiempo en la arquitectura de Rafael Moneo". *El Croquis,* 20 + 64 + 98= Omnibus (2004), pp. 534-550.

Outdoor Domesticity

Books

Bachelard, Gaston; Jean Baudrillard; Michel de Certeau; Jacques Herzog; Amédée Ozenfant; Christopher Reed; George Perec; Charles Rice; Felicity Scott; Georges Teyssot; Bernard Tschumi. *Intimus: Interior Design Theory Reader.* Edited by Mark Taylor; Julieanna Preston. Chichester, England; Hoboken, NJ: Wiley-Academy, 2006.

Ábalos, Iñaki. *La Buena Vida. Visita guiada a las casas de la modernidad.* Barcelona: Gustavo Gili, 2000.

Ackerman, James S. *La Villa. Forma e ideología de las casas de campo.* Madrid: Akal, 2006.

Alday, Iñaki. *Aprendiendo de todas sus casas: Aalto, Asplund, Barragan, Bottoni, Breuer.* Sant Cugat del Vallès; Barcelona: ETSAV; Edicions UPC, 1996.

Alexander, Christopher; Howard Davis; Julio Martínez, Donald Corner. *The Production of Houses.* New York: Oxford University Press, 2005.

Azara, Pedro. *La última casa.* Barcelona: Gustavo Gili, 1999.

Benevolo, Leonardo. *La casa dell'Uomo.* Roma: Laterza, 1976.

Benton, Tim. "The Twentieth-Century Architectural Interior: Representing Modernity", in *Imagined Interiors. Representing the Domestic Interior Since the Renaissence.* Edited by Jeremy Aynsley; Charlotte Crant; Harriet McKay. London: V&A Publications, 2006.

Blaser, Werner. *Patios: 5000 años de evolución desde la antigüedad hasta nuestros días.* Barcelona; Naucalpan: Gustavo Gili; Amadora, 2004.

Brunskill, R.W. *Vernacular Architecture: An Illustrated Handbook.* London: Faber, 2000.

Bryson, Bill. *En casa: Una breve historia de la vida privada.* Barcelona: RBA, 2011.

Camesasca, Ettore; Santiago Alcolea; Daniel Alcouffe; P. M. Bardi; Anne Berendsen; Mario Bussagli; Gianfilippo Carettoni; Segio Coradeschi; John Drummond; José Gudiol Ricart; Mihail Iljin; "ojciech Kalino2ski; Gianni K. Koenig; Adam Jerzy Milobedzki; charles F. Montgomery Jr.; Michelangelo Muraro; G. Opresco; P. Petresco. *Historia ilustrada de la casa.* Barcelona: Editorial Noguer, 1971.

Cevedio, Mónica. *Arquitectura y género. Espacio público / Espacio privado.* Barcelona: Icaria, 2003.

Colomina, Beatriz. *Domesticity at War.* Barcelona: Actar, 2006.

— *Privacidad y publicidad. Arquitectura moderna como medio de comunicación de masas.* Murcia: Cendeac, 2011.

Díaz-Y. Recasens, Gonzalo. *Recurrencia y herencia del patio en el movimiento moderno.* Sevilla: Universidad de Sevilla; Consejería de Obras Públicas y Transportes, 1992.

Duby, Georges; Philip Airès. *Historia de la vida privada. Vol. 6. Comunidad, el Estado y la familia en los siglos XVI-XVIII.* Edited by Roger Chartier. Madrid: Taurus, 1991.

Espuelas Cid, Fernando. *El claro en el bosque: Reflexiones sobre el vacío en arquitectura.* Barcelona: Fundación Caja de Arquitectos, 1999.

Friedman, Alice T. *Women and the Making of the Modern House: a Social and Architectural History.* New York: Harry N. Abram, 1998.

Gili Galfeti, Gustau. *Casas refugio = Private retreats.* Barcelona: Gustavo Gili, 1995.

— *Mi casa, mi paraíso: La construcción del universo doméstico ideal.* Barcelona: Gustavo Gili, 1999.

Hejduk, John. *Such Places as Memory.* Cambridge, London: MIT Press, 1998.

Jarauta, Francisco; François Lyotard; Massimo Cacciari; Michael Nyman; Luis Fernández-Galiano; José Quetglas; José M. Torres Nadal; Paolo Deganello; Kevin Power. *Pensar-componer, construir-habitar.* Edited by Francisco Jarauta. San Sebastián: Arteleku, 1994.

Jones, E. Michael. *Living Machines. Bauhaus Architecture as Sexual Ideology.* San Francisco: Ignatius Press, 1995.

Lleó, Blanca. *Sueño de habitar.* Barcelona: Gustavo Gili, 1998.

Melchionne, Kevin. "Living in Glass Houses: Domesticity, Interior Design, and Environmental Aesthetics", in *Aesthetics of Human Environments.* Edited by Arnold Berleant; Allen Carlson. Peterborough, Ont. New York, NY: Orchard Park; Broadview Press, 2007.

Monteys, Xavier; Pere Fuertes. *Casa collage: Un ensayo sobre la arquitectura de la casa.* Barcelona: Gustavo Gili, 2001.

Moore, Charles; Gerald Allen; Donkyn Lyndon. *La casa: forma y diseño.* Barcelona: Gustavo Gili, 1999.

Morales, José. *La disolución de la estancia: transformaciones domésticas (1930-1960).* Madrid: Rueda, 2005.

Oliver, Paul. *Dwelling: The Vernacular House World Wide.* Edited by Lindsay Asquith y Marcel Vellinga. London: Phaidon, 2003.

Parodi, Aníbal. *Puertas adentro: interioridad y espacio doméstico en el s. XX.* Barcelona: Edicions UPC, 2005.

Pasquinelli, Carla. *El vértigo del orden. La relación entre el yo y la casa.* Buenos Aires: Libros de la Aucaria, 2006.

Prost, Antoine; Gérard Vincent. *Historia de la vida privada / T. 10, Siglo XX: diversidades culturales.* Edited by Roger Chartier. Madrid: Taurus, 1991.

Quetglas, Josep. "Habitar, segunda parte", in *International property = Propietat internacional.* Barcelona: Col·legi d'Arquitectes de Catalunya, 1994.

— "Habitar", in *Escritos Colegiales. Escrits Col·legials.* Barcelona: Actar, 1997.

— *La Casa de Don Giovanni.* Madrid: Exit L.M.I., 1997.

Rapoport, Amos. *Vivienda y cultura.* Barcelona: Gustavo Gili, 1972.

Rice, Charles. *The Emergence of the Interior: Architecture, Modernity, Domesticity.* London: Routledge, 2007.

Rykwert, Joseph. *La casa de Adán en el paraíso.* Barcelona: Gustavo Gili, 1999.

Sack, Florentine. *Open House: Towards a New Architecture = Das offene Haus: für eine neue Architektur.* Berlin: Jovis, 2006.

Scully, Vincent. *The Shingle Style Today or the Historian's Revenge.* New York: George Braziller, 1974.

Smithson, Alison; Peter Smithson. *Cambiando el arte de habitar.* Barcelona: Gustavo Gili, 2001.

Torres Cueto, Jorge. *Casa por casa: reflexiones sobre el habitar.* Valencia: Ediciones Generales de la Construcción, 2009.

Trías, Eugenio. "El templo", in Félix Duque; Ferran Lobo; Simón Marchán; Josep Maria Montaner; José Luis Pardo; Piedad Solans; Federico Soriano. *Pensar,*

Construir, Habitar. Aproximación a la arquitectura contemporánea. Edited by Piedad Solans. Mallorca: Fundación Pilar i Joan Miró, 2000.

Wigley, Marc. "The Housing of Gender", in Sexualitat i espai: el disseny de la intimitat. Edited by Beatriz Colomina. Barcelona: Edicions UPC, 1997.

– White Walls, Designer Dresses: The Fashioning of Modern Architecture. Cambridge Mass.: MIT Press, 1995.

Wright, Frank Lloyd. The Natural House. New York: Horizon Press, 1954.

Magazines

Banham, Reyner. "A Home is not a House". Art in America 2 (1965, April), pp. 109-118.

Herreros, Juan. "Espacio doméstico y sistema de objetos". Exit L.M.I 1 (1994), pp. 82-99.

Somol, Robert E. "My Mother the House". The Princeton Journal: Thematic Studies in Architecture 4 (1992), pp. 50-71.

Sources of the Images

Actar publisher has made every effort to contact those people and institutions that own the copyright of the images published in this book. In some cases, their location has not been possible, and, for this reason, we suggest to owners of such copyrights contact the publisher.

Page 3: photograph ©Ricardo Devesa

Introduction

01 Gastón, Cristina. *Mies: el proyecto como revelación del lugar*. Barcelona: Fundación Caja Arquitectos, 2005.

02 López-Peláez, José Manuel. *La arquitectura de Gunnar Asplund*. Barcelona: Fundación Caja de Arquitectos, 2002.

03 Neuhart, Marilyn. *Eames House*. Berlin: Ernst & Sohn, 1994.

04 Hoffmann, Donald. *Frank Lloyd Wright's Fallingwater. The House and Its history*. New York: Dover Publications, 1993.

05 Montaner, Josep María, edt. *Coderch. Casa Ugalde*. Barcelona: COAC, 1998.

06 Carvalho Ferraz, Marcelo, edt. *Vilanova Artigas*. Lisboa: Editorial Blau, 1997.

07 Rykwert, Joseph. *La casa de Adán en el paraíso*. Barcelona: Gustavo Gili, 1999

La Casa, Bernard Rudofsky

01, 03, 05, 07, 09, 15, 17, 18, 21, 22, 25, 26, 27, 32, 33, 34, 36, 42, 46, 49, 52
Bocco Guarneri, Andrea. *Bernard Rudofsky. A Humane Designer*. Viena; New York: Springer, 2003.

02, 29, 37, 38, 39, 41, 43, 44, 45, 47, 50, 51
Platzer, Monica (edt.); *Bernard Rudofsky. Lessons from Bernard Rudofsky: Life as a Voyage*. Basel; Boston; Berlin: Birkhäuser, 2007.

04 Instituto cartográfico Nacional. Portal SIGNA (Sistema de Información Geográfica Nacional de España).

06 Collection: Bernard Rudofsky Papers. Research Library, The Getty Research Institute. Los Angeles, EE.UU.

08, 13, 14
Abercrombie, Stanley. "With Summer in View: the Spanish Retreat of Architect-Author Bernard Rudofsky". Interior Design vol. 55 n°8 (1984, agosto), pp. 138- [145].

10, 24
Rudofsky, Bernard. *Architecture without Architects: An Introduction to Nonpedigreed Architecture*. New York: Museum of Modern Art, 1964.

11, 12, 28, 30, 40
Rudofsky, Bernard. *Behind the Picture Window. An Unconventional Book on the Conventional Modern House and the Inscrutable Ways of its Inmates*. New York: Oxford University Press, 1955.

16, 23, 31, 53, 54, 55
Rudofsky, Bernard. *The Prodigious Builders. Notes Toward a Natural History of Architecture with Special Regard to Those Species That Are Traditionally Neglected or Downright Ignored*. New York: Harcourt Brace Jovanovich, 1977.

19, 20
La Pietra, Ugo (edt.). *Gio Ponti*. New York: Rizzoli, 1995.

35 Rudofsky, Bernard. "Vivienda en Nerja". *Arquitectura* 206-207 (1977, 2° cuatrimestre), pp. 96-99.

48 Monteys, Xavier. *Le Corbusier: Obras y proyectos = obras e projectos*. Barcelona: Gustavo Gili, 2005.

Cottage Caesar, Marcel Breuer

01, 12, 13, 16, 18, 19, 20
Cranston, Jones. *Marcel Breuer. Buildings and projects 1921-1962*. London: Thames & Hudson, 1962.

02, 09, 10
Breuer, Marcel; Peter Blake (ed.). *Marcel Breuer: Architect and Designer*. New York: Architectural Record, MoMA, 1949.

03, 04
Hitchcock, Henry Russell. *Built in USA: Post-war Architecture*. New York: Museum of Modern Art, 1952.

08, 11
"The House in the Museum Garden: Marcel Breuer, architect". New York: Museum of Modern Art Bulletin Vol. XV, nº 4, (1948, primavera).

05, 06, 07, 27
Breuer, Marcel; Peter Blake (ed.). *Marcel Breuer. Sun and Shadow. The Philosophy of an Architect*. New York: Dodd, Mead & Company, 1956.

14, 21
Hyman, Isabelle. *Marcel Breuer, Architect: The Career and the Buildings*. New York: Harry N. Abrams, 2001.

15, 17
Yorke, F.R.S. *The Modern House*. London: Architectural Press, 1957.

22 Klee, Paul; Sibyl Moholy-Nagy. *Pedagogical Sketchbook*. London: Faber and Faber, 183-?.

23 Ford, Edward R. *The Details of Modern Architecture. Volume II. 1928 to 1988*. Cambridge, Mass.; London: MIT Press, 1996.

24 Driller, Joachim. *Breuer Houses*. London: Phaidon, 2000.

25, 26
Remmele, Mathias; Alexandra Pioch. *Marcel Breuer: diseño y arquitectura*. Weil am Rhein: Vitra Design Museum, 2003.

28 Geelhaar, Christian. *Paul Klee et le Bauhaus*. Neuchatel: Editions Ides et Calendes, 1972.

Villa La Roche, Le Corbusier and Pierre Jeanneret

01, 17
Le Corbusier; W. Boesiger, O. Stonorov, M. Bill (edts.). *Le Corbusier et Pierre Jeanneret. V. 1, Oeuvre complète 1910-1929*. Berlin: Birkhäuser, 1995.

02 Le Corbusier. *Puerta de hielo*. *L'Esprit Nouveau, 1920-1925*. Castellón: Ellago, 2005.

03, 04, 05, 06, 07, 08, 11, 12, 13, 14, 28, 29
Le Corbusier. *Early Buildings and Projects, 1912-1923 / Le Corbusier*. New York; London; Paris: Garland; Fondation Le Corbusier, 1982.

16, 30, 39, 40
Le Corbusier. *Almanach d'architecture moderne: Documents, théorie, pronostics, histoire, petites histoires, dates, propos standarts, apologie et idéalisation du standart, organisation, industrialisation du bâtiment*. Paris: Connivences, 1987.

09, 10, 15
Benton, Tim. *The Villas of Le Corbusier et Pierre Jeanneret, 1920-1930*. Basel; Boston; Berlin: Birkhäuser, 2007.

19 Monteys, Xavier. *Le Corbusier: Obras y proyectos = obras e projectos*. Barcelona: Gustavo Gili, 2005.

20 Le Corbusier. *La Ville Radieuse. Éléments d'une doctrine d'urbanisme pour l'équipement de la civilisation machiniste*. Paris: Vincent, Fréal, 1964.

21, 22, 23, 24, 25, 26, 27, 31, 33, 34, 36, 42
Le Corbusier. *Une Petite Maison: 1923*. Zurich: Girsberger, 1954.

28 Sbriglio, Jacques. *Le Corbusier. Les Villas La Roche-Jeanneret = Le Corbusier : the Villas La Roche-Jeanneret*. Paris; Basel; Boston; Berlin: Fondation Le Corbusier; Birkhäuser, 1997.

32 Reichlin, Bruno. " 'Une Petite Maison' sul lago Lemano: la controversia Perret-Le Corbusier = 'Une Petite Maison' on Lake Leman: the Perret-Le Corbusier controversy". *Lotus* 60 (1988), pp. 58-83.

35, 41 Ricardo Devesa.

37 Olalla, Pedro. *Atlas mitológico de Grecia*. Atenas: Road Editions, 2001.

38 Le Corbusier. *Hacia una arquitectura*. Buenos Aires; Barcelona: Poseidón, 1978.

43 Quetglas, Josep. *"Point de veu dans l'axe de l'arbre"*. *Massilia* 2004bis. *Annuaire d'études corbuséennes: Le Corbusier y el paisaje*. Xavier Monteys (ed.). Sant Cugat del Vallés: Associació d'Idees Centre d'Investigacions Estètiques, 2004, pp. 144-149.

44 Le Corbusier; François de Pierrefeu. *La casa del hombre*. Barcelona: Apóstrofe, 1999.

Villa Pepa, Juan Navarro Baldeweg

01 Navarro Baldeweg, Juan; Erica Witschey, Raúl Rispa (edts.). *Juan Navarro Baldeweg*. Corte de Madera, Calif.: Gingko Press, 2001.

02, 03, 04, 05, 06, 08, 09, 10, 11, 12, 14, 15, 17, 18, 19, 20, 21, 22, 23, 32, 42 Estudio Juan Navarro Baldeweg.

07, 38, 39, 40 Bonet, Juan Manuel; Enrique Granell; Ángel González. *Juan Navarro Baldeweg*. Valencia: IVAM Institut Valencià d'Art Modern, 1999.

13 Lupano, Mario. *Juan Navarro Baldeweg. Il ritorno della luce*. Milan: Federico Motta Editrice, 1996.

16, 41 González García, Ángel; Juan José Lahuerta; Juan Navarro Baldeweg; Mirko Zardini (ed.). *Juan Navarro*

Baldeweg. Obras y proyectos. Madrid: Electa España, 1993.

24, 25, 26, 27, 28, 29, 30, 31, 33, 34, 35, 36, 37, 43 Juan Navarro Baldeweg.

Hexenhaus, Alison and Peter Smithson

01, 22 Sicmemi, Maddalena. "Un'opera aperta degli Smithson a Bad Karlshafen". *Cassabella* 726 (2004), pp. 6-20.

02, 04 Allen, Isabel; Deborah Singmaster. "Interiors and fit-outs". *Architects' Journal* 205 (1997, junio), pp. 39-40, 42, 45-46, 48, 50, 52.

03, 26, 29, 31 Roland Halbe.

05, 32 Smithson, Alison; Peter Smithson; Marco Vidotto; Aquil·les González. St. Hilda's College, Oxford: la arquitectura del entramado. Madrid: Colegio Oficial de Arquitectos de Madrid, 2001.

06, 08, 12, 13, 14, 27, 33, 34, 35, 36, 37 Smithson, Alison; Peter Smithson. *The Charged Void: Architecture*. New York: Monacelli Press, 2000.

07, 10, 11, 15, 16, 17, 18, 19, 20, 21, 23, 24, 25, 28 Heuvel, Dirk van den; Max Risselada; Beatriz Colomina. *Alison and Peter Smithson: From the House of the Future to a House of Today*. Rotterdam: 010 Publishers, 2004.

09 Ricardo Devesa.

30 Smithson, Alison; Peter Smithson. *Italienische Gedanken, weitergedacht*. Basel, Boston: Birkhäuser, Gütersloh: Bertelsmann Fachzeitschriften, 2001.

Theoretical Contributions

01 Cranston, Jones. *Marcel Breuer. Buildings and projects 1921-1962*. London: Thames & Hudson, 1962.

02, 03
   Ricardo Devesa.
04 Allen, Isabel; Deborah Singmaster.
   "Interiors and fit-outs". *Architects' Journal* 205 (1997, junio).
05 Juan Navarro Baldeweg.
06 Benton, Tim; et alt. *Le Corbusier et la Méditerranée*. Marsella: Parenthèses; Musées de Marseille, 1987.
07 Geelhaar, Christian. *Paul Klee et le Bauhaus*. Neuchatel: Editions Ides et Calendes, 1972.
08 Smithson, Alison; Peter Smithson. *Changing the Art of Inhabitation*. London: Artemis, 1994.
09 Alexander, Christopher; Sara Ishikawa; Murray Silverstein. *A Pattern Language* = *Un lenguaje de patrones: ciudades, edificios, construcciones*. Barcelona: Gustavo Gili, 1980.

10 Smithson, Alison; Peter Smithson. *Upper Lawn: Folly Solar Pavillion*. Barcelona: Edicions de la Universitat Politècnica de Catalunya, D.L., 1986.
11, 14
   Rudofsky, Bernard. *Constructores prodigiosos: Apuntes sobre una historia natural de la arquitectura*. México: Pax México, 2008.
12 Smithson, Alison; *Peter Smithson. The Charged Void: Architecture*. New York: Monacelli Press, 2000.
13 Rudofsky, *Bernard. Behind the Picture Window*. New York: Oxford University Press, 1955

Colophon

Smithson, Alison; Peter Smithson. *The Charged Void: Architecture*. New York: Monacelli Press, 2000.

Acknowledgements

First of all, I would like to thank my parents for their whole-hearted support of my desire to pursue architecture. Without them, I would never have had the resources or the time to complete the research that went into this book. Likewise, my thanks to Marina Romero for believing in me and in the doctoral dissertation that is condensed in this book Thank you also to my most loyal friend, Fernando Guerrero, who designed the layout of my dissertation and now this book, for his exacting and tasteful designs. I am especially grateful to my wife, Rosa J. Devesa for knowing how to wait for me, encourage me, and listen to me so sweetly and patiently over the years. Armed with her love, this has been a delightful and beautiful journey.

A sincere thanks to all the librarians who kindly responded to my requests, in particular from the library of the Architects' Association of Catalonia (COAC), the National Library of Catalonia, the library at the Barcelona School of Architecture (ETSAB) and Avery Library at Columbia University. I am also grateful for the documentation provided by the archives of the Getty Research Institute, Avery Archives, Juan Navarro Baldeweg, Monika Platzer, Axel Bruchhäuser and Roland Halbe.

In addition to the books and documentation, however, it was fundamental to have been able to visit most of the houses that appear in this book. Thank you, thus, to the people who gave me the chance to have them to myself for a few hours, especially to Axel Bruchhäuser (Hexenhaus), Juan Navarro and Pepa Ríos (Villa Pepa) and David Diao (Wolfson Cottage, built at the same time as the disfigured Caesar Cottage). Thanks also to the Le Corbusier Foundation (Villa La Roche and Villa Le Lac) and Carola Hohenlohe (La Casa).

My thanks to everyone who listened to the public presentations and discussed the progress in my research; they were essential to the subsequent reworking and revision of the texts.

Special acknowledgment goes to my colleagues from the seminars organized for PhD students whose dissertations were directed by Professor Antonio Armesto. Likewise, thank you to everyone who listened and contributed ideas during my lectures at the Barcelona School of Architecture, the València School of Architecture, ESARQ-UIC, the Portuguese Catholic University of Viseu, the Centro Mediterráneo at the University of Granada, the Institute for Advanced Architecture of Catalunya and the School of Architecture of La Salle in Barcelona. Finally, thank you to my undergraduate students at ETSAB and postgraduate students in Design, Environment and Architecture at ELISAVA.

I was also given magnificent opportunities to continue correcting and improving this material, afforded by journals that published excerpts of the text, including CIRCO, Quaderns d'Arquitectura i Urbanisme, ADE (Arquitectura en dibuixos exemplars) and Palimpsesto. Similarly, parts of this research were presented and subsequently published in the proceedings of the following conferences: the third International Seminar Arquitectonics Network (Barcelona 2010), the third CIAE conference (Centro Investigación Arte y Entorno, Valencia 2011), Tourbanism – the sixth conference of the IFOU (Barcelona 2012) and the first AURS conference (Arquitectura, Universitat, Recerca i Societat, Barcelona 2012). To all the organizers, thank you for your confidence.

Unquestionably, this book would not have been possible without the valuable contributions, directly or indirectly, from the people I consider my mentors: Cecilio Sánchez-Robles, Manuel Gausa, Carlos Martí, Josep Quetglas, Beatriz Colomina, Mark Wigley, Iñaki Ábalos, Enrique Walker, Jorge Otero-Pailos, Felicity D. Scott, Reinhold Martin, Joan Ockman and Juan Navarro Baldeweg. Each of them has been, in their own time and their own way, a beacon and guide for my theoretical, analytical and methodological work. That also includes my dissertation advisor, Antonio Armesto, whom I thank for his analytical and theoretical precision.

Publishing this book with Actar, the publishing house that shaped me as an editor and has helped me grow intellectually every day, would not have been possible without Ramon Prat and the trust he has placed in me during all these complicated and difficult years dedicated to the beautiful and risky business of publishing books.

Finally, I would like to extend my utmost gratitude to two colleagues and unconditional friends who followed along with the entire process of completing my dissertation: Francisco Llinares and Eduard Sancho. They were both attentive, available and generous with their contributions, and their comments were incisive and invaluable. Thank you both for your honest and productive conversations. Finally, thank you to my dear friend Erica Sogbe, who from the dissertation stages through to the concretion of the texts published here, has guided me with her intellectual acuity, her stubborn argumentative perfection, her artistic sensitivity and, above all, her support as the ideal companion throughout the long and wonderful personal journey that has brought me here.

My sincere gratitude to all these wonderful people!

Outdoor Domesticity
On the Relationships between Trees, Achitecture and Inhabitants

Published by
Actar Publishers
New York, Barcelona
www.actar.com

Author
Ricardo Devesa

Editor
Érica Sogbe

Graphic Design
Fernando Guerrero C&D

With contributions by
**María Teresa Muñoz,
Iñaki Ábalos**

*Translation, copy editing
and proofreading*
Angela Kay Bunning

Printing and binding
Arlequín & Pierrot

Distribution
Actar D, Inc.

440 Park Avenue South,
17th Floor
New York, NY 10016, EE. UU.
T +1 212 966 2207
salesnewyork@actar-d.com

Roca i Batlle 2-4
08023 Barcelona, España
T +34 933 282 183
eurosales@actar-d.com

Indexing
ISBN 978-1-948765-71-8
Library of Congress Control
Number 2021942604

Printed in Spain
Publication date: Sept. 2021

Available in Spanish
Domesticidad a la intemperie
ISBN: 978-1-948765-72-5

Drawing for *Jubilee Sign*, Battersea Park, 1977,
Alison and Peter Smithson